Establishing Monetary Stability in Emerging Market Economies

The Political Economy of Global Interdependence
Thomas D. Willett, Series Editor

Establishing Monetary Stability in Emerging Market Economies, edited by Thomas D. Willett, Richard C.K. Burdekin, Richard J. Sweeney, and Clas Wihlborg

Closure in International Politics: The Impact of Strategy, Blocs, and Empire, John A. Kroll

Toward a North American Community? Canada, the United States, and Mexico, edited by Donald Barry with Mark O. Dickerson and James D. Gaisford

Seeking Common Ground: Canada-U.S. Trade Dispute Settlement Policies in the Nineties, Andrew D.M. Anderson

The Challenge of European Integration: Internal and External Problems of Trade and Money, edited by Berhanu Abegaz, Patricia Dillon, David H. Feldman, and Paul F. Whiteley

The Political Economy of European Monetary Unification, edited by Barry Eichengreen and Jeffry Frieden

International Economic Sanctions, William H. Kaempfer and Anton D. Lowenberg

The European Monetary System and European Monetary Union, Michele Fratianni and Jürgen von Hagen

Profit-Making Speculation in Foreign Exchange Markets, Patchara Surajaras and Richard J. Sweeney

The Political Economy of International Organizations: A Public Choice Approach, edited by Roland Vaubel and Thomas D. Willett

Speculation and the Dollar: The Political Economy of Exchange Rates, Laurence A. Krause

Crossing Frontiers: Explorations in International Political Economy, Benjamin J. Cohen

# Establishing Monetary Stability in Emerging Market Economies

EDITED BY

Thomas D. Willett
Richard C. K. Burdekin
Richard J. Sweeney
Clas Wihlborg

Westview Press
BOULDER • SAN FRANCISCO • OXFORD

The Political Economy of Global Interdependence

All rights reserved. No part of this publication may be reproduced or transmitted in any form or by any means, electronic or mechanical, including photocopy, recording, or any information storage and retrieval system, without permission in writing from the publisher.

Copyright © 1995 by Westview Press, Inc.

Published in 1995 in the United States of America by Westview Press, Inc., 5500 Central Avenue, Boulder, Colorado 80301-2877, and in the United Kingdom by Westview Press, 12 Hid's Copse Road, Cumnor Hill, Oxford OX2 9JJ

Library of Congress Cataloging-in-Publication Data
Establishing monetary stability in emerging market economies / [edited by] Willett ... [et al].
   p. cm.
  Includes bibliographical references and index.
  ISBN 0-8133-8905-4 (alk. paper)
  1. Monetary policy. 2. Inflation (Finance) 3. Economic stabilization—Government policy. I. Willett, Thomas D.
HG230.3.E86 1995
332.4'91724—dc20   95-14104
                                                                                       CIP

Printed and bound in the United States of America

The paper used in this publication meets the requirements of the American National Standard for Permanence of Paper for Printed Library Materials Z39.48-1984.

10   9   8   7   6   5   4   3   2   1

Contents

Acknowledgments vii
About the Contributors ix

Introduction: The Political Economy of Establishing Monetary Stability, *Thomas D. Willett, Richard C. K. Burdekin, Richard J. Sweeney and Clas Wihlborg* 1

PART ONE
Aspects of the Political Economy of Inflation

1 The High Costs of Monetary Instability, *Richard C. K. Burdekin, Suyono Salamun and Thomas D. Willett* 13

2 Budget Deficits and Inflation: The Importance of Budget Controls for Monetary Stability, *Richard C. K. Burdekin* 33

3 Inflation and Optimal Seigniorage in the CIS and Eastern Europe, *King Banaian* 63

4 The Politics of Inflation: An Empirical Assessment of the Emerging Market Economies, *Marina Arbetman and Jacek Kugler* 81

PART TWO
Institutional Mechanisms for Promoting Economic Stability

5 Guidelines for Constructing Monetary Constitutions, *Thomas D. Willett* 103

6 Designing Central Bank Arrangements to Promote Monetary Stability, *Richard C. K. Burdekin and Thomas D. Willett* 115

7 Central Banking in Economies in Transition, *Eduard Hochreiter*   127

8 Alternative Approaches to Monetary Reform in the Formerly
   Communist Countries: A Parallel Strategy, *Annelise Anderson*   145

PART THREE
Case Studies

9 The Russian Central Bank and the Conduct of Monetary Policy,
   Stephen Lewarne   167

10 Impediments to the Macroeconomic Stabilization of Russia,
    Manuel Hinds   193

11 The Collapse of the Ruble Zone, 1991–93, *King Banaian
    and Eugenue Zhukov*   209

12 The Latvian Monetary Reform, *George J. Viksnins and Ilmars
    Rimshevitchs*   231

13 Fiscal and Monetary Policies in the Transition: Searching for
    the Credit Crunch, *Pierre Siklos and István Ábel*   237

About the Book   269

Acknowledgments

This is the first of a series of volumes that have been generated by a collaborative research effort on economic reform in the former communist countries among the Claremont Colleges, Georgetown University and the Gothenburg School of Economics and Commercial Law. The Claremont portion of the project was administered through the Claremont Institute for Economic Policy Studies at the Claremont Graduate School and the Lowe Institute of Political Economy at Claremont McKenna College and was funded primarily through a generous grant from the Lincoln Foundation.[1]

The Georgetown School of Business at Georgetown University provided further support through faculty summer grants, and workshop funding was provided from Georgetown's Finance/Accounting seminar series. Professor Sweeney also wishes to thank the Georgetown University Center for International Business Education and Research for travel and workshop funds, and the Georgetown University Center for Business-Government Relations for supplying summer research assistance.

Activities of the Swedish research group and conferences in Gothenburg, Sweden, and Tallinn, Estonia, were funded by the Royal Academy of Sciences, the Research Council for Humanities and Social Research, and the School of Economics and Commercial Law at Gothenburg University, Sweden. Additional funding for conferences in Tallinn was provided by the Bank of Keila and the Open Estonian Foundation in Estonia.

A major purpose of the project was to establish economic policy dialogues between Western economists and economists and policy officials from the former communist countries. The emphasis was not on having Western economists tell Eastern economists how they should do things, but rather to enter into discussions which would culminate in shared analysis about the nature of the key issues—even if there was not always agreement about policy recommendations. To this end we organized a substantial number of conferences and workshops which brought economists and officials from the former communist countries to Claremont, Georgetown, and Gothenburg and brought groups of Western economists to locations in Central Europe and the former Soviet Union. We especially appreciate the cooperation of local host institutions: the Czech National Bank in Prague, the Czech Republic; Tallinn

Technical University in Tallinn, Estonia; the Institute for World Economics in Budapest, Hungary; and the Institute for Advanced Studies and the Austrian National Bank in Vienna, Austria.

The papers in this and the companion volumes evolved out of this series of conferences and workshops. We are pleased at the number of authors from the former communist countries as well as from the West. A major unanticipated benefit of the project was the dialogues that were promoted among economists from the former communist countries. It quickly became clear that the tradition of international interaction among economists which is so common in the West had been stifled in the East under communism. There were not-infrequent interactions among economists in Moscow and local capitals, but little contact between economists across the satellite countries and republics. We are pleased to have been able to contribute to the breaking down of these walls between economists of different nations.

Special thanks go to Pamela Martin of the Claremont Institute of Economic Policy Studies and Jane Williams of the Lowe Institute of Political Economy for their excellent work in preparing the manuscript for publication.

Thomas D. Willett
Richard C. K. Burdekin
Richard J. Sweeney
Clas Wihlborg

1. The Lincoln Foundation places particular emphasis on the work of the nineteenth century American economist Henry George. A major focus of the Claremont portion of the project was on the relevance of Henry George's ideas to economic reform in the former communist countries. George was a strong advocate of the market and would undoubtedly have been pleased with the breakdown of communism. As our project developed, it became clear that a major priority in these countries was to bring inflation under control. George wrote little on inflation per se; it was not a major problem in his time. But his most famous proposal—that of a single tax on land—followed directly from his desire to promote economic growth through minimizing the damage done to the operation of the economy by inefficient taxation. This volume argues that inflation is one of the most damaging forms of taxation. The logic of George's approach would clearly put control of inflation high on the policy agenda.

About the Contributors

István Ábel, General Manager, Budapest Bank, and Professor of Economics, Budapest University of Economics.

Annelise Anderson, Senior Research Fellow, Hoover Institution, Stanford University.

Marina Arbetman, Associate Professor of Political Science, Tulane University.

King Banaian, Associate Professor of Economics, St. Cloud State University and Pitzer College.

Richard C. K. Burdekin, Associate Professor of Economics, Claremont McKenna College and The Claremont Graduate School.

Manuel Hinds, Private Consultant: Advisor to the Central Bank of El Salvador, the World Bank and in Eastern Europe and Russia.

Eduard Hochreiter, Chief of Foreign Research Division, Austrian National Bank.

Jacek Kugler, Elisabeth Helm Rosecrans Professor of International Relations, The Claremont Graduate School.

Stephen Lewarne, Advisor, State Committee for Economics, Kyrgyz Republic.

Ilmars Rimshevitchs, Vice President of the Bank of Latvia.

Suyono Salamun, Economist, Government of Indonesia.

Pierre Siklos, Associate Professor of Economics, Wilfrid Laurier University.

Richard J. Sweeney, Sullivan Dean Professor of International Finance at Georgetown University.

George Viksnins, Professor of Economics, Georgetown University and Senior Advisor to the Bank of Latvia.

Clas Wihlborg, Felix Neubergh Professor of Banking and Financial Economics at Gothenburg University.

Thomas D. Willett, Horton Professor of Economics, Claremont McKenna College and The Claremont Graduate School.

Eugenue Zhukov, Ph.D. candidate, Rice University.

Introduction: The Political Economy of Establishing Monetary Stability

Thomas D. Willett, Richard C. K. Burdekin, Richard J. Sweeney and Clas Wihlborg

Reform has gone badly wrong in many of the formerly centrally planned economies. Economists did not think that the reform process would be easy, but few anticipated how difficult the transition would prove for so many of the countries of central and eastern Europe and the former Soviet Union. There are bright spots, however; the performance of the Baltic nations and such countries as the Czech Republic, Hungary and Poland stand out in comparison with most of the economies in transition from centrally planned to market systems. The different degrees of success are perhaps most visible in the vast dispersion of rates of inflation, reported in the table below. Russia and many of the republics of the former Soviet Union have flirted with hyperinflation, but other countries, such as the Czech Republic and Hungary, have reduced inflation to industrial-country levels, and Estonia, Lithuania, Poland, and Slovenia have managed to keep inflation within a range of 20 to 50 percent a year—not ideal, but far better than the annual rates in the hundreds and thousands of percent per year that have characterized a majority of the formerly centrally planned economies. (For analysis of the role of inflation in the economic reform process in these countries, see the papers in this volume by Arbetman and Kugler, Banaian, Lewarne, Hinds, Viksnins and Rimshevitchs, and Siklos and Ábel.)

These differences in inflation performance largely mirror the progress of reform in these countries; in our judgment this is not coincidental. Though much debate among professional economists has focused on technical disputes

Selected Economic Indicators

Country	Inflation (1992)[a]	Currency[b]	Exchange Rate Arrangements
Russia	1341	Ruble	Flexible
Ukraine	2733	Karbovanets (11/93)	Flexible
Uzbekistan	699	Ruble and Coupons	
Kazakhstan	944	Ruble and Tanga	
Belarus	1116	Ruble and Ruble	
Azerbeijan	1174	Manat	Flexible
Georgia	1278	Ruble and Coupon	Coupon floats vs ruble
Tajikistan	1013	Ruble	
Kyrygystan	1006	Som (6/93)	Flexible
Moldova	1044	Ruble and Coupon	
Turkmenistan	931	Ruble	
Armenia	829	Ruble	
Estonia	41	Kroon (6/92)	Pegged at 8 Kr:1DM
Latvia	53	Lat (3/93)	Pegged to basket of currencies
Lithuania	36	Litas (6/93)	Currency board pegged to dollar
Bulgaria	61	Lev	Flexible
Czech Republic	11	Koruna	Pegged
Hungary	19	Forint	Frequently adjusted peg
Poland	47	Zloty	Preannounced crawl
Slovenia	23	Tolar	Flexible

[a] First quarter of 1993 at annual rate for Estonia, Latvia and Lithuania. 1993 annual data for Bulgaria and Slovenia.
[b] Dates of adoption for new currencies given in parentheses.
Source: Adapted from Willett and Al-Marhubi (1995).

about the optimal content and sequencing of reforms, economists actually working on reform efforts have become increasingly aware of the extent to which political considerations both drive and impede economic reform. There have been examples of bad policies adopted on the basis of bad economics—such as the fueling of inflation by central bank officials who denied that there was any connection between the massive credits they were creating and the inflation that raged around them. We have been impressed, however, by how deeply economists from the formerly centrally planned economies understand mainstream Western economics.

The contribution of bad economic policy advice to the failures of the economic reform process has generally been far outweighed by failures of political reform that have generated pressures to slow economic liberalization and to follow highly inflationary budget policies.

Economic analysis was slow to recognize the detrimental effects of inflation. For years economists popularized the notion that a little inflation might be good for growth. Today, however, we have a much better, though still incomplete, understanding of the longer-run costs of inflation. Unanticipated inflation can help reduce unemployment and increase economic growth in the short run, but these favorable effects are temporary: they disappear as expectations adjust. Moreover, because high inflation rates tend to be more unstable and generate greater uncertainty, the longer-run effects of inflation on growth are typically negative. Indeed, the empirical estimates that Burdekin, Salamun and Willett present in this volume suggest that in the case of developed market systems the growth costs of inflation can be substantial.

A central tenet of the analysis in this volume is that successful economic liberalization is virtually impossible when inflation is not under control. Countries do not run high, stable rates of inflation; almost inevitably high rates of inflation are quite variable as new stabilization efforts are launched and abandoned. This generates tremendous uncertainty and undermines the effectiveness of the price system. Such effects are especially pernicious in countries where a substantial proportion of the public is just learning to use markets in the first place. Perhaps even worse is the danger that the public will come to falsely associate inflation with the operation of the market system itself, rather than recognize that inflation is primarily the result of poor government policies. Under such a scenario, not only is the performance of the economy undermined in the short run, but over the longer term the outlook for the sustainability of the liberalization process is worsened.

Economists generally agree that inflation is in an important sense a monetary phenomenon. Though many types of developments can influence prices and inflation rates in the short run (crop failures, oil shocks, major financial innovations, etc.), any major sustained inflation has to be accommodated, if not initiated, by excessive monetary expansion. Thus, at the technical level economists certainly know how to prevent major, sustained inflation and how to end it. But knowing the relevant economics is only part of the answer to controlling inflation.

For some time economists have recognized that we also need to understand the forces that generate monetary expansions. Thus, analysis of the political economy of monetary policy and inflation has become a prominent subfield in both economics and political science.[1] Some sociological and political analyses of inflation go so far as to treat inflation primarily as the outcome of social conflicts. We agree that the more serious are the underlying social, cultural, and political conflicts within a country, the more likely is inflation. It is important to carefully relate such underlying conflicts to the nature of the monetary process, however. The authors in this volume see institutional arrangements as important, though often not dominant. The adoption of a good set of monetary institutions will not save a deeply divided society from economic policy problems. Modern political economy analysis suggests, however, that even where the underlying social and political situation is relatively stable, as in most Western democracies, the disaggregated nature of the operation of our political and economic systems often creates incentives for particular groups to pursue ends that are detrimental to the overall operation of the economy. The push of workers, managers, and owners in particular industries to secure tariffs and quotas to protect themselves from foreign competition is a classic example in public choice analysis.[2]

An analog for macroeconomic policy is that the push for credits for various industries results in overexpansion of the money supply. (See Manuel Hinds's chapter in this volume for the case of Russia.) Problems are not limited to the general jockeying for special favors on the expenditure and credit side and less taxation on the revenue side, with resulting budget deficits; often a substantial difference in the short-run and long-run effects of macroeconomic policies creates another important bias toward inflation. When more expansionary policies are adopted, particularly if the changes are surprises, the favorable effects of expanding employment and output tend to show up first; the costly effects of increased inflation lag behind. With contractionary policies to fight inflation the opposite happens: the politically costly effects of falling output and employment tend to show up first, the beneficial effects of lower inflation later. If the political process operates with a short time horizon, then even though the employment and output effects are temporary and the changes in inflation often lasting, there is a bias towards overexpansion that cuts against anti-inflationary macroeconomic policies.[3]

Short-run political pressures, frequent in the relatively stable democracies, are likely to be even greater in newly emerging democracies. Large numbers of parties and rapid turnover can make it extremely difficult for politicians to focus on the broader picture and take adequate account of longer-run considerations. In such situations the adoption of monetary institutions that reduce the impact of short-run political pressures on monetary policymaking becomes even more important. A major portion of this volume analyzes ways in which monetary policymaking may be at least partially depoliticized: the objective is not to override the democratic process but to base monetary policymaking on long-run rather than short-run interests.

Our contributors bring with them considerable understanding of the ways that institutional arrangements can be circumvented. They are not satisfied with preaching that central banks should be made independent, but give careful consideration to the types of institutional details that seem likely to make arrangements more or less effective in practice. (For analysis of the importance of the details of central bank arrangements, see the chapters by Burdekin and Willett, Hochreiter, and Lewarne.) We should add that while all of the contributions to this volume refer to monetary issues in Central and Eastern Europe and the former Soviet Union, the issues are largely the same in many developing countries that are engaged in substantial liberalization. Thus the reference in the title of the volume to emerging market economies is not limited to formerly communist states.

The authors believe reforms such as central bank independence are insufficient in themselves to guarantee that inflation will be avoided. Rather, central bank independence should be a complement to a wide array of measures designed to resist pressures toward inflationary policies. As Richard Burdekin stresses in his discussion of budget deficits, it is virtually impossible for economies without developed capital markets to avoid financing a substantial part of a large deficit with money creation.[4] Thus, progress on budget control is especially important for economies in transition. In a similar vein the chapters by Hinds and by Siklos and Ábel stress the importance of how the financing of state enterprises and the development of the private banking and financial systems influences the pressure for accommodative monetary policies. Eduard Hochreiter emphasizes how the process of wage bargaining can help or hinder the task of the monetary authorities. In this regard, one of the most hotly debated issues concerns what type of exchange rate regime best complements domestic efforts to create monetary stability. As is discussed in the overview chapter by Willett, "Guidelines for Constructing Monetary Constitutions," there is no simple answer to this question. Given the complicated nature of this issue we have devoted a companion volume to its exploration (Sweeney, Wihlborg, and Willett; forthcoming).

The theory of optimum currency areas demonstrates that the type of exchange rate regime that is good for one country may be bad for another, thereby providing an example of the need for economists to tailor their policy proposals to the particular situation of the country in question.[5] Of course there are many basic economic principles that hold over almost any kind of economy. Reducing inflation requires reducing the rate of growth of the money supply, and promoting the optimum level of market transactions requires equilibrium prices. But, as we move to the political economy underpinnings of economic policies, specific knowledge of the country in question is increasingly important. The danger of thinking that institutions developed in the West will work the same way in the East is particularly emphasized in the chapter by Annelise Anderson in this volume. Study of the economies in transition is having a healthy effect on Western economists, forcing attention to the important economic roles played by underlying legal and political frameworks—roles economists have often tended to take for granted.[6]

Recognition of the potential costs of inflation increases the case for giving substantial priority to anti-inflationary policies, not just in those economies where inflation is running in the hundreds and thousands of percent, but also for those relative success stories, such as Hungary and Poland, where inflation is running in the range of 20 to 40 percent a year. Though virtually all economists worry about inflation in the upper ranges, a number of economists are relatively sanguine about the costs of more moderate inflation. Indeed, the literature on the optimal inflation tax suggests that such rates of inflation may be part of an optimal regime of public finance: that is, moderate inflation may not reflect a failure to control the budget and money growth but may instead represent a reasonable form of taxation that recognizes the costs of other ways of raising government revenue. Because tax collection is often particularly difficult in transition economies, some observers argue that these countries should rely more on the inflation tax than the industrial democracies. As King Banaian discusses in his paper in this volume, there is some truth to this argument. There is a major problem, however, with the standard literature on the optimal inflation tax: this literature has assumed that inflation is perfectly anticipated, and by doing so, it has assumed away the uncertainty effects of inflation, the most important part of inflation's economic cost. Taking these uncertainty costs into account drastically reduces optimal inflation taxes.

The recent research on this issue does not conclusively show that continued inflation in the 20 to 40 percent range will seriously retard the medium- and long-term growth prospects of economies in transition, but it raises the prospect that this is a serious risk. Prudence suggests that transition economies continue efforts to reduce inflation, at least until a single-digit level is hit. This will not be easy, but the experience of countries like the Czech Republic show that it is possible.[7]

Even after completing such initial adjustments as decontrolling prices and recalculating the weights in price indices to reflect the changing composition of economic activity, however, countries that succeed in keeping their prices of internationally traded goods constant relative to those in low-inflation trading partners will likely face inflation in sectors of their economy where productivity is growing less rapidly. The greater is productivity growth in the most dynamic sectors, the more important will be such differential price trends. As productivity grows in the tradeable goods sector, wages and other factor rewards will rise even with constant tradeables prices. These higher factor rewards in the tradeables sector will push up rewards in the non-tradeables sector where productivity is likely growing more slowly. Thus, unit costs are likely to rise in the non-tradeables sector, pushing up prices there even though tradeables prices and unit costs are more or less constant.

Because consumer price indices include both tradeables and non-tradeables, inflation as measured by the CPI is likely to be positive; therefore, as liberalizing countries have greater potential for productivity growth than developed countries, simply by catching up to developed countries, CPI inflation may be higher in liberalizing than in developed countries. Indeed, the faster is growth in the liberalizing country, the higher may CPI inflation be. Still, for the average factor owner, this inflation will be more than offset by rising factor incomes.[8] While it is, of course, possible that all this could be handled without overall inflation through price declines in the sectors of greatest productivity growth—think, for example, of what has happened to the price of computers—this would require exchange-rate appreciation.

There is a substantial body of literature suggesting that rates of consumer price inflation tend to be greater in economies with more rapid productivity growth.[9] As this relationship is inevitable for countries that maintain fixed exchange rates against a non-inflationary trading partner with slower productivity growth, some economists have spoken of inflation as the price of rapid development.[10] This argument is basically correct, but it should be stressed that it is quite different from the traditional type of Keynesian argument that a little inflation is good for growth, and it can be used to explain (justify) only limited rates of inflation in overall price indices. It does suggest, however, that monetary authorities should pay particular attention to the rate of inflation in their home-produced traded-goods sectors and should worry less about moderate rates of inflation in the consumer price index. Many economists in emerging market economies understand this point; they are sanguine about domestic price increases that leave their international sectors competitive.

This volume is organized into three parts. The first considers a number of the most important aspects of the political economy of inflation. The second focuses on proposals for the development of monetary institutions that will help combat the political and economic pressures to generate inflation. Part three presents case studies that highlight a number of the key factors which have contributed to success in controlling inflation in some countries and to failure in many more.

Notes

1. See, for example, the analysis and references in Alesina (1988), Willett (1988), Haggard and Kaufman (1992), and Havrilesky (1993). The paper by Arbetman and Kugler in this volume applies a new quantitative measure of the political strength of governments to the analysis of inflation.

2. For public choice analysis of protectionist policies see the analysis and references in Odell and Willett (1990).

3. See the analysis and references in Willett (1988).

4. To be sure, foreign grants and loans can help finance government spending in noninflationary ways while the government is reducing the budget deficits; examples are "stabilization" loans proposed for Russia and Ukraine.

5. For recent treatments of the theory of optimum currency areas see Wihlborg and Willett (1991) and Tavlas (1993), and for applications to the formerly centrally planned economies see Willett and Al-Marhubi (1995). Such analysis will be a major focus of Sweeney, Wihlborg, and Willett (forthcoming).

6. We should emphasize that law and economics, public choice and political economy scholars have long recognized the importance of institutions. Indeed, a recent movement in economics has been labeled the new institutional economics. For examples and references see North (1990), Vaubel and Willett (1991), and Yarbrough and Yarbrough (1992).

7. One important caveat concerns the measurement of inflation. As controlled prices are liberalized there are often substantial price increases. These adjustments to market clearing prices are not true inflation, although they are often reported as such. This is a form of "inflation" that helps promote growth.

8. In the early stages of price liberalization, there may often be catch-up inflation. Suppose tradeables prices are liberalized first. As non-tradeables prices are then liberalized, measured inflation continues. Further, if some non-tradeables prices are sluggish, it may take several months or quarters for non-tradeables prices to achieve an equilibrium relative to the tradeables prices determined in world markets (subject to transportation and trade-barrier costs).

9. See Balassa (1964), Officer (1976) and Sweeney and Willett (1976). For recent analysis see Kravis and Lipsey (1988).

10. Sepp (1994).

References

Alesina, Alberto. 1988. "Macroeconomics and Politics" in Stanley Fischer, ed., *NBER Macroeconomics Annual 1988*. Pp. 13–52. Cambridge, Mass.: The MIT Press.

Balassa, B. 1964. "The Purchasing Power Parity Doctrine: A Reappraisal." *Journal of Political Economy* 72: 584–96.

Haggard, Stephan, and Robert R. Kaufman, eds. 1992. *The Politics of Economic Adjustment—International Constraints, Distributive Conflict, and the State*. Princeton, N.J.: Princeton University Press.

Havrilesky, Thomas. 1993. *The Pressures on American Monetary Policy*. Boston, Mass.: Kluwer Academic Publishers.

Kravis, Irving B., and Richard E. Lipsey. 1988. "National Price Levels and the Prices of Tradables and Nontradables." *American Economic Review Papers and Proceedings* 78: 474–78.

Odell, John S., and Thomas D. Willett. 1990. *International Trade Policies: Gains from Exchange Between Economics and Political Science*. Ann Arbor, Mich.: The University of Michigan Press.

Officer, Lawrence H. 1976. "The Purchasing Power Parity Theory of Exchange Rates: A Review Article." *International Monetary Fund Staff Papers* 23: 1–60.

North, Douglass C. 1990. *Institutions, Institutional Change and Economic Performance*. Cambridge: Cambridge University Press.

Sepp, Urmas. 1994. "Inflation in Estonia: The Cost of Development." Paper for the conference on Restructuring Financial Institutions in Emerging Market Economies in Tallinn, Estonia, October 17–18, 1994.

Sweeney, Richard J., Clas Wihlborg and Thomas D. Willett, eds. forthcoming. *Currency Policies for Emerging Market Economies*. Boulder, Colo.: Westview Press.

Sweeney, Richard J., and Thomas D. Willett. 1976. "The International Transmission of Inflation," in Michele Fratianni and Karel Tavevnier, eds., *Bank Credit, Money, and Inflation in Open Economies*. Pp. 441–517. Supplement to *Kredit und Kapital*.

Tavlas, George S. 1993. "The 'New' Theory of Optimum Currency Areas." *World Economy* 16: 663–85

Vaubel, Roland, and Thomas D. Willett, eds. 1991. *The Political Economy of International Organizations: A Public Choice Approach*. Boulder. Colo.: Westview Press.

Wihlborg, Clas, and Thomas D. Willett. 1991. "Optimum Currency Areas Revisited on the Transition Path to a Currency Union," in Clas Wihlborg, Michele Fratianni and Thomas D. Willett, eds., *Financial Regulation and Monetary Arrangements After 1992*. Pp. 270–97. Amsterdam: Elsevier.

Willett, Thomas D., ed. 1988. *Political Business Cycles: The Political Economy of Money, Inflation, and Unemployment*. Durham, N.C.: Duke University Press.

Willett, Thomas D., and Fahim Al-Marhubi. 1995. "Currency Policies for Inflation Control in the Formerly Centrally Planned Economies." *World Economy*, forthcoming.

Yarbrough, Beth, and Robert Yarbrough. 1992. *Cooperation and Governance in International Trade: The Strategic Organizational Approach*. Princeton: Princeton University Press.

PART ONE

Aspects of the Political Economy of Inflation

1

The High Costs of Monetary Instability

*Richard C. K. Burdekin, Suyono Salamun
and
Thomas D. Willett[1]*

Why is control of inflation given such emphasis by most economists working on economic reform? The answer has less to do with the direct effects of rising prices themselves—uncomfortable as these may be—than with the uncertainties generated by high rates of inflation.

In the following section we discuss the nature of these costs. While many inflation costs are not quantifiable, several empirical studies have investigated the effects of inflation on economic growth and per capita incomes. Contrary to the old Phillips curve view that increasing inflation is good for employment and growth, recent research finds that this type of relationship tends to hold only in the short run and that, over the longer term, inflation is harmful to growth. In sections 3 and 4 we discuss this literature and present new empirical work of our own. In section 5 we consider the implications of this research for the economies in transition.

Why Is Inflation Costly?

Conceptually, we can conceive of a steady annual rate of inflation of 100 percent. The effects of such a high but stable inflation would be relatively modest. There would, of course, be distortions from the corresponding tax on the holding of non-interest bearing currency—the consideration emphasized in the misleadingly named literature on the optimal rate of inflation[2]—and costs from changing prices using more complicated price schedules. But the real economy could continue to operate reasonably effectively up to the point where high inflation gives way to hyperinflation. What undermines the operation of the economy most is uncertainty about whether inflation next year will again be 100 percent or will fall to 50 percent or rise to 150 percent. In such circumstances much of the value of the information communicated in a well-functioning price system is destroyed.[3]

Consideration of the real economic factors that should determine the allocation of resources over time becomes secondary to guessing the future rate of inflation. Under stable monetary conditions, expected real rates of interest for different classes of borrowers typically range between 0 and 20 percent, with real rates for long-term borrowing to finance capital investment typically ranging between 2 and 10 percent. Variations in the rate of inflation in high-inflation countries become far more important. For example, if the best estimate of next year's inflation is 100 percent and this forecast is held with confidence, then a one-year loan might carry a nominal interest rate of say 110 percent. High inflation rates are seldom steady, however. Suppose (realistically) that with a best forecast inflation rate there is a good chance of the actual inflation rate turning out to be 75 percent or 125 percent. With the former the borrower would pay a real rate of interest of 35 percent. With the latter, the ex post real rate of interest would be -15 percent, and the lender would lose considerable money on the loan.

As a result of this uncertainty, market-determined interest rates tend to build in a substantial risk premium that discourages investment. This risk premium will also generally be greater the longer the maturity of the loan as the cumulative risk of unanticipated changes in the price level mounts. Longer-term lending for capital investments may virtually come to a halt. Indexing loans and wage contracts to inflation can reduce some of this risk, but not eliminate it. The problem is that not all prices move together: there can be considerable variability in relative prices. Borrowers would like to have loans indexed to changes in the prices of their particular inputs and output, but this would be much less attractive to the lender who would be exposed to the risk of variability in relative prices.

At high rates of inflation, even making comparisons of prices for immediate sale or purchase can become difficult. Inflation, and the uncertainties it tends to bring, can greatly impede the operation of the price system and hence seriously damage the ability of people and firms to engage in the extensive levels of specialization and exchange needed to produce high levels of output and income. The costs of inflation are more than just economic in nature. Severe inequities can be generated through capricious income redistribution caused by unanticipated changes in the rate of inflation. With high inflation, the fabric of societal relationships and the operation of the political system itself can be severely strained. It is ironic that in the initial stages a little bit of unanticipated inflation may be a low-cost way of resolving distributional conflicts in society.

But history shows that the risk is high that a little bit of inflation will lead to a little bit more and so on, until soon inflation will be generating rather than relieving social tensions. As Ottmar Emminger, former Bundesbank president, once pointed out: "In the long run, an economy cannot have 'just a little inflation,' for if you start flirting with inflation, it will end up marrying you."[4]

While the reasons why higher rates of inflation tend to be more variable and hence generate more uncertainty are not entirely clear, the historical association is strong.[5] There is, however, little reason to expect a simple mechanical relationship between average rates of inflation and their variability. Much of the resulting variability is likely due to political pressures and policy reactions as well as to fluctuations in economic variables such as investment and velocity. Critics of a strong positive link between inflation and its variability have pointed to substantial instability in the estimates of these relations across different time periods and have suggested that, for example, the tendency for high inflation rates to be more variable over the postwar period in the United States was due to the timing of major supply shocks from OPEC that happened to coincide with the high-inflation period of that decade. These criticisms have validity in that the supply shocks of the 1970s did contribute to the positive correlation between inflation and its variability in the 1970s. Yet substantial correlation remains even after the effects of the supply shocks are removed.[6] In our view, these critiques make a valid point in that one should not expect a precise relationship to hold between inflation rates and their variability. But this does not contradict the large body of statistical evidence supporting the view that if the average rate of inflation increases substantially, the variability of inflation and the resulting inflation uncertainty is also likely to increase.

A better understanding of the political and economic underpinnings is certainly an important area for research, but one need not wait for the outcomes of such research to argue it would be highly imprudent for policymakers to believe that inflation rates can be stabilized at high levels in such a way as to obviate inflation uncertainty. Thus, while we applaud the substantial progress made by Russia in reducing its inflation rates during 1993 and 1994, we read with dismay press reports of President Yeltsin's statement that inflation was to be stabilized in the 5 to 7 percent per month range.[7] Due to compounding, this would imply an annual rate of inflation between 79.6 and 125.2 percent. While there are examples of inflation rates in this range being kept fairly stable for a year or two, the odds that this could be accomplished are not great. It is much more likely that short-term stabilization in this range would be followed by a renewed acceleration of inflation within a few years. Furthermore, even if inflation were stabilized within this monthly range, there is a 45.6 percent spread between the annualized effects of 5 percent monthly inflation and the annualized effects of 7 percent monthly inflation. This difference would carry with it the potential for high variability in annual inflation rates and implies considerable uncertainty for ex post real interest rates and the real value of contracts.

Empirical Estimates of the Economic Costs of Inflation

It is virtually impossible to accurately measure many of the various types of economic costs generated by inflation. We know that, at the microeconomic level, greater inflation uncertainty will tend to lead not only to a reduction in the volume of activity but also to more mistakes in economic transactions as economic agents' expectations turn out to be incorrect. Although we do not have estimates of the full magnitude of these misallocation effects, there is a substantial literature on the costs arising from the incentives generated by inflation to economize excessively on the use of cash balances. These costs are discussed in the accompanying chapter in this volume by Banaian (1995).

There remains, however, a growing empirical literature on the effects of inflation on economic growth and levels of production. Unfortunately, in addition to all of the standard problems involved with drawing causal inferences from estimated correlations, especially the possibility that third factors are affecting both inflation and growth, there are two particular statistical problems in this area of research. One is that it is primarily the variability or uncertainty associated with inflation that is expected to have a detrimental effect on growth. Measures of variability or uncertainty typically require the use of measures based on relationships over a number of periods such as standard deviations. As a consequence, studies using such measures are primarily cross sectional in nature, with perhaps the addition of a few observations over time based on, say, decade averages. With such cross-sectional data one worries about spurious correlations resulting from country-specific factors, even when many other determinants of growth are included in the regression equations.

An alternative approach is to use inflation rates directly and rely upon the type of positive relationships between rates and variability of inflation found in previous studies. This reduced-form approach allows one to use time-series analysis on data for each country. Since the costs of inflation are expected to flow largely from the uncertainty generated, we have reservations about attempting to include measures for both inflation and inflation variability in the same equation. Where this is done one typically finds a significant effect for one variable or the other but not for both (see, for example, Cooper 1992). In such cases, one needs to be careful about the interpretation offered. Where the variability-of-inflation measure is significant and the inflation variable in the same equation is insignificant, we do not believe that this warrants the interpretation that inflation does not adversely affect growth. In particular, Cooper (1992:94), having found a significant adverse effect from the variability of inflation on growth in a large sample of developing countries, may not have been justified in concluding that, because the inflation rate was not also significant in his equations, "the proposition that inflation is a serious drag on growth does not stand up empirically."

A second major problem with simply regressing annual rates of growth on annual rates of inflation is that for many countries the short-run statistical

Phillips curve is alive and well. Where aggregate demand rather than supply shocks dominate, an unanticipated increase in the rate of inflation is frequently associated with a short-run increase in the rate of growth—while a reduction in inflation may well be associated with a short-run decrease in the rate of growth. Thus, the old-fashioned idea that a little inflation is good for growth still holds for many economies in the short run with respect to unanticipated inflation.

To gain an accurate picture of the harmful medium- and longer-run effects of inflation on growth, the short-run effects of unanticipated changes in the rate of inflation need to be purged from the analysis. Grimes (1991) suggests a simple method by which this may be at least partially accomplished. By entering the change in the inflation rate in the growth equation along with the actual rate of inflation, one has a proxy for the first-period effects of unanticipated shifts in the inflation rate. While the simple change form used assumes that people expect this year's inflation rate to be the same as last year's, one could of course develop more sophisticated approaches for proxying the unanticipated component of the current inflation rate and consider short-run effects over multiple periods. Nevertheless, Grimes finds that, with annual data, his simple formulation—which also includes an import price variable to account for the effects of supply shocks—provides strong empirical results for the industrial countries.

Grimes uses wholesale prices for his inflation variable. We estimated the same pattern of equations using consumer prices and got similar results. Our findings are reported in Table 1.1. (See the Appendix for details of our data sources and estimation techniques.) We find considerable evidence of a short-run Phillips curve tradeoff. The coefficient of the change in the rate of inflation on the rate of growth is positive for eighteen of the twenty-three countries and significantly so for ten. More importantly for our purposes, we find significant negative effects of the rate of inflation on growth for fifteen countries and the signs are also negative for seven of the eight countries whose coefficients are not significant. Furthermore, the estimated effects for many of the countries are quite large. The coefficients for the United States, Sweden, Switzerland, Japan, and Luxembourg all lie between -0.5 and -0.6, and those for Denmark, Germany, Finland, Greece, and Australia all fall between -0.3 and -0.5. France, Italy, Portugal, the United Kingdom, and Spain also all have significant coefficients of -0.14 or above. The latter coefficients would imply that a 10 percent increase in the rate of inflation would reduce the average annual rate of growth by 1.5 to 2.5 percentage points, while for the larger estimated effects a negative rate of growth would be implied for most economies.

The use of Grimes's simple formulation allows us to also combine time-series and cross-section data. Using a panel approach on this pooled data (see Burdekin et al. 1994) we find a highly significant coefficient of -0.123 for the full sample and one of -0.232 for the sample of fifteen industrial countries for which the coefficients from the individual time-series equations were found to be

TABLE 1.1 Effects of Inflation on Growth in the Industrial Countries

Countries	Time Periods	Number Observ.	Inflation	Change in Inflation	Time	Oil Price	R^2
1. United States	1961-1990	30	-0.51***	0.25*	-0.02	0.006	0.39
2. United Kingdom	1961-1990	30	-0.17***	-0.04	0.10***	-0.03***	0.45
3. Belgium	1961-1990	30	-0.23	0.39*	0.01	-0.03***	0.55
4. Denmark	1961-1990	30	-0.42***	0.03	-0.16***	0.01	0.44
5. France	1961-1990	30	-0.14*	0.15	-0.07**	-0.01*	0.71
6. Germany	1961-1990	30	-0.45***	0.28	-0.003	0.03***	0.39
7. Italy	1961-1990	30	-0.23**	0.38***	-0.09**	-0.01	0.43
8. Netherlands	1961-1990	30	-0.12	0.27	-0.12	0.27	0.49
9. Norway	1961-1990	30	0.32	-0.15	-0.04	-0.04	0.13
10. Sweden	1961-1990	30	-0.55***	0.28***	-0.09***	0.02**	0.62
11. Switzerland	1961-1990	30	-0.59***	0.85***	-0.10**	-0.01	0.58
12. Canada	1961-1990	30	-0.19	0.56***	-0.03	-0.01	0.31
13. Japan	1961-1990	30	-0.51***	0.21***	-0.31***	-0.03***	0.76
14. Finland	1961-1990	30	-0.34***	0.32***	-0.05	0.01	0.18
15. Greece	1961-1990	30	-0.37***	0.08	0.01	0.004	0.62
16. Iceland	1961-1990	30	-0.05	-0.08	-0.09	-0.02	0.20
17. Ireland	1961-1990	30	-0.01	0.02	0.08	-0.03	0.11
18. Spain	1961-1990	30	-0.22***	0.14**	-0.07*	-0.03***	0.76
19. Australia	1961-1990	30	-0.34***	-0.13	-0.06	-0.01	0.59
20. New Zealand	1961-1990	30	-0.19	-0.20*	-0.22***	0.03*	0.27
21. Austria	1965-1990	26	-0.11	0.32*	-0.0004	-0.03	0.43
22. Portugal	1967-1990	24	-0.24**	0.02	-0.03	-0.02	0.42
23. Luxembourg	1961-1990	30	-0.56**	0.78***	0.10	-0.02	0.10

*** significant at 1% level ** significant at 5% level * significant at 10% level
For details of the data and estimation techniques see the Appendix

significant. These results suggest that inflation has a very substantial adverse effect on growth rates in the industrial countries.

We also investigated the effects of inflation on growth in a large sample of developing countries. Here the individual country results were much weaker (see Table 1.2). We found significant negative coefficients on inflation for only fifteen of the forty-nine countries investigated. Relatively large coefficients were found for some countries (for example, -0.15 for the Philippines, -0.27 for Thailand, -0.20 for Mexico, and -0.23 for South Korea) but most of the estimated coefficients were quite small. Using the panel approach, the estimated coefficient for the full sample was a highly significant, but small, -0.001. For the sample of fifteen countries where significant negative coefficients were found in the individual time-series regressions, the estimated panel coefficient was substantially larger (-0.03) but was still roughly an order of magnitude below the coefficients found for the industrial countries.

Qualitatively similar findings with respect to the relative coefficients in industrial and developing countries are reported by Cozier and Selody (1992) and Motley (1994). It is not entirely clear what should be made of these findings. Given their much greater use of the price system and financial markets, we find it plausible that the industrial countries would be more susceptible to the adverse effects of inflation than would most developing countries (see Burdekin et al. 1994). In effect, the very types of factors that allow the industrial countries to engage more effectively in specialization and exchange, and thus enjoy higher incomes, may also make them more sensitive to the effects of inflation. Such an interpretation is consistent with the findings of Cozier and Selody that the adverse effects of inflation fall more strongly on levels of per capita income than they do on growth rates.

There has been much debate about what types of country experiences are most relevant as lessons for the economies in transition. With respect to many issues, the consensus has been that lessons from the developing countries are the most relevant. We would be quite cautious, however, in using our estimates of the cost of inflation in developing countries as grounds for arguing that the economies in transition can take a relatively relaxed attitude toward bringing inflation under control. For one thing, a number of these countries have not-unrealistic expectations of coming close to industrial country standards of living within a decade or two and are currently laying the infrastructure for market economies. For such countries as the Czech Republic, Hungary, and Slovenia, estimates of the costs of inflation in industrial countries are surely of some relevance.

Furthermore, there is good reason to believe that our estimating procedures underestimate the costs of inflation in a developing country sample that evinces a far greater range of inflation rates than our industrial country sample. Bolivia, for example, went through a period of hyperinflation while some other countries experienced single-digit or low double-digit inflation rates. As is typical of

TABLE 1.2 Effects of Inflation on Growth in the Developing Countries

Countries	Time Periods	Number Observ.	Inflation	Change in Inflation	Time	Oil Price	R^2
1. Argentina	1961-1990	30	-0.0001	-0.002***	-0.04	-0.05*	0.33
2. Bolivia	1961-1990	30	-0.001***	0.001***	-0.05	-0.07***	0.83
3. Costa Rica	1961-1990	30	-0.05***	-0.03**	0.09*	-0.06***	0.75
4. El Salvador	1961-1990	30	-0.14	0.07	0.20	-0.10***	0.55
5. Guatemala	1961-1990	30	0.03	-0.04	0.01	-0.06***	0.54
6. Honduras	1961-1990	30	-0.25*	0.01	0.01	-0.02	0.22
7. Panama	1961-1990	30	-0.16	0.31	-0.79***	0.09**	0.44
8. Paraguay	1961-1990	30	-0.02	0.02	0.05	-0.006	0.00
9. Peru	1961-1990	30	0.008***	-0.02***	-0.02	-0.36	0.52
10. Uruguay	1961-1990	30	0.03	-0.05***	0.18	-0.05**	0.28
11. Venezuela	1961-1990	30	-0.10***	-0.09***	0.27***	-0.09***	0.62
12. Syria	1961-1990	30	0.12	-0.18	-0.46	0.04	0.12
13. India	1961-1990	30	-0.10	0.09	0.11	0.004	0.05
14. Pakistan	1961-1990	30	0.07	0.04	0.12	0.03	0.34
15. Philippines	1961-1990	30	-0.15*	-0.01	0.03	-0.03**	0.42
16. Sri Lanka	1961-1990	30	0.41**	-0.22	0.06	-0.10**	0.17
17. Singapore	1961-1990	30	-0.04	0.06	0.05	-0.03	0.10
18. Thailand	1961-1990	30	-0.27***	0.13**	0.14*	-0.03	0.18
19. South Africa	1961-1990	30	-0.42***	0.21	0.01	0.01	0.39
20. Turkey	1961-1990	30	-0.09***	-0.01	0.24***	-0.03*	0.35
21. Jamaica	1961-1989	29	-0.30***	0.07	0.09	-0.02	0.45
22. Guyana	1961-1988	28	-0.38**	0.26*	0.18	-0.02	0.18
23. Brazil	1964-1990	27	0.003	-0.012	0.07	-0.07**	0.47
24. Chile	1964-1990	27	-0.02**	0.005	0.24	-0.06	0.26

(continues)

TABLE 1.2 (continued)

25. Dominican Republic	1964-1990	27	-0.28***	0.12***	-0.17	-0.05**	0.42
26. Mauritius	1964-1990	27	-0.12	-0.04	0.14	-0.07**	0.39
27. Mexico	1961-1986	26	-0.20***	-0.03*	0.41***	0.01	0.87
28. Zambia	1962-1987	26	0.22	0.006	-1.06	0.07	0.12
29. Ecuador	1966-1990	25	0.26**	-0.23***	-0.39	-0.05	0.13
30. Indonesia	1966-1990	25	0.02	0.03***	-0.07	-0.004	0.09
31. Nepal	1966-1990	25	-0.04	0.06	0.15	-0.001	0.09
32. Ghana	1966-1990	25	0.03	-0.006	0.41**	-0.11**	0.20
33. Morocco	1966-1990	25	0.44**	0.26	0.13	-0.06**	0.25
34. Tanzania	1966-1990	25	-0.01	0.03	0.02	-0.04**	0.36
35. South Korea	1967-1990	24	-0.23***	0.04	-0.04	-0.03	0.48
36. Haiti	1967-1990	24	0.03	0.17*	-0.02	-0.04	0.30
37. Iran	1965-1988	24	-0.17	0.16	-0.88*	0.07	0.27
38. Trinidad and Tobago	1968-1990	23	0.01	0.09	-0.87	0.05	0.24
39. Liberia	1965-1987	23	-0.03	0.31	0.31	-0.08**	0.05
40. Colombia	1969-1990	22	-0.03	-0.08	0.001	-0.04***	0.57
41. Israel	1969-1990	22	-0.02	0.04**	0.47	-0.08	0.03
42. Tunisia	1969-1990	22	-2.35***	0.61**	-0.54**	0.15***	0.39
43. Kenya	1968-1989	22	0.02	0.06	0.16	-0.06***	0.37
44. Myanmar	1968-1989	22	-0.10**	-0.10**	-0.47***	0.06***	0.68
45. Jordan	1970-1990	21	0.84***	-1.16***	0.73*	-0.03	0.63
46. Saudi Arabia	1969-1989	21	0.04	0.61***	-0.57	-0.10	0.39
47. Zaire	1971-1990	20	-0.06	0.12*	0.45	-0.06	0.34
48. Malaysia	1971-1990	20	-0.21	0.55***	-0.51***	0.03	0.58
49. Burundi	1971-1990	20	-0.13	-0.18	-0.03	0.03	0.12

*** significant at 1% level ** significant at 5% level * significant at 10% level
For details of the data and estimation techniques see the Appendix

the literature in this area, our basic equations assumed a linear relationship for the effects of inflation. In other words, the effects of a one percentage point increase in the rate of inflation are assumed to be the same whether the increase was from 0 to 1 or 10 to 11 or 100 to 101 or even 100,000 to 100,001.

For the range of inflation rates experienced by the industrial countries during the postwar period, this linearization appears to be a reasonable approximation except perhaps at very low rates of inflation. Using our panel approach, we do not begin to find a negative relationship between inflation and growth until one includes data with inflation above 5 percent, and the estimates do not become significant until observations of inflation rates of up to 7 percent are added (see Table 1.3). Given this minimum threshold applies even to the industrial countries, it likely reflects, in part, the problems of constructing price indices that adequately reflect quality improvements and the introduction of new products. Thus, for many countries, measured rates of inflation of the consumer price index of, say, 1 to 3 percent per year may not reflect true inflation. Note, however, that as data on increasingly high rates of inflation are added to the analysis, there is relatively little change in the estimated coefficients. This suggests that above some low threshold value, the effects of inflation in the industrial countries have been approximately linear.

For the developing countries, though, we find a quite different story. As inflation rises to quite high levels, we would expect its total cost to continue to mount but the marginal costs of an additional percentage point of inflation to fall. Going from 10 to 11 percent inflation surely represents a greater increase in uncertainty than is caused by going from 100,000 to 100,001 percent inflation. Indeed, the high average coefficients estimated for the industrial countries could not possibly hold for countries with annual inflation rates in the hundreds or even thousands of percent a year. If taken literally, these estimates would imply that some high-inflation countries should have had negative GDPs.

In Table 1.4, we test for nonlinearity for the developing countries by progressively dropping lower rates of inflation from our panel analysis. Note that as we raise the cut off from 10 to 45 percent inflation there is virtually no change in the estimated coefficients. As we move above 50 percent, however, a fall in the estimates becomes detectible, and above 80 percent this fall becomes quite sizeable. Above 120 percent the coefficients remain small but are positive. The coefficients stop being statistically significant once the 48 percent level is passed. This is not surprising as, by then, the initial sample of over 1000 observations has been reduced to a little over 100. We interpret this evidence as suggesting that the effects of inflation are indeed nonlinear. In other words, the marginal costs of inflation fall at high rates of inflation. We do not, however, conclude that these costs disappear entirely.

TABLE 1.3 Inflation Rate Thresholds from Panel Estimation: Industrial Countries

Inflation Rate (%)	Inflation	Change in Inflation	Number of Observations	Number of Countries
Less than 3	0.23	0.34***	128	21
Less than 4	0.35***	0.11	207	22
Less than 5	-0.06	0.19***	284	23
Less than 6	-0.07	0.16**	339	23
Less than 7	-0.13**	0.13**	400	23
Less than 8	-0.05	0.10**	445	23
Less than 9	-0.04	0.08	475	23
Less than 10	-0.05	0.09**	513	23
Less than 11	-0.10**	0.08	537	23
Less than 12	-0.11***	0.10**	557	23
Less than 13	-0.13***	0.07**	573	23
Less than 14	-0.11***	0.05	592	23
Less than 15	-0.13***	0.06	600	23
Less than 16	-0.14***	0.05	613	23
Less than 17	-0.14***	0.06	623	23
Less than 18	-0.15***	0.05	630	23
Less than 19	-0.14***	0.05	634	23
Less than 20	-0.13***	0.06**	641	23
Less than 21	-0.15***	0.09***	650	23
Less than 22	-0.14***	0.08**	652	23
Less than 23	-0.15***	0.07**	655	23
Less than 24	-0.15***	0.06**	658	23
Less than 25	-0.16***	0.06**	662	23
Less than 26	-0.16***	0.06**	664	23
Less than 27	-0.17***	0.05	665	23
Less than 28	-0.17***	0.05	667	23
Less than 29	-0.17***	0.05	667	23
Less than 30	-0.16***	0.01	669	23
Less than 31	-0.14***	0.007	670	23
Less than 32	-0.14***	0.008	671	23
Less than 33	-0.14***	0.007	672	23
Less than 34	-0.14***	0.007	672	23
Less than 35	-0.14***	0.007	672	23
Less than 36	-0.14***	0.007	672	23
Less than 37	-0.14***	0.007	672	23
Less than 38	-0.14***	0.007	672	23
Less than 39	-0.14***	0.007	672	23
Less than 40	-0.14***	0.007	672	23

*** significant at 1% level
** significant at 5% level
* significant at 10% level

TABLE 1.4 Linearity of the Coefficient Estimates Across Different Inflation Levels: Developing Countries

Inflation Rate (%)	Inflation	Change in Inflation	Number of Observations	Number of Countries
Greater than 3	-0.00132***	0.0005	1032	49
Greater than 4	-0.00128***	0.0005	959	49
Greater than 5	-0.00125***	0.0005	899	49
Greater than 6	-0.00121***	0.0005	842	49
Greater than 7	-0.00117***	0.0005	787	49
Greater than 8	-0.00118**	0.0005	730	49
Greater than 9	-0.00117**	0.0005	684	49
Greater than 10	-0.00115**	0.0005	642	49
Greater than 11	-0.00112**	0.0004	601	49
Greater than 12	-0.00114**	0.0004	545	49
Greater than 13	-0.00113**	0.0005	513	49
Greater than 14	-0.00115**	0.0005	478	48
Greater than 15	-0.00113**	0.0005	447	48
Greater than 16	-0.00115**	0.0005	419	48
Greater than 17	-0.00116**	0.0005	388	47
Greater than 18	-0.00113**	0.0004	366	45
Greater than 19	-0.00118**	0.0005	348	44
Greater than 20	-0.00120**	0.0005	321	42
Greater than 21	-0.00115**	0.0005	307	41
Greater than 22	-0.00113**	0.0004	298	41
Greater than 23	-0.00114**	0.0004	283	39
Greater than 24	-0.00113**	0.0004	268	38
Greater than 25	-0.00117**	0.0005	258	37
Greater than 26	-0.00116**	0.0005	246	36
Greater than 27	-0.00117**	0.0005	237	33
Greater than 28	-0.00121**	0.0005	224	33
Greater than 29	-0.00124**	0.0005	209	30
Greater than 30	-0.00123**	0.0005	200	30
Greater than 31	-0.00123**	0.0004	194	30
Greater than 32	-0.00116**	0.0004	182	28
Greater than 33	-0.00115*	0.0004	178	28
Greater than 34	-0.00112*	0.0004	174	27
Greater than 35	-0.00115*	0.0004	166	25
Greater than 36	-0.00116*	0.0004	164	25
Greater than 37	-0.00120**	0.0005	158	23
Greater than 38	-0.00120**	0.0005	154	23
Greater than 39	-0.00120*	0.0005	150	22
Greater than 40	-0.00118*	0.0005	145	21
Greater than 41	-0.00115*	0.0005	142	21
Greater than 42	-0.00114*	0.0005	139	19

(continues)

TABLE 1.4 (continued)

Inflation Rate (%)	Inflation	Change in Inflation	Number of Observations	Number of Countries
Greater than 43	-0.00112*	0.0005	137	19
Greater than 44	-0.00113*	0.0005	136	19
Greater than 45	-0.00113*	0.0005	133	19
Greater than 46	-0.00113*	0.0005	129	19
Greater than 47	-0.00097*	0.0004	127	19
Greater than 48	-0.00096	0.0004	126	19
Greater than 49	-0.00095	0.0003	121	19
Greater than 50	-0.00094	0.0003	120	19
Greater than 60	-0.00095	0.0004	99	15
Greater than 70	-0.00090	0.0003	86	15
Greater than 80	-0.00057	0.0002	73	14
Greater than 90	-0.00032	0.0001	63	13
Greater than 100	-0.00018	0.00005	56	12
Greater than 120	0.00015	-0.00016	42	9
Greater than 125	0.00005	-0.00012	39	8
Greater than 150	0.00043	-0.0004	32	6
Greater than 175	0.00061	-0.00049	29	6
Greater than 200	0.00058	-0.00047	25	6
Greater than 225	0.00063	-0.00046	24	6
Greater than 250	0.00058	-0.00036	22	6
Greater than 300	0.0013	-0.0015	20	6
Between 0 and 50	-0.06234***	0.0089	1124	49
Between 50 and 100	-0.05400	-0.01546*	64	18
Between 100 and 150	0.07589	-0.06525*	24	11
Greater than 150	0.00043	-0.0004	32	6

*** significant at 1% level
** significant at 5% level
* significant at 10% level

When Does Inflation Hurt Economic Growth in Developing Countries?

We believe that the costs of high rates of inflation have been well documented. For countries with inflation in the triple-digit range and above, the need to reduce inflation is clear. But what about countries whose inflation rates are running in, say, the 20 to 40 percent a year range? Clearly lower is better, but is the temporary pain incurred in reducing inflation to single-digit levels greater than the likely benefits? There is no consensus within the economics profession on this question. It is not uncommon, for example, for economists analyzing developing countries to judge that policies that have brought inflation rates down to 15 to 20 percent a year have been successful.[8] For the industrial countries it is clear that such rates of inflation would be very costly, but for developing countries is there some higher threshold before the adverse effects of inflation become substantial?

This is an under-researched issue which deserves considerable attention. In Tables 1.5 and 1.6 we present evidence from a panel analysis of, first, our full set of developing countries and, then, of the set of fifteen developing countries for which we found significant negative effects of inflation in the earlier time-series analysis of the individual countries. For the full set of countries, at inflation rates of less than 10 percent we find a significant positive association between inflation and growth. The coefficient does not turn negative until inflation rates above 23 percent are included in the analysis, and the coefficients do not become consistently negative until inflation rates in the high thirties are added. These results are consistent with the view that inflation rates in, say, the 20 percent range should not be a major concern.

TABLE 1.5 Inflation Rate Thresholds from Panel Estimation: Developing Countries

Inflation Rate (%)	Inflation	Change in Inflation	Number of Observations	Number of Countries
Less than 3	0.26	-0.02	264	39
Less than 4	0.25**	-0.04	338	41
Less than 5	0.28**	-0.07	397	42
Less than 6	0.21**	-0.06	445	44
Less than 7	0.15	-0.07	510	45
Less than 8	0.15**	-0.06	567	46
Less than 9	0.19***	-0.04	613	46
Less than 10	0.13**	-0.009	655	47
Less than 11	0.09	-0.009	696	48
Less than 12	0.05	0.03	752	48
Less than 13	0.05	0.03	784	49
Less than 14	0.07	0.03	818	49
Less than 15	0.05	0.02	850	49
Less than 16	0.05	0.02	877	49
Less than 17	0.03	0.02	909	49
Less than 18	0.04	0.02**	931	49
Less than 19	0.03	0.02	948	49
Less than 20	0.02	0.02	976	49
Less than 21	0.02	0.01	990	49
Less than 22	0.006	0.01	999	49
Less than 23	0.005	0.06	1014	49
Less than 24	-0.01	0.02	1028	49
Less than 25	-0.01	0.01	1039	49
Less than 26	-0.02	0.01	1051	49

(continues)

The High Costs of Monetary Instability

A different story emerges, however, when we focus on the panel analysis of the fifteen developing countries for which we did find significant negative effects in the individual country results (see Table 1.6). Here, the coefficient becomes negative when inflation rates above 6 percent are included and becomes significantly negative when rates above 7 percent are added. Furthermore, the size of the estimated effects is substantial, averaging around -0.2.

Both these and the industrial country results raise substantial doubts about the wisdom of officials and decision makers in the transition economies adopting the view that inflation rates in the 20 percent range are acceptable. Our findings suggest that even those developing, or transitional, countries, such as the Czech Republic and Slovenia, that already have brought inflation down to this "moderate" level should strive to make further progress toward lowering their inflation rates to the single-digit levels typical of the industrial countries in the 1990s.

TABLE 1.5 (continued)

Inflation Rate (%)	Inflation	Change in Inflation	Number of Observations	Number of Countries
Less than 27	-0.02	0.01	1060	49
Less than 28	-0.02	0.01	1073	49
Less than 29	-0.03	0.01	1087	49
Less than 30	-0.04	0.01	1097	49
Less than 31	-0.04**	0.01	1103	49
Less than 32	-0.03	0.01	1115	49
Less than 33	-0.03	0.01	1119	49
Less than 34	-0.03	0.01	1123	49
Less than 35	-0.03	0.01	1131	49
Less than 36	-0.03	0.01	1133	49
Less than 37	-0.04**	0.01	1139	49
Less than 38	-0.04**	0.01	1143	49
Less than 39	-0.04**	0.01	1147	49
Less than 40	-0.04**	0.01	1152	49
Less than 41	-0.03**	0.01	1155	49
Less than 42	-0.04**	0.01	1158	49
Less than 43	-0.04**	0.01	1160	49
Less than 44	-0.04**	0.01	1161	49
Less than 45	-0.04**	0.01	1164	49
Less than 46	-0.04**	0.01	1168	49
Less than 47	-0.05***	0.01	1170	49
Less than 48	-0.05***	0.01	1171	49
Less than 49	-0.05***	0.01	1176	49
Less than 50	-0.05***	0.01	1177	49

*** significant at 1% level
** significant at 5% level
* significant at 10% level

TABLE 1.6 Inflation Rate Thresholds from Panel Estimation: Developing Countries with a Negative and Significant Coefficient on Inflation

Inflation Rate (%)	Inflation	Change in Inflation	Number of Observations	Number of Countries
Less than 3	0.10	0.08	90	15
Less than 4	0.24	0.04	124	15
Less than 5	0.20	-0.01	150	15
Less than 6	0.06	0.03	175	15
Less than 7	-0.02	0.02	191	15
Less than 8	-0.02	-0.01	213	15
Less than 9	-0.04	0.001	231	15
Less than 10	-0.11	0.02	246	16
Less than 11	-0.11	0.01	256	16
Less than 12	-0.12	0.006	269	16
Less than 13	-0.10	0.001	281	16
Less than 14	-0.10	-0.0002	288	16
Less than 15	-0.09	0.006	300	16
Less than 16	-0.04	0.006	317	16
Less than 17	-0.08	0.008	327	16
Less than 18	-0.08	0.01	337	16
Less than 19	-0.08*	0.01	344	16
Less than 20	-0.07	0.01	352	16
Less than 21	-0.07	0.01	354	16
Less than 22	-0.09**	0.01	358	16
Less than 23	-0.07**	0.01	360	16
Less than 24	-0.09**	0.01	364	16
Less than 25	-0.10***	0.01	367	16
Less than 26	-0.10***	0.01	372	16
Less than 27	-0.10***	0.01	375	16
Less than 28	-0.10***	0.01	383	16
Less than 29	-0.10***	0.01	387	16
Less than 30	-0.10***	0.01	390	16
Less than 31	-0.10***	0.01	394	16
Less than 32	-0.09***	0.01	397	16
Less than 33	-0.09***	0.01	400	16
Less than 34	-0.08***	0.01	401	16
Less than 35	-0.07***	0.01	404	16
Less than 36	-0.07***	0.01	405	16
Less than 37	-0.07***	0.01	406	16
Less than 38	-0.08***	0.004	408	16
Less than 39	-0.08***	0.004	409	16
Less than 40	-0.08***	0.004	410	16

*** significant at 1% level
** significant at 5% level
* significant at 10% level

Concluding Remarks

There is overwhelming empirical evidence that increases in rates of inflation will, on average, lower the rate of economic growth and the level of per capita real income over the long term. The temptation to inflate continues to be fueled, however, by the fact that increasing rates of inflation often tend to stimulate output in the short run. Consequently, we believe that there is a strong case for adopting institutional structures that emphasize a long-term perspective in the formulation of monetary policies and so offset the inflationary bias that has characterized the world economy since the demise of the gold standard.

Evidence on the strength of the adverse effects of inflation on growth is not entirely clear cut. While quite substantial harmful effects have been well documented in the industrial countries, the empirical research to date does not find adverse effects as consistently for the developing countries. Even when statistically significant effects are found, the estimated effects are typically much smaller than for the industrial countries. There is also some evidence to suggest that the threshold levels at which inflation starts to have a serious adverse effect on economic performance may be higher on average in developing countries.

Why such differential effects might exist is an important topic for further research. Countries cannot put monetary and fiscal policy decisions on hold until such research is completed, however. We have suggested that the apparent differential effects of inflation across countries may reflect, in substantial part, differences in the degree of utilization of the price system and financial markets. In our view, greater use of markets will lead to increases in per capita income but will also make economic performance more sensitive to inflation.

This suggests a further need for the economies in transition to take a longer-run perspective with respect to decisions that influence inflation. As these economies come to make greater use of markets, the costs of inflation will rise and high initial inflation will make the transition toward the more effective use of markets more difficult. Thus, while there is considerable uncertainty about just how costly continued high or even "moderate" rates of inflation would be, to settle for continuing rates of inflation in the double-digit range is likely to be a risky strategy for many countries, especially those which have the best medium-term prospects for approaching the standards of living of the industrial countries in the West.

Appendix:
Regressing Inflation on Economic Growth

Grimes (1991) emphasizes that simple correlations of inflation and growth rates may be misleading because they fail to take into account other important influences on growth such as supply shocks (proxied here by oil prices) and short-term Phillips-curve-type effects of changes in the rate of inflation. Following Grimes, we correct for some of the most important of these effects as follows:

$$GROWTH = B_0 + B_1 INF + B_2 CHINF + B_3 TIME + B_4 OIL + \epsilon$$

where

$GROWTH$	is the growth rate of real GDP at time t,
INF	is the inflation rate of the consumer price index at time t,
$CHINF$	is the first difference of the inflation rate,
$TIME$	is a time trend,
OIL	is the Venezuelan oil price (Venezuela being the only country for which a continuous oil price data series is available over our sample period),
ϵ	is a white-noise error term.

We estimate individual equations for each country in our post-1960 sample using seemingly unrelated regression analysis. We also pool the annual data using a panel estimation technique that combines the information from the individual regressions and limits the influence of outliers. All data are from the *International Financial Statistics* published by the International Monetary Fund. (For further documentation, see Salamun 1994).

Notes

1. The authors thank Eduard Hochreiter, Sung Kim, Tamara Mast and Tom Mayer for helpful comments.

2. See McClure and Willett (1988) and chapter 3 of this volume.

3. For discussions of the various costs of inflation, see Frohman, Laney and Willett (1981); Fischer (1981, 1984); Leijonhufvud (1984); Driffill, Mizon and Ulph (1990); Ball and Romer (1992); Heymann and Leijonhufvud (1994); and Tommasi (1994a, 1994b).

4. Quoted by Schlesinger (1984:98).

5. See, for example, Logue and Willett (1976); Taylor (1981); Holland (1984); Evans (1991); Evans and Wachtel (1993); and Ungar and Zilberfarb (1993). A part of the association is likely due to policy variability generated by periodic stabilization efforts. The economic and political reasons for higher inflation rates being more variable remain an important topic for research.

6. Karras (1993) finds evidence supporting long-run neutrality in the effects of money growth on output growth and attributes his finding of an overall negative relationship between inflation and output entirely to the 1970s oil shocks. Our empirical analysis reported below suggests, however, that the negative inflation-output

relationship remains even when the regressions control for the effects of oil price shifts. While such findings do not prove causality, they at least appear to be more than just a figment of the 1970s (see also Frohman, Laney and Willett 1981).

7. In a subsequent statement, President Yeltsin cited a more reasonable objective of bringing inflation down to 2 to 3 percent a month.

8. For example, see Kiguel and Liviatan (1988:296–7); Ortiz (1991:283); and Dornbusch and Fischer (1993).

References

Ball, Laurence, and David Romer. 1992. "Inflation and the Informativeness of Prices." NBER Working Paper No. 4267.

Banaian, King. 1995. "Inflation and Optimal Seigniorage in the CIS and Eastern Europe," this volume.

Burdekin, Richard C. K., Thomas Goodwin, Suyono Salamun and Thomas D. Willett. 1994. "The Effects of Inflation on Economic Growth in Industrial and Developing Countries: Is There a Difference?" *Applied Economics Letters* 1: 175–77.

Cooper, Richard N. 1992. *Economic Stabilization and Debt in Developing Countries*. Cambridge, Mass.: MIT Press.

Cozier, Barry, and Jack Selody. 1992. "Inflation and Macroeconomic Performance: Some Cross-Country Evidence." Department of Monetary and Financial Analysis, Bank of Canada, Ottawa.

Dornbusch, Rudiger, and Stanley Fischer. 1993. "Moderate Inflation." *World Bank Economic Review* 7: 1–44.

Driffill, John, Grayham E. Mizon, and Alistair M. Ulph. 1990. "Costs of Inflation," in Benjamin M. Friedman and Frank H. Hahn, eds. *Handbook of Monetary Economics*. Volume II. Amsterdam: North Holland.

Evans, Martin. 1991. "Discovering the Link Between Inflation Rates and Inflation Uncertainty." *Journal of Money, Credit, and Banking* 23: 169–84.

Evans, Martin, and Paul Wachtel. 1993. "Inflation Regimes and the Sources of Inflation Uncertainty." *Journal of Money, Credit, and Banking* 25: 475–511.

Fischer, Stanley. 1981. "Towards an Understanding of the Costs of Inflation: II." *Carnegie-Rochester Conference Series on Public Policy* 15: 5–42.

──────. 1984. "The Benefits of Price Stability," in *Price Stability and Public Policy*. Kansas City, Mo.: Federal Reserve Bank of Kansas City.

Frohman, Deborah A., Leroy O. Laney, and Thomas D. Willett. 1981. "Uncertainty Costs of High Inflation." *Voice of the Federal Reserve Bank of Dallas*, July: 1–9.

Grimes, Arthur. 1991. "The Effects of Inflation on Growth: Some International Evidence." *Weltwirtschaftliches Archiv* 127: 631–44.

Heymann, Daniel, and Axel Leijonhufvud. 1994. *High Inflations*. New York: Oxford University Press.

Holland, A. Steven. 1984. "Does Higher Inflation Lead to More Uncertain Inflation?" *Federal Reserve Bank of St. Louis Review* 66: 15–26.

Karras, Georgios. 1993. "Money, Inflation, and Output Growth: Does the Aggregate Demand-Aggregate Supply Model Explain the International Evidence?" *Weltwirtschaftliches Archiv* 129: 662–74.

Kiguel, Miguel A., and Nissan Liviatan. 1988. "Inflationary Rigidities and Orthodox Stabilization Policies: Lessons from Latin America." *World Bank Economic Review* 2: 273–98.

Leijonhufvud, Axel. 1984. "Inflation and Economic Performance," in Barry N. Siegel, ed., *Money in Crisis: The Federal Reserve, the Economy, and Monetary Reform*. San Francisco, Calif.: Pacific Institute for Public Policy Research.

Logue, Dennis E., and Thomas D. Willett. 1976. "A Note on the Relation Between the Rate and Variability of Inflation." *Economica* 43: 151–58.

McClure, J. Harold, Jr., and Thomas D. Willett. 1988. "The Inflation Tax," in Thomas D. Willett, ed., *Political Business Cycles: The Political Economy of Money, Inflation, and Unemployment*. Pp. 177–85. Durham, N.C.: Duke University Press.

Motley, Brian. 1994. "Growth and Inflation: A Cross-Country Study." Paper presented at the Federal Reserve Bank of San Francisco Conference on Monetary Policy in a Low Inflation Regime, San Francisco, Calif.

Ortiz, Guillermo. 1991. "Mexico Beyond the Debt Crisis," in Michael Bruno, Stanley Fischer, Elhanan Helpman and Nissan Liviatan, eds., *Lesson of Economic Stabilization and Its Aftermath*. Cambridge, Mass: MIT Press.

Salamun, Suyono. 1994. *The Effects of Different Levels of Inflation on Economic Growth: An Empirical Study for Industrial and Developing Countries*. Unpublished Ph.D. dissertation, Claremont Graduate School.

Schlesinger, Helmut. 1984. "The Role of the Central Bank in Achieving Price Stability: An International Perspective," in *Price Stability and Public Policy*. Kansas City, Mo.: Federal Reserve Bank of Kansas City.

Taylor, John B. 1981. "On the Relation Between the Variability of Inflation and the Average Inflation Rate." *Carnegie-Rochester Conference Series on Public Policy* 15: 57–86.

Tommasi, Mariano. 1994a. "High Inflation: Resource Misallocations and Growth Effects." Unpublished manuscript, Department of Economics, UCLA.

_____. 1994b. "The Consequences of Price Instability on Search Markets: Towards Understanding the Costs of Inflation." *American Economic Review* 84: 1385–96.

Ungar, Meyer, and Ben-Zion Zilberfarb. 1993. "Inflation and Its Unpredictability —Theory and Empirical Evidence." *Journal of Money, Credit, and Banking* 25: 709–20.

2

Budget Deficits and Inflation: The Importance of Budget Controls for Monetary Stability

Richard C. K. Burdekin[1]

This fundamental cause of the inflation ... is the unlimited growth of the [government's] floating debt and its transformation into currency through the discounting of treasury bills at the Reichsbank ... But ... the Reich must live, and an actual refusal to discount, in the face of expenditures set in the budget, would have led to chaos.
                                    Reichsbank President Havenstein 1923[2]

For countries with very limited or underdeveloped capital markets,... government borrowing needs may effectively determine the rate at which the domestic assets of the central bank grow, because the government has no alternative to compelling the central bank to monetize its deficits.
                                    Farhadian and Dunn 1986:66–67

There are factors that make the Soviet economy especially vulnerable [to hyperinflation]. There are, above all, the enormous state expenditures, the budget deficit, and the state debt. What is more, of late the union government has been losing many sources of income, but it retains control over the printing of money because the central bank is in fact not independent.
                                    Chirkova 1992:75–76

Introduction

Russia's budget deficit reached an estimated 15 percent of gross domestic product (GDP) in 1992 before declining to approximately 9–10 percent of GDP in 1993. The 1993 deficit was substantially above the year-end deficit target of 5 percent of gross national product (GNP) agreed with the International Monetary Fund. Moves toward fiscal stringency had, however, been opposed by the Russian parliament, which, in July 1993, passed legislation aimed at fixing the budget deficit at 22 trillion rubles, or 25 percent of GNP. Following the dissolution of the Russian parliament in September 1993, the monthly inflation rate for consumer prices declined from 25 percent in October to 15 percent in November and 12 percent in December 1993. Nevertheless, Russia's financial problems remain severe. Prices increased approximately ninefold for 1993 as a whole. The Russian central bank set an inflation target for 1994 of 10 percent a month. Central Bank Chairman Viktor Gerashchenko—previously derided by Jeffrey Sachs as perhaps "the worst central-bank governor in history"—won praise for getting inflation below 10 percent a month in early 1994 even though, as Goldman Sachs International Vice President Roger Hormats put it, "he's not quite Alan Greenspan yet" (see Ignatius 1994:A11).

The Russian deficit must be financed either by printing money or by issuing bonds. In contrast to countries such as the United States, which are able to fund the majority of their deficits through bonds, Russian bond issuance has financed only a trivial percentage of the nation's deficit. Indeed, government bonds outstanding stood at only 0.02 trillion rubles in September 1993, accounting for less than one-tenth of one percent of Russia's 25.3 trillion M3 money supply measure (Lewarne 1995). Unless the government can substitute foreign borrowing for domestic borrowing, the only remaining option is to finance the deficit through money issue. As with the famous hyperinflations in Austria, Germany, Hungary, and Poland after World War I (Sargent 1993:chp. 3), the recent Russian experience with double-digit monthly price inflation reveals a key role for government fiscal policy actions in driving both the rate of monetary expansion *and* the inflation process.

The next section of this chapter focuses on the many factors that could theoretically be expected to influence the relationship between budget deficits and inflation. This section includes an analysis of tax-backing theory, deficit sustainability and the optimal seigniorage literature.

The third section discusses some of the factors accounting for the development of large budget deficits. The experiences of the economies that have undergone hyperinflation are compared with the large postwar budget deficits experienced in the United States and Latin America.

In the fourth section, some international evidence is provided on the link between fiscal policies and inflation performance. A comparison of failed and successful stabilization attempts reveals that fiscal reform may be a necessary, but not sufficient, condition for restoring price stability. Success depends upon confidence in the durability of the reform; and the fiscal correction must be credible and sustainable in the eyes of the public.

The fifth section draws some conclusions regarding the prevalent deficit-inflation cycles among the less-developed economies of Latin America and discusses the role played by the institutional arrangements for monetary and fiscal policy. The potential benefits arising from recent institutional reforms, such as the movement towards an independent central bank in Mexico, are addressed.

The sixth section focuses on the implications of the international evidence for the emerging market economies of Central and Eastern Europe. The divergent experiences of Russia, the Ukraine and Estonia are used to illustrate the importance of fiscal factors in the former Soviet Republics.

Theoretical Perspectives on Deficit Finance

In order to remain solvent, governments must raise sufficient revenue from current debt and money issue to cover today's budget deficit *plus* interest payments and principal payments due on *past* debt issue. If the government continues to run deficits, the rising debt burden can be offset, for a time, by "rolling over" the debt and issuing new debt to pay off the old debt. However, if there is no prospect of the government levying future taxes or cutting spending to reverse the progressive buildup of debt, this rolling over of the debt must eventually be regarded as a nonsustainable Ponzi scheme. At this point, no one will be willing to hold the government's debt, leaving monetization of the debt, or money finance, as the only remaining option.

The government's dynamic budget constraint can be expressed as follows:

(1) $$P_t(G_t - T_t) + D_{t-1} = D_t + M_t$$

where

P_t is the price level,
G_t is real government spending,
T_t is real tax revenue,
D_t is current debt issuance,
D_{t-1} is the cost of servicing past debt issue, and
M_t is current base money issuance.

While the form of this budget constraint is uncontroversial, the sustainability issue is not. At what point will individuals refuse to hold the government bonds and force the government to monetize the debt—that is, to inflate it away? We know that in the United States government debt can rise well above 50 percent of GNP without triggering this result. On the other hand, countries like Russia may hardly be able to use bond finance at all, both because of the less developed nature of the country's capital markets and because of less confidence in the government's capacity to eventually redeem the debt.

There is certainly no theoretical rationale for inflation and deficits always going hand in hand. The relationship depends upon public perception of the government's willingness and/or ability to avoid resorting to the money financing option. Unless the public believes that current debt will eventually be redeemed out of future taxes, then bond issuance has inflationary effects today because of money issue expected in the future (see Sargent 1993, chapter 2 on this point).[3] What matters, then, is not just the size of the current deficit but perceptions about the government's ability to redeem its obligations through *future* taxes and/or cuts in government spending. That is, if even large issues of currency or bonds are considered "backed" by future taxes, these issues need not be inflationary (see Smith 1985a, 1985b; Bernholz 1988a; Calomiris 1988; and Siklos 1990). Moreover, any fiscal "news" relevant to the perceived ability of the government to reduce expenditures or raise taxes in the future can influence inflation *now*.[4]

Monetization of the deficit has often occurred in the midst of crises brought on by war or revolution, where the government has essentially used monetization as a financing method of last resort. The effects of this policy during the American War of Independence gave rise to the expression "not worth a continental" as the former national currency was inflated away and eventually used as wallpaper by some disgruntled citizens. In Imperial Germany, monetization of the outstanding government debt by the Reichsbank both during and after World War I (Balderston 1989; Webb 1989) was a key element in the ensuing hyperinflation. By the end of 1923, the German government's real debt burden had shrunk to approximately zero as had the value of all obligations denoted in paper assets. At the time of the November 1923 stabilization, one prewar gold mark exchanged for one trillion paper marks (Sargent 1993:50).

It is sometimes argued, however, that it is "optimal" for the government to finance part of its expenditures through money creation. Indeed, the revenue from money creation can be thought of as a lump-sum tax that avoids the deadweight loss arising from traditional income taxes that reduce the incentive to work and invest. The problem is that the "inflation tax" brings with it many distortions and adverse effects of its own, including uncertainty costs. As pointed out by Banaian (1995) in this volume, traditional optimal inflation rate calculations are typically overstated because they ignore these costs. Taking these costs into account, Banaian finds, for example, that the estimated optimal inflation rate for the former Yugoslavia during the 1980s is reduced from more than 70 percent per year to close to zero.

It is, in fact, doubtful that optimal finance explanations can account for even moderate inflations of say, 15–30 percent per year (Dornbusch and Fischer 1993:5). Certainly, the extremely rapid inflation experienced recently in Russia, and the hyperinflation that developed in the Ukraine and the former Yugoslav republics of Croatia and Serbia, go far beyond the pale even of the optimal inflation calculations that ignore uncertainty costs entirely. It remains to be seen whether the emerging market economies of Central and Eastern Europe will be able to eschew reliance on the inflation tax, or whether we will see the ongoing cycles of inflation that have characterized many of the Latin American economies in the postwar period. Already, however, countries like the Czech Republic and Estonia have demonstrated that budget balance is not impossible in these economies. Hungary, meanwhile, provides an example where bond financing has been used to limit the inflationary consequences of short-run budget deficits. The demand for Hungarian government bonds by banks can be explained by the fact that the government is seen as a better credit risk than the private sector and is willing to offer a realistic rate of return (Dezséri 1993).

Whatever the type of economy one is considering, the key issue surely remains belief in the *future* restoration of budgetary stability. Even in the United States, the almost unbroken succession of federal government budget deficits in the post-1960 period has called into question the government's ability to restore fiscal balance and cast doubt on its very solvency. Hakkio and Rush (1991), for example, find that government revenues and expenditures are not cointegrated over the 1964–1988 period. This failure of the revenue and spending flows to converge implies that, if these same policies are continued, the debt to GNP ratio must rise without limit as "the government is bubble-financing its expenditures, in which old debt that matures is financed by issuing new debt" (Hakkio and Rush:431). Hoover and Sheffrin (1992) further obtain evidence that, in contrast to the early postwar period, federal tax and spending processes became causally independent after the late 1960s. These results suggest that the present U.S. situation may, in the long run, be no more sustainable than the unfavorable fiscal imbalances currently faced by Russia and the less fortunate emerging market economies of Central and Eastern Europe.

Factors Accounting for the Development of Non-Sustainable Budget Deficits, Past and Present

The pre-World War II experiences with high inflation generally developed as a result of war or civil disorder. The same is true of such early post-World

War II hyperinflations as those experienced by China and Greece in the 1940s (Capie 1986). In each case, the government reacted to the crisis by raising spending but could not fund these expenditures without resorting to widespread issue of unbacked paper currency. Most of these inflationary episodes lasted for no more than a few years, however. The Chinese inflation is perhaps the longest lasting. The inflationary spiral began in 1937 and degenerated into true hyperinflation by 1949, with the monthly inflation rate reaching 82 percent a month in April of that year.[5]

The much more persistent, if generally less extreme, inflations experienced in Latin America and elsewhere in the postwar period clearly cannot be explained in terms of the temporary crises that marked the earlier episodes of high inflation. Rather, the fiscal imbalances and chronic inflation that have plagued many of the less developed countries in the postwar era seem to derive from a continued pattern of political instability, polarization of society and distributional conflicts. Moreover, the degree to which the governments in such countries have resorted to seigniorage as a means of financing government spending has been found to be positively related to the degree of political instability (Edwards and Tabellini 1991; Roubini 1991; Cukierman, Edwards and Tabellini 1992).

In Latin America, in particular, despite the many attempted stabilizations in the postwar era—as discussed in the next section—the solutions to the fiscal problems have generally proved to be only temporary in nature. One rationale for the longstanding fiscal and monetary problems faced by many of the Latin American nations concerns the way in which distributional conflict may be channelled through the budget deficit as different groups seek tax breaks or social expenditures that increase their share in national income (for further analysis of the implications of distributional conflict, see Willett and Banaian 1988; Burdekin and Burkett 1989). Unless the stabilization program is able to alleviate the strains on the budget arising from such pressures, the government will be unable to enact a lasting reduction in the budget deficit and the inflation process will continue (Baer 1991; Feijo and de Carvalho 1992).[6] Bresser Pereira and Dall'Acqua (1991:36) further state that

> fiscal austerity has too often been rejected because of the difficulties in reducing interest payments associated with a huge public debt and the fear that cuts in social expenditures will provoke widespread social conflict and political unrest. As a result, Latin American governments have failed to adopt decisive fiscal correction measures, and large budget deficits have become a major obstacle to stabilization.

Naturally, adverse external factors like the debt crisis and declining primary product prices exacerbated the problems experienced by the Latin American governments. Pazos (1990) points out that governments faced with severe declines in foreign income generally applied expansionary policies aimed at softening the resultant declines in output and employment. In Chile, such expansionary policies were followed in 1970–1973, culminating in 1973 in a 378 percent increase in public spending, a 606 percent inflation rate and -5.6 percent real growth. While the government did succeed in boosting output during the first two years of the program, the results of the expansionary policies appear to be a classic example of short-run benefits vs. long-run costs. As shown by Pazos (1990:124), the Peruvian expansionary policies of 1985–1988 suffered a similar fate, with inflation reaching 1722 percent in 1988.

It is easy to say that the governments in Chile and Peru should have maintained tight fiscal and monetary policies despite the external shocks. However, even in countries like Japan, the United Kingdom and the United States, the respective national governments followed inflationary policies when faced with the 1973 oil shock. What is at issue here is probably not so much the fact that Latin American governments followed expansionary policies to dampen the effects of external shocks, but rather the *magnitude* of this response and the degree to which this fueled the inflation process. Perhaps the most plausible explanation for the apparent overreaction is simply that the pressures to inflate were greater in Latin America than was true in Europe or Japan. That is, as declines in national income exacerbated the pre-existing distributional conflicts and struggle over income shares, it is probably not surprising that an already precarious fiscal situation rapidly deteriorated to near-hyperinflation levels (or, in Bolivia's case, to true hyperinflation).

International Evidence on the Link Between Fiscal Solvency and Inflation Performance

The available evidence on high inflation (defined by Capie 1986 as annual rates of price increase that exceed 100 percent) reveals that large, money-financed deficits appear to lie behind not only the pre-World War II and pre-twentieth century inflationary episodes (Sargent 1993:chp. 3; Capie 1986; Burdekin and Langdana 1992:chp. 2–3) but also most, if not all, of the more recent experiences with high inflation in Latin America and elsewhere. Table 2.1 (from Dornbusch, Sturzenegger and Wolf 1990:34) shows the relative debt and deficit levels in low-inflation developing countries vs. high-inflation developing countries over the 1983–1989 period. Strikingly, the average fiscal deficit in low-inflation countries over this period was 1.3 percent of GNP; for the high-inflation countries the average level was 7.5 percent of GNP.[7]

Individual stabilization attempts in the postwar period also seem to corroborate Sargent's (1993:chp. 3) finding of a strong link between inflation and budget deficits. The remainder of this section focuses on eleven major

TABLE 2.1 Deficits, Debt and Inflation in Developing Countries, 1983–89

	Low Inflation Countries	High Inflation Countries
Debt/GNP	39.5	45.9
Debt Service/GNP	7.3	5.8
Budget Deficit/GNP	1.3	7.5
Annual Money Growth	12.0	187.8

Notes: The sample includes eighty-eight net-debtor developing counties. All numbers are weighted averages over the period calculated with GDP weights. Countries with less than 6 percent annual (CPI) inflation were classified as low-inflation countries, while countries with more than 15 percent annual inflation were considered high-inflation countries.
Source: Dornbusch, Sturzenegger and Wolf (1990:34)

postwar stabilization programs that are documented by Végh (1992:670–91).

These episodes span the major stabilization programs attempted in the 1960s, 1970s, and 1980s in Latin America plus the 1985 Israeli plan.[8] Data on inflation and budget deficits for these stabilization experiences are given in Table 2.2. Each of the three Argentinean stabilization programs and both of the Uruguayan programs achieved temporary reductions in the inflation rate, but ended amid a combination of rising budget deficits and rising inflation. The second Brazilian stabilization program (the Cruzado plan) did lower inflation temporarily, but the budget deficit was not reduced and within a year the inflation rate rose above the 246 percent rate registered just prior to the implementation of the program.

Of the more successful stabilization programs, the Bolivian stabilization of 1985 brought inflation down from 38,803.3 percent in the third quarter of 1985 to double-digit rates in 1986. Subsequent inflation rates varied between 3.1 percent and 34.7 percent in the period prior to the end of 1990. At the same time, the budget deficit was reduced from 29.4 percent of GDP at the end of 1984, to 10.1 percent at the end of 1985 and 3.4 percent in 1986. Following a temporary increase in the deficit to 7.7 percent of GDP in 1987, it was gradually reduced again, declining to 3.3 percent of GDP in 1990. While the Bolivian plan clearly did not entirely eliminate inflation, the drastic decline that was achieved in combination with equally drastic deficit reduction contrasts with the less successful experiences discussed above (none of which involved any lasting reduction in the size of the budget deficit).

The 1985 Israeli stabilization reveals a pattern similar to the Bolivian case. The deficit was reduced from 13 percent of GDP in 1984 to 2.8 percent of GDP at the end of 1985, following which the budget moved into surplus. As in Bolivia there was a subsequent temporary increase in the deficit, but this was reversed by 1989. Inflation meanwhile was reduced from triple digits to

TABLE 2.2   Budget Deficits and Inflation Rates During Eleven Postwar Stabilization Attempts

Year/ Quarter	Inflation Rate	Budget Deficit/GDP
1. Argentina (1967:1–1970:2)		
1966:1	29.2	
1966:2	22.6	
1966:3	16.0	
1966:4	48.4	4.6
1967:1	21.8	
1967:2	24.3	
1967:3	39.2	
1967:4	34.7	1.9
1968:1	10.8	
1968:2	-1.4	
1968:3	3.4	
1968:4	27.4	2.1
1969:1	1.8	
1969:2	-0.9	
1969:3	6.7	
1969:4	23.8	1.6
1970:1	6.0	
1970:2	11.7	
1970:3	14.4	
1970:4	51.6	1.7
1971:1	42.8	
1971:2	23.7	
1971:3	43.7	
1971:4	38.5	4.3
1972:1	98.1	
1972:2	58.6	
1972:3	47.0	
1972:4	64.4	5.2
2. Argentina (1979:1–1981:1)		
1978:1	196.3	
1978:2	185.1	
1978:3	126.3	
1978:4	166.9	3.2
1979:1	204.3	
1979:2	138.4	
1979:3	169.5	
1979:4	96.7	2.7
1980:1	97.1	

(continues)

TABLE 2.2 (continued)

Year/Quarter	Inflation Rate	Budget Deficit/GDP
1980:2	98.2	
1980:3	73.2	
1980:4	87.6	3.6
1981:1	71.6	
1981:2	129.8	
1981:3	177.2	
1981:4	125.0	8.1
1982:1	161.8	
1982:2	71.3	
1982:3	324.5	
1982:4	342.6	7.2

3. Argentina (1985:2–1986:3)

Year/Quarter	Inflation Rate	Budget Deficit/GDP
1984:1	508.6	11.0
1984:2	650.7	9.3
1984:3	827.4	6.9
1984:4	810.0	9.3
1985:1	1004.4	10.1
1985:2	1687.8	6.5
1985:3	258.5	3.0
1985:4	31.6	2.0
1986:1	40.4	4.7
1986:2	63.9	2.2
1986:3	113.0	1.5
1986:4	107.2	8.7
1987:1	113.9	5.1
1987:2	88.9	5.7
1987:3	215.7	8.1
1987:4	336.1	5.9
1988:1	179.9	9.3
1988:2	480.0	5.1
1988:3	954.8	3.5
1988:4	220.2	6.1

4. Bolivia (1985:3–1990:4)

Year/Quarter	Inflation Rate	Budget Deficit/GDP
1984:1	682.5	
1984:2	4518.3	
1984:3	407.0	
1984:4	7860.6	29.4
1985:1	123,729.9	
1985:2	4217.9	
1985:3	38,803.3	

(continues)

TABLE 2.2 (continued)

Year/Quarter	Inflation Rate	Budget Deficit/GDP
1985:4	508.6	10.1
1986:1	498.8	
1986:2	38.4	
1986:3	27.3	
1986:4	10.3	3.4
1987:1	16.7	
1987:2	11.0	
1987:3	3.1	
1987:4	12.1	7.7
1988:1	6.4	
1988:2	34.7	
1988:3	33.3	
1988:4	12.3	6.5
1989:1	8.1	
1989:2	4.9	
1989:3	16.7	
1989:4	33.8	5.1
1990:1	12.5	
1990:2	6.4	
1990:3	19.2	
1990:4	33.1	3.3
5. Brazil (1964:2–1968:3)		
1963:1	73.4	
1963:2	85.5	
1963:3	78.7	
1963:4	92.4	4.2
1964:1	128.5	
1964:2	89.2	
1964:3	67.3	
1964:4	62.8	3.2
1965:1	99.0	
1965:2	67.9	
1965:3	30.6	
1965:4	25.0	1.6
1966:1	51.8	
1966:2	53.0	
1966:3	38.6	
1966:4	24.1	1.1
1967:1	34.8	
1967:2	34.1	
1967:3	20.1	
1967:4	13.6	1.7

(continues)

TABLE 2.2 (continued)

Year/Quarter	Inflation Rate	Budget Deficit/GDP
1968:1	20.9	
1968:2	28.7	
1968:3	25.0	
1968:4	19.0	1.2
1969:1	22.0	
1969:2	20.1	
1969:3	25.3	
1969:4	28.5	0.6
1970:1	16.8	
1970:2	18.4	
1970:3	28.6	
1970:4	23.9	0.4
6. Brazil (1986:1–1986:4)		
1984:1	195.3	
1984:2	190.2	
1984:3	216.9	
1984:4	214.8	5.8
1985:1	273.6	
1985:2	170.8	
1985:3	258.0	
1985:4	246.4	13.0
1986:1	419.6	
1986:2	36.4	
1986:3	9.0	
1986:4	26.1	14.5
1987:1	268.1	
1987:2	862.5	
1987:3	347.6	
1987:4	262.5	14.4
7. Chile (1978:1–1982:2)		
1977:1	90.4	
1977:2	74.7	
1977:3	53.5	
1977:4	49.9	1.1
1978:1	33.0	
1978:2	34.7	
1978:3	33.4	
1978:4	27.2	0.2
1979:1	25.4	
1979:2	34.6	

(continues)

TABLE 2.2 (continued)

Year/Quarter	Inflation Rate	Budget Deficit/GDP
1979:3	51.8	
1979:4	41.1	-4.9
1980:1	29.5	
1980:2	33.3	
1980:3	28.1	
1980:4	34.4	-5.5
1981:1	18.4	
1981:2	11.7	
1981:3	9.3	
1981:4	6.7	-2.4
1982:1	2.9	
1982:2	-0.8	
1982:3	26.1	
1982:4	55.8	2.3
1983:1	18.7	
1983:2	25.4	
1983:3	26.8	
1983:4	26.5	2.6
8. Israel (1985:3–1990:4)		
1984:1	334.2	
1984:2	447.8	
1984:3	426.5	
1984:4	710.9	13.0
1985:1	180.7	
1985:2	365.8	
1985:3	375.4	
1985:4	40.7	2.8
1986:1	5.2	
1986:2	29.2	
1986:3	12.6	
1986:4	29.0	-0.7
1987:1	22.5	
1987:2	18.0	
1987:3	9.3	
1987:4	17.5	3.3
1988:1	17.7	
1988:2	21.8	
1988:3	7.3	
1988:4	22.0	8.1
1989:1	30.7	
1989:2	19.2	
1989:3	12.8	

(continues)

TABLE 2.2 (continued)

Year/Quarter	Inflation Rate	Budget Deficit/GDP
1989:4	19.4	3.9
1990:1	12.6	
1990:2	21.1	
1990:3	19.0	
1990:4	20.0	4.4
9. Mexico (1988:1–1991:4)		
1987:1	139.1	
1987:2	142.7	
1987:3	143.3	
1987:4	169.5	-1.8
1988:1	272.3	
1988:2	54.3	
1988:3	19.4	
1988:4	12.9	3.6
1989:1	24.6	
1989:2	17.2	
1989:3	13.7	
1989:4	19.6	1.7
1990:1	46.0	
1990:2	23.6	
1990:3	24.3	
1990:4	25.8	-2.3
1991:1	32.7	
1991:2	15.3	
1991:3	11.4	
1991:4	19.6	-3.3
10. Uruguay (1968:2–1971:4)		
1967:1	119.3	
1967:2	61.8	
1967:3	191.1	
1967:4	130.9	3.0
1968:1	268.5	
1968:2	105.7	
1968:3	46.8	
1968:4	5.3	1.7
1969:1	16.6	
1969:2	19.6	
1969:3	10.9	
1969:4	14.8	2.5
1970:1	19.7	

(continues)

TABLE 2.2 (continued)

Year/Quarter	Inflation Rate	Budget Deficit/GDP
1970:2	18.1	
1970:3	11.5	
1970:4	19.9	1.3
1971:1	27.4	
1971:2	19.0	
1971:3	28.3	
1971:4	60.6	5.8
1972:1	90.1	
1972:2	124.4	
1972:3	59.4	
1972:4	130.6	2.6
1973:1	160.3	
1973:2	33.4	
1973:3	134.0	
1973:4	38.0	1.4
11. Uruguay (1978:4–1982:4)		
1978:1	23.7	
1978:2	52.5	
1978:3	47.6	
1978:4	49.4	0.8
1979:1	68.9	
1979:2	73.2	
1979:3	90.0	
1979:4	86.9	-0.2
1980:1	66.7	
1980:2	41.8	
1980:3	57.4	
1980:4	34.6	-0.2
1981:1	25.1	
1981:2	29.7	
1981:3	40.4	
1981:4	25.2	1.4
1982:1	7.7	
1982:2	11.4	
1982:3	22.7	
1982:4	18.8	9.0
1983:1	139.6	
1983:2	31.6	
1983:3	36.0	
1983:4	47.2	3.9

Source: Végh (1992).

single digits by 1986, following which the inflation rate varied between 7.3 percent and 30.7 percent through the end of 1990.

Another case in which a sustained decline in the deficit was accompanied with a sustained decline in inflation is that of the first Brazilian stabilization program of 1964:2–1968:3. Over this time period the deficit was reduced from 4.2 percent of GDP to 1.2 percent of GDP. In contrast to the ill-fated Cruzado plan, this earlier stabilization program achieved a lasting budget deficit reduction that left the deficit at only 0.4 percent of GDP at the end of 1970. The inflation rate was brought down from 128.5 percent in the first quarter of 1964 to 25 percent in 1968:3. Inflation later declined to 12.7 percent in 1973 before rising again after the oil crisis.

The Chilean and Mexican stabilizations both involved fiscal restraint that moved the budget into surplus. In the Mexican case, however, the initial decline in inflation in 1988 from triple digits to 12.9 percent at the end of the year preceded the deficit reduction that took effect in 1989. The initial inflation reduction should therefore probably be attributed more to the wage/price controls and exchange rate stabilization than to deficit reduction. Nevertheless, the experience of other countries suggests that the inflation decline in Mexico could not have been sustained without the fiscal tightening that followed (see Edwards 1993 on the credibility of the Mexican stabilization program).

As with the Uruguayan stabilization that began at the same time, the Chilean stabilization program began in 1978 with inflation at around 50 percent a year but only a small budget deficit. Despite budgetary surpluses and substantial real exchange rate appreciation, inflation in both countries declined only slowly, reaching single digits in Chile in 1981 and in Uruguay in 1982. The output costs of the stabilization programs then led to a policy reversal and movement into deficit by the end of 1982. However, whereas in Uruguay the deficit rose to 9 percent of GDP and inflation soared to a high of 139.6 percent in early 1983, the Chilean budget deficit was kept below 3 percent of GDP and the upsurge in inflation was less drastic. At the end of 1983, inflation stood at 26.5 percent as compared to 49.9 percent just prior to the implementation of the stabilization program.

Nevertheless, the relationship between deficits and inflation suggested elsewhere leads one to question why the fiscal stringency adopted in Chile and Uruguay at the end of 1978 did not meet with more success. One major reason is likely the fact that each country pegged its exchange rate to the dollar at a time when the dollar was rising in value against most other currencies.[9] Friedman (1992:chp. 9) contrasts the Chilean stabilization with the seemingly more successful Israeli stabilization, and attributes the different outcomes chiefly to the fact that Israel pegged to the dollar when the dollar was falling

Budget Deficits and Inflation

and so avoided the drastic real exchange rate appreciation and output losses experienced in Chile (and also in Uruguay—Giorgi 1991).

This discussion of course focuses our attention on the fact that there is more to a stabilization program than just fiscal stringency. Still, of the eleven cases surveyed in this section, there is no example of a sustained inflation decline that was not accompanied by a reduction in the government's budget deficit. Moreover, in those instances where the inflation rate renewed its upward climb, this was again always accompanied by a similar renewed increase in the budget deficit. While the deficit increase in Chile and Uruguay in the 1980s may have been a consequence of the problems with the exchange rate policy, the comovement between deficits and inflation rates remains consistent with the other experiences described above.

Institutional Arrangements for Policy and the Inflation Process

While the Latin American experience with high inflation suggests that fiscal restraint is a prerequisite for a successful stabilization package, it is clear that it is not a sufficient condition for eliminating inflation. None of the stabilizations discussed in the preceding section kept inflation at a single-digit level for more than a quarter or two. Moreover, inflation has sometimes fallen very slowly despite the fiscal tightening that was implemented. For example, at the end of 1970, Brazilian inflation was still above 20 percent despite a budget deficit of only 0.4 percent of GDP and six years of fiscal stringency that had produced an average deficit of 1.1 percent of GDP.

The repeated failure of the Latin American countries to eliminate inflation stands in sharp contrast to the post-World War I hyperinflations where, in each case, the implementation of the stabilization program reduced inflation to single-digit levels and kept it there. Are these different results explained by the fact that most Latin American stabilizations occurred *before* the country entered hyperinflation? The Bolivian experience suggests otherwise. The monthly inflation rate of 57.6 percent for the year preceding Bolivia's October 1985 stabilization is higher than the inflation observed in post-World War I Austria and Hungary. Nevertheless, while in Austria and Hungary inflation quickly declined to monthly rates of 0.4 percent and 0.2 percent, respectively, Bolivian inflation continued at a monthly rate of 5.7 percent in the year following the stabilization (see Végh 1992:637).

In comparing the Bolivian case to earlier experiences with hyperinflation, Bernholz (1988b) points out that, after the 1985 currency reform, the Bolivian real money supply in 1987 still had not risen beyond 60 percent of its 1967 value. By contrast, in the post-World War I hyperinflations the decline in the real money supply during the inflationary period was followed by a return to normal, pre-inflation levels. Bernholz (1988b:766) suggests that the different pattern of behavior may be explicable in terms of "a general mistrust in Bolivian political institutions and in the stability of property rights." Moreover

> if the real stock of national money had grown to 100% instead of 60% or 70% because of more confident expectations concerning long-term stability, then the remaining inflation would have been wiped out as in the German and Austrian cases of the early 1920s. (Bernholz 1988b:767)

The costs of stabilization remain controversial. It appears that German production actually increased in the year following the November 1923 stabilization (Garber 1982:28). While Wicker (1986) has suggested that unemployment approximately doubled over the twelve months following the 1924 Hungarian and Polish stabilizations, in the Hungarian case output actually grew by 13.5 percent between 1924 and 1925—and the average growth rate from stabilization to the onset of the great depression was 8.4 percent (see Siklos 1993:287–88). In Austria, output fell initially following the October 1922 stabilization, but recovered the following year even though unemployment continued to rise until 1926. In Bolivia, unemployment and real output remained relatively stable after the 1985 stabilization. It is impossible to accurately disentangle the effects of the stabilization programs from other influences operative during these episodes, however. In cases of hyperinflation, the tradeoff between the costs of stabilization and the disruptions and dislocation associated with the hyperinflation process itself may help explain why such extreme disinflations did not have bigger unemployment effects.

The stabilizations from chronic but sub-hyperinflationary levels in many cases show gains in real output in the early stages of the program. This is true for eight of the ten chronic inflation cases discussed in the previous section, with the only obvious exceptions being the 1985 Argentinean stabilization and the 1987 Mexican stabilization. However, subsequent contractions in output and real consumption led to these gains being reversed in most cases. Significantly, however, Mexico, which is perhaps the country that has so far shown the greatest commitment to lasting stabilization, continued to enjoy rising real consumption, and the initial downturn was reversed as early as mid-1988 (see Végh 1992:649–52). The Mexican case, in fact, suggests that it is at least possible to end chronic inflation without prolonged costs for the real economy.

Certainly, the seemingly low costs of terminating past hyperinflations should not be taken to imply that one should go from chronic—or moderate—inflation to hyperinflation before attempting to introduce a stabilization program! The distortions of productive activity in Germany in 1923, for example, helped make it possible to stabilize without inducing any further rise in unemployment. However, the 23.4 percent unemployment rate in November

1923 reminds us that the relative improvement in 1924 still left the economy in very poor condition—and industrial production stood at only 77 percent of the 1913 level in 1924 (see Garber 1982:28, 30). Similarly, by the time the stabilization program was enacted in Bolivia, the unemployment rate had already risen above 15 percent (Bernholz 1988b:769).

It is not clear that either currency reform or international intervention is necessary for successful stabilization. While currency reform preceded the 1923 German stabilization, in cases such as Austria currency reform did not occur until much later (the Austrian stabilization was achieved in August 1922 but the new currency, the schilling, was not introduced until the end of 1924—Sargent 1993:59). Other more recent cases, notably Argentina and Brazil, demonstrate that currency reform alone is no more than a change in the unit of account against which the rate of inflation is measured. International protocols and loans do appear to have assisted the Austrian, German and Hungarian stabilizations. However, the fact that Poland stabilized without this assistance—just as Czechoslovakia avoided entering hyperinflation through domestic policy initiatives alone—suggests that international intervention (while potentially helpful) cannot be considered a necessary condition for stabilization.

Sargent (1993:chp. 3) does, however, emphasize the importance of the fact that the post-World War I stabilizations involved not only fiscal reform but also *monetary* reforms providing for an independent central bank. Until recently, monetary policy in the Latin American countries has remained under firm government control. This has left the government free to expand the deficit without any concern as to whether the central bank will consent to finance this deficit. Among the industrialized countries, central bank independence appears to have significantly constrained deficit expansion in Germany, Switzerland and the United States over the 1960–1983 period (Burdekin and Laney 1988; see also Burdekin and Langdana 1992:chp. 7). Thus, just as distributive conflicts may lead to added pressures on the government purse, the lack of an independent monetary policy maker may make it too easy for the government to accede to these demands through deficit spending.[10]

Recent institutional changes in Chile and Mexico promise to provide an opportunity to put this theory to the test. Chile's Pinochet government, by maintaining highly restrictive fiscal and monetary policies despite high unemployment costs, kept inflation in the 15–25 percent range even after abandoning the 1978–1982 exchange-rate-based stabilization program. In an attempt to maintain the hard-won disinflation achieved during the 1980s, the democratic government that came into power in 1990 established an independent central bank (see Dornbusch and Fischer 1993). The bank's legal charter includes responsibility for monetary stability without any requirement for the bank to pursue the potentially conflicting goals of growth and full employment. Dornbusch and Fischer (1993:17) characterize this institutional reform as "the final step in assuring that a disinflation process was locked in."

Recently, Mexico also introduced legislation making its central bank independent of the government (see Hall 1993). In common with the U.S. Federal Reserve System, the constitutional amendment passed by the Mexican Congress in June 1993 provides for staggered terms for the central bank's board so that no one president can readily "stack the deck" in his or her favor. Significantly, Mexico, like Chile, had moved its budget into surplus prior to implementing the legislation creating the independent central bank. An important reason why monetary autonomy has been so rare among less developed countries is that, in the absence of any significant market for government bonds, a commitment to an independent central bank is tantamount to a commitment to a balanced budget. While it remains to be seen whether the new legislation passed in Chile and Mexico will be effective in insuring against a return to the deficit spending policies of old, there is at least the possibility that these reforms mark a real break with the past.

Even if the Chilean and Mexican constitutional reforms are shown to be successful, they can only be emulated in other developing economies if the government is willing and able to commit to a sustainable fiscal policy and eschew seigniorage as a major revenue source.[11] Evidence from the postwar era suggests that most Latin American countries have, in the past, found such a commitment impossible to maintain. Political reform and/or measures aimed at defusing the rampant distributional conflicts in such countries are likely to remain a prerequisite for effective, and successful, economic reform.

Implications for the Emerging Market Economies of Central and Eastern Europe

In recent years, budget deficit and inflation problems have, in varying degrees, plagued not only Russia but all the other former Iron Curtain countries. Table 2.3 provides 1991 and 1992 budget deficit and inflation data for the members of the former Czechoslovak Federation (the Czech Republic and Slovakia) together with Hungary, Poland and three members of the former Soviet Union—Estonia, Russia and the Ukraine.[12] In the transition towards a market economy, the deficit and inflation figures have been heavily influenced by the output declines experienced in each of these countries, the effects of the price liberalization programs, shifting patterns of trade and so forth (for further discussion, see, for example, Bofinger 1993 and Gáspár 1993). Nevertheless, there is an apparent tendency for the countries with smaller deficits to have lower inflation rates.

Budget Deficits and Inflation 53

TABLE 2.3 Central and Eastern European Deficit and Inflation Data

	Budget Deficit/GDP		*Inflation Rate*	
	1991	1992	1991	1992
Czech Republic	1.0	1.0	52.0	12.7
Estonia	-4.9	-1.5	N/A	N/A
Hungary	5.0	7.0	33.8	21.8
Poland	5.0	8.0	60.3	44.5
Russia	11.3	15.0	160.6	2525.2
Slovakia	1.0	1.0	58.2	9.1
Ukraine	14.4	33.3	N/A	N/A

Notes: The budget deficit data for the Czech Republic and Slovakia reflect the fiscal position of the Czechoslovak Federation that was dissolved at the beginning of 1993. The 1992 Russian deficit data and the 1992 Ukrainian deficit data are estimates. The inflation data refer to the percentage change in the retail price index, except for Russia where the new consumer price index is used.

Sources: Bofinger (1993:4) for the Czechoslovakian, Hungarian and Polish budget deficit data. Goldman, Ickes and Ryterman (1993:28) for the 1991 Russian and Ukrainian budget deficit data. Lewarne (1993:27) for the Estonian budget deficit data. Gáspár (1993:2) for estimates of the 1992 Russian and Ukrainian budget deficits. *PlanEcon Report* (1993a, 1993b, 1993c, 1993d, 1993e) for the inflation data.

In the former Czechoslovakia, the relatively strong fiscal position enjoyed in 1991 with only a very small budget deficit was maintained in 1992. In 1992, the Czech and Slovak regions both enjoyed inflation rates close to 10 percent, lower than for any of the other countries represented in Table 2.3. Hungary and Poland had higher inflation rates of 21.8 percent and 44.5 percent in 1992 as well as bigger deficits equal to 7 percent and 8 percent of GDP, respectively. These trends continued into 1993. The Czech budget moved into surplus during the first five months of 1993, and the monthly inflation rate was as low as 0.5 percent a month (*PlanEcon* 1993f). Thus, while Hungary, Poland and Slovakia devalued their currencies, the Czech koruna was under pressure to revalue. In Hungary, meanwhile, the projected 1993 deficit of 6.4–6.7 percent of GDP (*PlanEcon* 1993g) suggested only a marginal gain from the 1992 ratio of 7.0 percent. Neither Hungary nor Poland has so far been able to meet the IMF's recommendation of a 5 percent deficit target.

It is Russia, however, that stands out with deficits estimated at 11.3 percent of GDP in 1991 and 15 percent of GDP in 1992 coupled with 160.6 percent inflation in 1991 and 2525.2 percent inflation in 1992.[13] Despite the improvements apparently registered for 1993, Russia's deficit and inflation performance has remained far worse than those of Hungary, Poland, and the former Czechoslovakia. Even though the 1991 inflation figures were influenced by the price liberalization that began at the end of that year, it seems that large deficits played an important role in the inflation process throughout this period. Resort to inflationary finance was fueled in 1991 by a sharp reduction in the contributions to the federal budget from the republics. Even prior to the adoption of the liberalization measures, Gaidar (1993:71) states that the first half-year budget for 1991 showed

> receipts totalled only 40 per cent of the planned amount ... Over half of federal expenses were covered through issuing money. The state bank increased loans for budgetary purposes by 80 billion roubles, or 12 per cent. In the meantime, both sides pointed an accusing finger at one [an]other arguing who was to blame for the high inflation rate ("Republicans dodge taxes." "The centre issues money.")

The data on Estonia and the Ukraine are insufficient to provide a full comparison with the countries discussed above. However, the available evidence suggests that, while Estonia had surpluses in both 1991 and 1992, the Ukraine suffered budget deficits even larger than those experienced in Russia. Indeed, the Ukraine's 1992 budget deficit is estimated by Gáspár (1993) to equal as much as one-third of the country's GDP.[14] Although an accurate price level comparison cannot be made at this point, exchange rate data on the movements of the Russian ruble against the Estonian kroon and the Ukrainian karbovanets enable some inferences to be drawn regarding relative inflation performance. In 1993, the Estonian kroon enjoyed substantial appreciation against the ruble. Meanwhile, the exchange rate of the Ukrainian karbovanets against the ruble depreciated from less than 3:1 in February 1993 to nearly 20:1 in September 1993. Indeed, by September 1993, the Ukraine appeared to have entered into hyperinflation—and, between mid-August and the beginning of September, the exchange rate with the U.S. dollar went from 6,000:1 to 19,000:1 (*The Economist* 1993). Black-market rates of 29,000:1 to 32,000:1 were reported in December 1993 (notwithstanding the fixed rates imposed by the Ukrainian government in November).

Once again, there is at least some indication of a linkage between a country's fiscal position and inflation performance. As in Latin America, emerging market economies that fail to control their deficit spending have also had trouble containing inflation and exchange rate depreciation. At the same time, it is not only the size of the deficit but the method of financing that helps account for the inflationary consequences of expansionary fiscal policies. In Russia, without a developed capital market to absorb government debt issues, and in the midst of severe doubts as to the government's political survival, money finance has been preeminent in covering the large shortfall of taxes below state expenditures.

In 1992, central bank credit creation accounted for 40 percent of Russia's GDP. An April 1993 agreement between the Russian finance minister, Boris Fyodorov, and the central bank governor, Viktor Gerashchenko, stipulated that the rate of central bank credit creation would be drastically cut back to no more than 10 percent a month by December 1993. Although Finance Minister Fyodorov claimed that the Russian central bank "continues to underwrite industry with its printing press" (Roth 1993:A12), Russia's inflation rate did begin to fall in late 1993 and dropped below 10 percent a month in March 1994. Yeltsin's decree to privatize land may help the fiscal situation by offsetting at least part of the subsidies to Russia's farm sector—subsidies that may have accounted for nearly 60 percent of the estimated 17 trillion ruble 1993 budget deficit (Roth 1993). However, in the midst of the continuing economic and political turmoil, the ruble exchange rate can be expected to remain highly sensitive to policy announcements, political events and other fiscal news (see Linda S. Goldberg 1992).

The importance of expectations and of public confidence in the government cannot be stressed too much. As discussed above, even drastic fiscal restraint often failed to put an end to the inflation process in Latin America. In Bolivia, for example, public reluctance to hold the new currency appears to have been instrumental in the fact that inflation—although greatly reduced—remained stubbornly at around the 20 percent level after the 1985 stabilization and currency reform. By contrast, where public perceptions are more favorable, the U.S. experience shows that a government can run large, and perhaps non-sustainable, budget deficits without inducing any short-run inflationary pressure (although the U.S. government may currently be pushing this possibility to its limit).

Perhaps the key issue is whether, once the present transition to a market economy is substantially complete, the Central and Eastern European nations will be able to surmount the factors that have led to the persistent inflation faced by the Latin American countries. The sharp output declines in these countries, coupled with the conflict over distributional shares that appears to lie behind the breakup of Czechoslovakia, will certainly make it extremely difficult for the Slovakian government, in particular, to maintain a policy of fiscal stringency.[15] Even Germany has resorted to deficit finance in an attempt to boost economic activity in the former East Germany and placate the workers displaced in the transition to a market economy.

There are, however, already some apparent success stories. Estonia, in particular, committed to a hard currency policy by introducing a currency board that pegged its new national currency, the kroon, to the Deutsche mark on June 20, 1992 (see Buyske 1993). This commitment to monetary stringency was accompanied by fiscal tightening, and tax hikes and reduced subsidies yielded budgetary surpluses in both 1991 and 1992. Since the rate of monetary expansion under the currency board cannot exceed the board's reserves of foreign currency and other hard assets, monetary finance of budget deficits is in any event severely constrained, if not eliminated, so long as this system remains in place. The credibility gains associated with these reforms may explain the rapid drop in Estonia's inflation rate from near 1000 percent at the beginning of 1992 to an estimated annual rate of 33 percent in 1993.

Furthermore, many of the transitional countries have passed legislation making their central banks statutorily independent of the government. The central banks of Bulgaria, the Czech Republic, Hungary, Slovakia and Slovenia all have limits on lending to the government. These central banks also have as their mandated objectives price and/or exchange rate stability (see Siklos 1994 and Hochreiter 1995 for further analysis of the respective institutional structures). The effective degree of independence may be less pronounced than the statutes suggest, however. The Act on the National Bank of Hungary 1991, for example, while designed to strengthen the independence of the central bank, includes a provision giving the prime minister the power to appoint (and replace) the head of the central bank. Immediately following the passage of this new law, the former head of the Hungarian central bank, György Suranyi—who had been openly critical of the government—was summarily dismissed and replaced by a former government minister (Dezséri 1993). Meanwhile, the original limits on fiscal financing laid down in both Bulgaria and Hungary have already been overruled by their parliaments (see Hochreiter 1995).

The intent of the institutional reforms in monetary policy in the former Communist countries nevertheless remains a positive sign. The phasing out of direct budget financing, if fully implemented, remains a potentially important step towards fiscal stringency in these economies. These reforms also come at a time when Latin American countries like Chile and Mexico are also making attempts to "lock in" the gains from recent stabilizations. It is certainly critical that policy makers in the emerging market-orientated economies recognize the longer-term cost of tolerating even the "moderate" inflation experienced in many of the Latin American countries, let alone chronic inflation of the levels still experienced in Brazil. Otherwise, it is likely that, as has been the case in nations like Argentina and Brazil, we will be faced, not with one lasting stabilization, but a series of short-lived "stabilizations," each less credible than the last.[16]

Notes

1. Associate Professor of Economics, Claremont McKenna College and the Claremont Graduate School. An earlier version of this paper was presented at the 1993 meetings of the Western Economic Association at Lake Tahoe, Nevada, June 20–24. The author thanks Tom Willett, Pierre Siklos, Steve Lewarne, Mike Kuehlwein, Kálmán Dezséri, Paul Burkett and King Banaian for helpful comments, and is also grateful to King Banaian for sharing data on the Central and Eastern European economies.

2. Quoted in Webb (1989:24).

Budget Deficits and Inflation 57

3. This contrasts with a Ricardian regime in which deficits are temporary and fully offset by future budget surpluses. In the Ricardian case, deficits have no effect on the path of base money growth—and government bonds are not net wealth so long as the value of the bonds is offset by the present value of the implied stream of future taxes (see Barro 1974).

4. Evidence of the link between inflation performance and fiscal news during the American and French Revolutions, and under the Southern Confederacy of 1861–1865, is provided in Burdekin and Langdana (1992:chp. 3).

5. See Chou (1963:chp. 8) for a comparison of the Chinese, German, Greek and (second) Hungarian hyperinflations.

6. Such pressures are, of course, not specific just to Latin America. In the German hyperinflation, distributional conflict between wages and profits combined with fiscal news in driving the spiralling inflation after World War I (see Burdekin and Burkett 1992).

7. Statistical support for a strong effect of the budget deficit on inflation in one such high-inflation country is provided by Choudhary and Parai (1991), using quarterly data for Peru over the 1973–1988 period. Consistent evidence of a link between deficits and inflation appears to arise only in more extreme cases, however. While De Haan and Zelhorst (1990) find that acute inflation years (where inflation is above 75 percent a year) are generally accompanied by higher than normal budget deficits across their sample of forty-six developing countries, there is much less support for a link between deficits and inflation for the sample taken as a whole.

8. For more detailed discussion of these stabilization experiences than can be provided here, the reader is referred to Giorgi (1991), Kiguel and Liviatan (1991, 1992), Feijo and de Carvalho (1992), Végh (1992), Patinkin (1993), and the references provided therein.

9. Argentina also adopted such a policy as part of its second stabilization attempt. However, Argentina never matched the fiscal stringency of Chile and Uruguay, and its budget remained in deficit while inflation continued at or near the three-digit level throughout.

10. Bresser Pereira and Dall'Acqua (1991:35) also point out that, during the 1970s, the "existence of easy foreign finance made it easier for Latin American countries practically to ignore budget deficits." However, once external funding began to dry up at the beginning of the 1980s, these same countries were then faced with excessively large budget deficits that could only be financed by money creation.

11. The prior importance of seigniorage revenue to Mexico is reflected in the fact that seigniorage accounted for an average of 23.9 percent of total Mexican government revenue over the 1971–1982 period—while Brazil, Chile, Colombia and Peru each averaged 17 percent or more over this same period (Cukierman, Edwards and Tabellini 1992:538).

12. These figures differ somewhat from the numbers reported by Lewarne (1993:27) over this same time period. However, the relative standings of the countries based on deficit and inflation performance remain the same. The Czech Republic, for example, has deficits of 2.0 percent of GDP in 1991 and 3.3 percent in 1992 based on Lewarne's figures (as compared to the 1 percent estimate for each year given in Table 2.3), yet retains the same relative ranking ahead of all other countries besides Estonia.

13. The ruble's high rate of depreciation has met with increasing rejection of the currency by the Russian public. By November 1992, there were already nearly 1,000 dollar stores in Moscow alone, and it was estimated that more than $10 billion worth of dollars circulated in Russia as a whole (Carey Goldberg 1992).

14. In consultation with the Ukrainian Embassy in Moscow, Lewarne (1993:27) estimates that the ensuing 1993 Ukrainian budget deficit exceeded 35 percent—with inflation running between 7,000 and 10,000 percent for the year.

15. Slovakia also appears to have evidenced the important role of expectations in determining price and exchange rate behavior. Despite inheriting the near-balanced budget pursued in 1991 and 1992 by the now-defunct Czechoslovak Federation, the Slovak koruna was already exchanging at a discount relative to the Czech koruna in early 1993 (*PlanEcon* 1993e). Slovakia seems to have suffered from the fact that the loss of the transfers previously received from the Czechs, and perceived structural problems with the Slovak economy, were fueling expectations of *future* deficits—even though the actual Slovak deficit, at that time, remained quite low.

16. See, for example, Kiguel and Liviatan (1991) on the erosion of credibility following the failure of the Austral and Cruzado plans.

References

Baer, Werner. 1991. "Social Aspects of Latin American Inflation." *Quarterly Review of Economics and Business* 31: 45–57.

Balderston, T. 1989. "War Finance and Inflation in Britain and Germany, 1914–1918." *Economic History Review* 42: 222–44.

Banaian, King. 1995. "Inflation and Optimal Seigniorage in the CIS and Eastern Europe," this volume.

Barro, Robert J. 1974. "Are Government Bonds Net Wealth?" *Journal of Political Economy* 82: 1095–1117.

Bernholz, Peter. 1988a. "Inflation, Monetary Regime and the Financial Asset Theory of Money." *Kyklos* 41: 5–34.

―――. 1988b. "Hyperinflation and Currency Reform in Bolivia: Studied from a General Perspective." *Journal of Institutional and Theoretical Economics* 144: 747–71.

Bofinger, Peter. 1993. "The Output Decline in Central and Eastern Europe: A Classical Explanation." Discussion Paper No. 784, Centre for Economic Policy Research, London.

Bresser Pereira, Luiz, and Fernando Dall'Acqua. 1991. "Economic Populism versus Keynes: Reinterpreting Budget Deficit in Latin America." *Journal of Post Keynesian Economics* 14: 29–38.

Burdekin, Richard C. K., and Paul Burkett. 1989. "Conflict Inflation and the Institutionalisation of Nonactivist Monetary Policy." *British Review of Economic Issues* 11: 103–20.

―――. 1992. "Money, Credit, and Wages in Hyperinflation: Post-World War I Germany." *Economic Inquiry* 30: 479–95.

Burdekin, Richard C. K., and Leroy O. Laney. 1988. "Fiscal Policymaking and the Central Bank Institutional Constraint." *Kyklos* 41: 647–62.

Burdekin, Richard C. K. and Farrokh K. Langdana. 1992. *Budget Deficits and Economic Performance*. London: Routledge.
Buyske, Gail. 1993. "Estonia, Monetary Model for Russia." *Wall Street Journal*, June 29: A14.
Calomiris, Charles W. 1988. "Institutional Failure, Monetary Scarcity, and the Depreciation of the Continental." *Journal of Economic History* 48: 47–68.
Capie, Forrest. 1986. "Conditions in which Very Rapid Inflation Has Appeared," in Karl Brunner and Allan Meltzer, eds., *The National Bureau Method, International Capital Mobility and Other Essays*. Pp. 115–68. Amsterdam: North-Holland.
Chirkova, E. 1992. "Where the Government Is Looking: An Attempt at a Popular Account of the Nature of Hyperinflation." *Problems of Economic Transition* 35: 63–76.
Chou, Shun-Hsin. 1963. *The Chinese Inflation: 1937–1949*. New York: Columbia University Press.
Choudhary, Munir A. S., and Amar K. Parai. 1991. "Budget Deficit and Inflation: The Peruvian Experience." *Applied Economics* 23: 1117–21.
Cukierman, Alex, Sebastian Edwards, and Guido Tabellini. 1992. "Seignorage and Political Instability." *American Economic Review* 82: 537–55.
De Haan, Jakob, and Dick Zelhorst. 1990. "The Impact of Government Deficits on Money Growth in Developing Countries." *Journal of International Money and Finance* 9: 455–69.
Dezséri, Kálmán. 1993. Personal interview, Claremont McKenna College, October 27.
Dornbusch, Rudiger, and Stanley Fischer. 1993. "Moderate Inflation." *World Bank Economic Review* 7: 1–44.
Dornbusch, Rudiger, Federico Sturzenegger, and Holger Wolf. 1990. "Extreme Inflation: Dynamics and Stabilization." *Brookings Papers on Economic Activity* No. 2: 1–84.
The Economist. 1993. "Ukraine over the Brink." September 4: 45–46.
Edwards, Sebastian. 1993. "Exchange Rates as Nominal Anchors." *Weltwirtschaftliches Archiv* 129: 1–32.
Edwards, Sebastian, and Guido Tabellini. 1991. "Fiscal Policies and Inflation in Developing Countries." *Journal of International Money and Finance* 10: S16–S48.
Farhadian, Ziba, and Robert M. Dunn, Jr. 1986. "Fiscal Policy and Financial Deepening in a Monetarist Model of the Balance of Payments." *Kyklos* 39: 66–84.
Feijo, Carmem Aparecida, and Fernando J. Cardim de Carvalho. 1992. "The Resilience of High Inflation: Recent Brazilian Failures with Stabilization Policies." *Journal of Post Keynesian Economics* 15: 109–24.
Friedman, Milton. 1992. *Money Mischief: Episodes in Monetary History*. New York: Harcourt Brace Jovanovich.
Gaidar, Egor T. 1993. "Inflationary Pressures and Economic Reform in the Soviet Union," in Michael Ellman, Egor T. Gaidar and Grzegorz W. Kolodko, *Economic Transition in Eastern Europe*. Pp. 63–90. Oxford : Basil Blackwell.
Garber, Peter M. 1982. "Transition from Inflation to Price Stability," in Karl Brunner and Allan H. Meltzer, eds., *Monetary Regimes and Protectionism*. Pp. 11–42. Amsterdam: North-Holland.

Gáspár, Pál. 1993. "The Fiscal Consequences of Economic Transition in Eastern-European Economies." Working Paper, Institute for World Economics, Budapest, Hungary.

Giorgi, Eduardo. 1991. *Inflation Under Different External Regimes: The Case of Uruguay*, Arne Bigsten, ed. Aldershot, England: Avebury.

Goldberg, Carey. 1992. "As 'Dollarization' Grows, Russians Disdain the Ruble." *Los Angeles Times*, November 27: A1, A14, A16.

Goldberg, Linda S. 1992. "Moscow Black Markets and Official Markets for Foreign Exchange: How Much Flexibility in Flexible Rates?" Working Paper No. 4040, National Bureau of Economic Research, Cambridge, Mass.

Goldberg, Linda S., Barry Ickes, and Randi Ryterman. 1993. "Departures from the Ruble Area: The Political Economy of Adopting Independent Currencies." Paper presented at the Conference on "Markets, States and Democracy: The Transformation of Communist Regimes in Eastern Europe and the Former Soviet Union." University of California at Berkeley.

Hakkio, Craig S., and Mark Rush. 1991. "Is the Budget Deficit 'Too Large?'" *Economic Inquiry* 29: 429–45.

Hall, Kevin G. 1993. "Experts Laud Mexico's Proposal for Autonomous Central Bank." *Journal of Commerce and Commercial*, Pacific Edition, May 19: 3A.

Hochreiter, Eduard. 1995. "Central Banking in Economies in Transition," this volume.

Hoover, Kevin D., and Steven M. Sheffrin. 1992. "Causation, Spending, and Taxes: Sand in the Sandbox or Tax Collector for the Welfare State?" *American Economic Review* 82: 225–48.

Ignatius, Adi. 1994. "Russia's Top Banker Wins New Respect." *Wall Street Journal*, April 20: A11.

Kiguel, Miguel A., and Nissan Liviatan. 1991. "The Inflation-Stabilization Cycles in Argentina and Brazil," in Michael Bruno, Stanley Fischer, Elhanan Helpman and Nissan Liviatan, eds., *Lessons of Economic Stabilization and Its Aftermath*. Pp. 191–232. Cambridge, Mass.: MIT Press.

_____. 1992. "When Do Heterodox Stabilization Programs Work? Lessons from Experience." *World Bank Research Observer* 7: 35–57.

Lewarne, Stephen. 1993. "Assessment and Analysis of the Macroeconomic, Financial, and Fiscal Sector Environment in the Kyrgyz Republic." Report submitted to the United States Agency for International Development, Almaty, Kazakhstan.

_____. 1995. "The Russian Central Bank and the Conduct of Monetary Policy," this volume.

Patinkin, Don. 1993. "Israel's Stabilization Program of 1985, or Some Simple Truths of Monetary Theory." *Journal of Economic Perspectives* 7: 103–28.

Pazos, Felipe. 1990. "Runaway Inflation: Experiences and Options." *CEPAL Review* 42: 115–30.

PlanEcon Report. 1993a. Washington, D.C., March 10.

PlanEcon Report. 1993b. Washington, D.C., March 22.

PlanEcon Report. 1993c. Washington, D.C., April 5.

PlanEcon Report. 1993d. Washington, D.C., April 20.

PlanEcon Report. 1993e. Washington, D.C., April 30.

PlanEcon Report. 1993f. Washington, D.C., July 23.

PlanEcon Report. 1993g. Washington, D.C., September 17.

Roth, Terence. 1993. "Fyodorov Aims for Top Post at Russia's Bank." *Wall Street Journal*, November 1: A12.
Roubini, Nouriel. 1991. "Economic and Political Determinants of Budget Deficits in Developing Countries." *Journal of International Money and Finance* 10: S49–S72.
Sargent, Thomas J. 1993. *Rational Expectations and Inflation*, 2nd ed. New York: Harper Collins.
Siklos, Pierre L. 1990. "Hyperinflations: Their Origins, Development and Termination." *Journal of Economic Surveys* 4: 225–48.
―――――. 1993. "Interpreting a Change in Monetary Policy Regimes: A Reappraisal of the First Hungarian Hyperinflation and Stabilization, 1921–28," in Michael D. Bordo and Forrest Capie, eds., *Monetary Regimes in Transition*. Pp. 274–311. New York: Cambridge University Press.
―――――. 1994. "Central Bank Independence in the Transitional Economies: A Preliminary Investigation of Hungary, Poland, the Czech and Slovak Republics," in István Székely and John P. Bonin, eds., *Development and Reform of the Financial System in Central and Eastern Europe*. Brookfield, Vt: Edward Elgar, forthcoming.
Smith, Bruce D. 1985a. "American Colonial Monetary Regimes: The Failure of the Quantity Theory and Some Evidence in Favour of an Alternate View." *Canadian Journal of Economics* 18: 531–65.
―――――. 1985b. "Some Colonial Evidence on Two Theories of Money: Maryland and the Carolinas." *Journal of Political Economy* 93: 1178–1211.
Végh, Carlos A. 1992. "Stopping High Inflation: An Analytical Overview." *International Monetary Fund Staff Papers* 39: 626–95.
Webb, Steven B. 1989. *Hyperinflation and Stabilization in Weimar Germany*. New York: Oxford University Press.
Wicker, Elmus. 1986. "Terminating Hyperinflation in the Dismembered Hapsburg Monarchy." *American Economic Review* 76: 350–64.
Willett, Thomas D., and King Banaian. 1988. "Explaining the Great Stagflation: Toward a Political Economy Framework," in Thomas D. Willett, ed., *Political Business Cycles: The Political Economy of Money, Inflation, and Unemployment*. Pp. 35–62. Durham, N.C.: Duke University Press.

3

Inflation and Optimal Seigniorage in the CIS and Eastern Europe

King Banaian[1]

Current joke in Russia: What is the difference between inflation and hyperinflation? Scenario 1: Your purse is stolen, the thief takes your rubles and throws away your purse; this is inflation. Scenario 2: Your purse is stolen, the thief throws away your rubles and takes your purse; this is hyperinflation.

from a computer bulletin board, June 1993

Introduction

Recent writings on inflation policy have recognized the public finance role of central banking policy. A public finance view recognizes that money creation generates revenue—*seigniorage*—for the government. The rule of taxation (usually attributed to Ramsey 1927) is that policymakers equalize the marginal cost of raising the tax rate on any base. In countries where the costs of income taxation are high, asset taxation may be a useful alternative; and money is a readily identifiable asset. There is also the desire to tax where the demand is inelastic. Simple principles of economics teach us that the welfare cost of taxation is reduced when taxation does not induce substitutions to other goods or assets. Thus, the optimal rate of the inflation tax will be a function of the elasticity of demand for money and the costs of taxing other bases. In countries where the tax system is inefficient and credit markets incomplete, an optimal mix of taxes on both income and money can imply a positive optimal inflation rate. That rate is below the rate of inflation that generates the maximum amount of seigniorage revenues.

The centrally planned economies of the former Soviet Union and Eastern Europe would appear to fit the criteria just laid out. Their tax systems were not developed, as the state simply claimed whatever share of state enterprise output it required for its plan. The financial system consisted of a monobank that offered only savings accounts to its citizens and transferred funds internally from one state enterprise to another. It printed currency and gave credit at the direction of the state plan.

Tax and financial systems take time to develop. In the interim, countries undergoing the transition from central planning to market economies might be expected to place some reliance on seigniorage. In 1989 Yugoslavia took in 12 percent of gross social product as seigniorage revenues, accounting for 35 percent of all fiscal revenues. Poland relied somewhat less on it, but financed a deficit of approximately 7 percent of its GDP by money creation.

One would expect such policies to draw criticism from economists. Yet economists' indifference towards, or perhaps even encouragement of, a heavy reliance on the inflation tax by developing economies is a profoundly disturbing feature of economic policy advice of the late twentieth century. Many of the economies of Eastern Europe, after the shock of price liberalization, have settled into inflation rates in the 30–50 percent range, and such policy statements as those of Pazos (1990) and Dornbusch and Fischer (1993) discussed above may lead some to conclude that no further attempts to lower inflation need be taken.[2]

This chapter describes the relevant factors in understanding whether these rates are efficient outcomes for the transitional economies. The optimal inflation rate is influenced strongly by three factors: the elasticity of money demand; the efficiency of the tax system; and the strength of the uncertainty effects of inflation in retarding growth. While a standard calculation of optimal and revenue-maximizing inflation rates would perhaps indicate differently, explicit recognition of the uncertainty costs of inflation suggests that the present rates of inflation in most of the transitional economies are too high. After some discussion of the special character of seigniorage in transitional economies, the differences in these views are highlighted. Then, using plausible estimates for key parameters in the transitional economies, the social welfare and revenue-maximizing rates of inflation for several of these economies are calculated.

What Is Seigniorage in a Transitional Economy?

Definitions of seigniorage depend largely on the context within which the analysis takes place. One approach is to view seigniorage revenues as an excise tax upon holders of base money.[3] If the Fisher relation holds, such that a rise in the inflation rate leads to an equal rise in the nominal rate of interest, the demand for (base) money diagram can be used to show a rectangle corresponding to government revenues, plus a welfare loss triangle. Klein and Neumann (1990) and Neumann (1992) refer to the welfare loss as *opportunity cost seigniorage*, and this is most applicable to studies of optimal inflation rates.[4] The real value of the seigniorage revenue can be measured as the product of the nominal rate of interest and the holdings of real base money.[5] There are several difficulties with calculation of such measures. There is of course the problem of specifying the demand for money function. In particular, economies in transition will have unstable money demand functions due to the (hopefully) rapid development of new financial instruments, changes in currency convertibility laws, and removal of interest rate ceilings. Additionally, one must determine the appropriate rate of interest to employ. But most importantly, perhaps, the standard seigniorage measure does not correspond to the actual revenues the central bank obtains from issuing currency. The value of assets on its own portfolio is affected by changes in interest rates, such that rising inflation gains operating revenues but imposes a capital loss on its holdings of government bonds.

An alternative measure, which Neumann calls *monetary seigniorage*, is obtained by simply measuring the change in base money, deflated by some price index. The central bank issues base money in return for some nonmoney asset. The real value of that asset is seigniorage. This calculation is straightforward once one defines what base money is. Typically, we treat the monetary base as consisting of two parts: currency and reserves. Certain modifications are necessary when discussing the central banks of the transitional economies. For example, consider this balance sheet for the National Bank of Moldova, one of the CIS countries:[6]

On 31 December, 1992 (in billions of rubles)

Assets:			Liabilities:		
Net International Reserves		-7.94	Currency		10.83
Convertible	1.01		Coupons	6.41	
Non-convertible	-8.95		Rubles	4.42	
Net Domestic Assets		57.11	Required reserves		9.43
Claims on govt.	51.64		Excess reserves		28.82
Credit to banks	3.37		Enterprise deposits		0.09
Other items (net)	2.10				
Total Assets		49.17	*Total Liabilities*		49.17

On 30 June, 1993 (in billions of rubles)			
Assets:		Liabilities:	
Net International Reserves	-27.12	Currency	40.23
Convertible	-9.46	Coupons	31.38
Non-convertible	-17.66	Rubles	8.85
Net Domestic Assets	125.41	Required reserves	17.79
Claims on govt.	78.45	Excess reserves	39.74
Credit to banks	30.39	Enterprise deposits	0.53
Other items (net)	16.57		
Total Assets	98.28	Total Liabilities	98.28

Source: IMF, *Country Report, Moldova*, May 1994.

The total change in central bank liabilities is Rb 49.11 billion, and by our definition this would be the value of monetary seigniorage for the first six months of 1993. But not all of this accrues to the Moldovan government. Direct lending to the government was only Rb 26.81 billion. The second use of these seigniorage revenues was lending to banks in the amount of Rb 27.02 billion. Many of these banks lend to state enterprises; enterprise losses funded by state subsidies or central bank credits are equivalent in discussing uses of seigniorage. One can see that these two items alone amount to more than 100 percent of the seigniorage revenues generated.[7]

The reason for this is that not all currency used in Moldova is printed by its national bank. The liabilities side shows that the quantity of rubles that are the responsibility of the national bank doubled. This increase of Rb 4.43 billion is offset on the asset side by a decrease in the bank's international reserves.[8] This, along with the rest of the change in international reserves, shows the degree to which Moldova's credit expansion is financed externally. In short, the change in the base can be described as base = (international reserves) + (domestic credit issued by central bank). The amount generated directly by the central bank is the amount of additional coupons printed (Rb 24.97 bn) and the additional reserves that commercial banks and state enterprises held with it (Rb 19.72 bn).[9] The sum of these numbers, 44.69 billion rubles, may be a better measure of the nominal value of monetary seigniorage obtained by Moldova. This value is about 5 percent of Moldovan GDP over the six-month period in question.

Two remaining points require clarification. First, in high-inflation economies, estimating real revenues requires determining the timing of base money creation, so as to know the appropriate price level. Were we to deflate the corrected seigniorage value above by the exchange rate in effect at the end of June, Rb 1100:$1, we would obtain $40.6 million as the real value. But this assumes that the entire increment to the monetary base was added on June 30. Alternatively, using balance sheet data for March 31 and the exchange rates for then and December 31 gives us real seigniorage revenues of $64.8 million. This assumes all the money is spent at the beginning of each quarter. The true figure lies somewhere between, and only higher frequency data will lead us to a more accurate assessment.

Last, we should consider the peculiar cases of the CIS countries, where there were dual currencies in circulation and a division of seigniorage revenues with the Central Bank of Russia. The other transitional economies of Eastern Europe for the most part use a single currency as a medium of exchange. The balance sheets of their central banks, however, are similar. Each issues money, usually by fiat, and funnels revenues to both the central government and state enterprises.[10]

Most of the transitional economies in Eastern Europe have stabilized their seigniorage revenues at about 1.5 percent of GDP, not much higher than in western Europe. This has occurred in spite of high and in some cases accelerating inflation. It has been accompanied by sharp declines in the real money supply (by 22 percent in Poland and 16 percent in Czechoslovakia in 1991). A way to reconcile these two developments is that if inflation promotes economic growth, implying a negatively sloped long-run Phillips curve, then the marginal cost of raising the inflation rate to the government is reduced by the additional income tax revenues produced by increased inflation. Banaian, McClure and Willett (1994) argue instead that higher inflation will reduce the rate of economic growth, reducing the amount of tax collected from the income base, and driving up the cost of raising revenue from that source. Friedman (1977) suggests that high and variable inflation causes economic agents to spend more of their time and resources bargaining for higher wages using shorter and shorter length contracts. The argument thus turns on the presence of transaction costs, in the form of work stoppages and time taken in wage bargaining.[11] These transactions costs generate a significant difference in the effect of anticipated and unanticipated inflation. Higher anticipated inflation begets more *variable* unanticipated inflation, causing firms and workers to divert resources to wage bargaining instead of producing goods and services.

The cost of using seigniorage is inflation. Note that Neumann's definition speaks of a demand for base money. As with any tax, increasing the rate of taxation on money reduces the demand for the monetary base. The increase in inflation in these economies can thus be considered a prime reason for the decline in real money balances. The concept of *optimal inflation* comes from the idea that governments should set an inflation rate that maximizes the social welfare of an economy through equalizing the marginal cost of raising tax revenues through different mechanisms. There will also be a revenue-maximizing inflation rate, since too high a rate of money creation may so reduce the demand for money that the fall in the base is proportionately greater than the increase in the tax rate.

Derivation of Revenue-Maximizing and Optimal Seigniorage Rates [12]

In high-inflation economies, Cagan (1956) suggests that a demand for money function may take the form of

$$\frac{M^d}{P} = a y^\alpha e^{-\beta \pi^e}$$

which states that the demand for real money balances is a semi-logarithmic function of output and expected inflation. The output term is usually ignored in high-inflation countries as dominated by movements in expected inflation. Cagan shows that the revenue-maximizing rate of inflation, $1/\beta$, is usually far less than the rate of inflation in hyperinflating economies. However, as argued elsewhere (McClure and Willett 1988, Burdekin et al. 1995), an increase in the level of inflation imposes uncertainty costs. If higher inflation reduces the rate of economic growth, the amount of tax collected from the income base is reduced, which increases the cost of using the inflation tax. Taking into account shrinking contract lengths and other increases in transactions costs, the revenue-maximizing and optimal rates of inflation are lower than those described by Cagan (1956), Bailey (1956), or Dornbusch and Fischer (1993). Consider the total derivative of the money demand function above with respect to inflation:

$$\frac{dM}{d\pi} = \frac{dM}{di} \bullet \frac{di}{d\pi} + \frac{dM}{dy} \bullet \frac{dy}{d\pi} = -\beta M \bullet \frac{di}{d\pi} + \frac{dM}{dy} \bullet \frac{dy}{d\pi}$$

The Fisher effect $i = r + \pi$ gives $di/d\pi = 1$ if real interest rates are not affected by fully anticipated inflation. The second expression yields the effect on real balances if inflation reduces the level of income in an economy. Let the last derivative $dy/d\pi = f$, which is less than zero.

A government may tax income at a flat rate of t or it may tax money balances at the rate of π. Its revenues are calculated to be $R = ty + \pi(M/P)$, where y is real income and M/P is real money balances. If raising revenue from each source reduces the size of the tax base, we set taxes such that $MC_t = MC_\pi$. Taking the derivative of this equation with respect to inflation:

$$\frac{dR}{d\pi} = M + \pi \bullet \frac{dM}{d\pi} + t \bullet f$$

This and the total derivative above can be used to solve for the revenue-maximizing rate of inflation:

$$\pi_{RM} = \frac{1+t(f/y)(y/M)}{-(\beta+a(f/y))} \tag{1}$$

This includes the traditional result of $-(100/\beta)$ percent as a special case where $f = 0$.

The marginal welfare cost of raising the inflation rate by one point can be viewed as

$$\frac{dW}{d\pi} = (\beta + a \bullet f/y) \bullet i \bullet M + f \bullet \phi < 0$$

where ϕ is the change in welfare resulting from a one-unit change in income, which we assume equals one. To simplify, we assume a social welfare function with output as the sole determinant. The traditional welfare cost of βiM thus understates the true welfare cost in two ways: (i) the traditional deadweight loss per point of inflation is increased by the lowering of money demand as demonstrated above (as given by the expression a(f/y)iM); and (ii) the inclusion of output reduction in the consideration of welfare losses (the value fϕ).

We can now calculate the marginal welfare cost of inflationary finance by taking the ratio of the (negative of the) welfare cost of inflationary finance to the revenues it can generate.

$$MC_\pi = \frac{-dW/d\pi}{dR/d\pi} = \frac{-i(\beta + a \bullet f/y) + \phi(f/y) \bullet (y/M)}{1 + (\beta + a \bullet (f/y)) + t(f/y) \bullet (y/M)}$$

Note again that the Bailey solution of $-i/(1+\beta)$ is obtained if $f = 0$. Using the Fisher relation for the value of i above, we can solve for the optimal inflation rate as

$$\pi^* = \frac{MC_\pi(1 + t \bullet (f/y)(y/M)) + \phi \bullet (f/y)(y/M)}{-(\beta + a \bullet f/y)(1 + MC_\pi)} - r \tag{2}$$

The optimal rate of inflation then depends positively upon the marginal cost of income taxation, since an increase in the cost of raising revenue from one source should induce increased reliance on other sources. A greater elasticity of money demand (β) lowers the optimal rate, just as we find for other excise taxes. The larger is the Friedman effect (f/y), the lower the optimal rate, as this implies greater output losses from inflation. Higher velocity also lowers the optimal rate, as lower output will cause a greater decline in the quantity demanded of money. And lastly, higher tax rates on income lower the optimal inflation rate, since inflation reduces the base on which the income tax is assessed. The last two effects are only valid as long as a Friedman effect is present.

The traditional estimate of $1/\beta$ produces estimates of a revenue-maximizing rate of inflation in the former Yugoslavia in the 1980s of slightly over 4.5 percent per month or more than 70 percent per year (suggesting that the hyperinflation there in 1993 was in the end damaging even the government's own budget—see Frenkel and Taylor 1993). If the marginal cost of raising one dinar of tax revenue there was an additional 0.4 dinars, the traditional optimal inflation rate calculation of $MC_\pi / (1+MC_\pi)$ would be 1.3 percent per month or 16.7 percent per year. This is very close to the range one often hears mentioned in popular discussions of optimal inflation rates for developing economies. For example, Pazos (1990:117) states, "We specialists in developing countries ... have accepted much higher inflation with the same passivity, as long as it did not surpass 40 percent to 50 percent annually." Dornbusch and Fischer (1993:6) meanwhile state that a game-theoretic view of inflation "could ... support the notion of equilibrium inflation rates in the 15 to 30 percent range." If there are uncertainty costs of inflation that are associated with higher average inflation rates, however, that rate is above the optimal level. With an average tax rate of 34 percent and velocity of 2.9 times per year, an output loss of .05 percent of GDP per 1 percent of inflation would give a revenue-maximizing rate of inflation of 4.3 percent per month (65 percent per year) and an optimal rate of 0.8 percent per month, or 9.5 percent per year.

The chapter in this volume by Burdekin, Salamun and Willett argues that the size of these uncertainty costs can be substantial. These costs can arise from contracting costs, from suppression of investment, or from declines in labor productivity. Burdekin and his coauthors find that the output costs are quite different for developing and industrialized economies. This raises the question of which values are appropriate when discussing the CIS. Their level of development has been retarded and their per capita output levels barely match those of the poorer European states such as Spain, Portugal or Turkey. However, one can argue that the output cost depends on the development not so much of physical capital, but upon the development of market relationships. Many developing economies also lack a commitment to market processes. If allocation is done by nonmarket mechanisms, the impact of inflation may not be great: the misallocations may persist in times of high and low inflation. The impact of high inflation will be most felt when resource allocation is left to the market, assuming that inflation leads to the misallocations discussed above.

Implications for Optimal and Revenue-Maximizing Rates of Seigniorage Taxation

The impact of the income effects of inflation reach to the government's own budget. The reductions in income reduce the income base on which the government can collect income taxes and decrease even further the demand for base money. Both of these effects are in addition to the traditional Bailey calculations, as shown above. The accompanying appendix presents the partial derivatives of the revenue-maximizing and optimal inflation rates with respect to the various parameters employed. The sign of all but one of these is unambiguous; the last, that of the impact of the optimal rate arising from the elasticity of money demand with respect to expected inflation, is most likely positive, turning negative only if the optimal inflation rate is negative.[13]

To calculate the magnitude of the effects requires parameter values for several economic variables, which we can estimate with varying degrees of precision. For some we have established base cases, and for others we have made estimates over a range of possible values. The relevant variables include the following:

The Elasticity of Money Demand with Respect to Inflation

The value of this is likely to be rapidly changing in a country undergoing the transition from a centrally planned to a market economy. One estimate for Yugoslavia during the 1980s sets this value at -1.5 (Frenkel and Taylor 1993). Phylaktis and Taylor (1991) compute values of -1.64 for Bolivia and -0.64 for Peru over the 1975–1987 period during which each country suffered high inflation. Bahmani-Oskooee and Malixi (1991) estimate similar functions for several developing countries, with elasticities ranging from -1 to -4. In Tables 3.1 and 3.2, I take -1.5 as a base case and present an alternative based on an elasticity of -3.

Marginal Tax Rates

Most transitional economies have adopted a broad-based value-added tax with tax rates near 30 percent. These have tended not to attain nearly the revenue expected, and many of the countries have opted to either increase that rate or continue to rely on turnover taxes that tend to have sharply higher effective rates (particularly for manufactured goods). There are a variety of excise taxes and some progressivity is introduced in some countries by an excess wage tax that is designed to limit wage-push inflationary pressures. Rather than try to calculate a marginal rate, the average rate is used. Only tax revenues appear in the numerator.

The Costs of Income Taxation

The transitional economies tend to have highly inefficient tax systems. In Russia in 1993, paratroopers, the elite of the Russian Army, were redeployed in tax collection efforts. Bird (1991) suggests that the collection costs of taxation in developing economies exceeds 30 percent. These costs are likely much higher in transitional economies, where governments previously expropriated whatever amount of revenue they desired. I use 50 percent collection costs as a base case, and compute alternatives for costs of 30 percent and 70 percent.

Velocity

The transitional economies also tend to have relatively low degrees of financial intermediation. There are few near-money substitutes available. Thus while high inflation and low nominal interest rates on deposits tend to force individuals to favor holding wealth in nonmoney form, there are significant transactions costs to portfolio shifting. This appears both in the velocity figures and the relatively low elasticities we expect these countries to have.

Table 3.1 shows results for revenue-maximizing and optimal inflation rates for some Eastern European economies, and provides a few comparison cases with other European economies. As confirmed by the derivatives in the appendix, the revenue-maximizing and optimal inflation rates both increase with increases in the cost of taxation from other sources. Thus inflationary finance may be attractive to countries with very poor income tax systems; transitional economies will reduce inflationary pressures by increasing the efficiency of tax collections (Edwards and Tabellini 1991). Also note that the optimal and revenue-maximizing rates are lower, the greater is velocity. This implies that increasing financial intermediation in the transitional economies will increase the pressures for price stability.

TABLE 3.1 Optimal and Revenue Maximizing Rates in Eastern Europe

Country	Velocity	Tax Rate	Actual π
Turkey	3.28	0.50	38.0
Portugal	1.13	0.38	17.4
Spain	1.38	0.44	9.3
Romania	3.03	0.38	216.0
Hungary	1.50	0.30	27.0
CSFR	1.59	0.27	15.0
Poland	2.03	0.41	63.0
Yugoslavia	2.87	0.34	134.0

(continues)

TABLE 3.1 (continued)

Revenue maximizing rate if f/y equals:

	0	-0.05	-0.1	-0.2
Turkey	33.9	30.6	27.4	21.3
Portugal	21.6	20.9	20.2	18.9
Spain	25.2	24.2	23.1	21.1
Romania	66.7	60.8	55.3	45.3
Hungary	66.7	63.1	59.7	53.5
CSFR	66.7	63.1	59.8	53.7
Poland	66.7	61.8	57.3	49.0
Yugoslavia	66.7	61.4	56.4	47.4

Critical f/y for zero optimal inflation given marginal cost equals:

	0.3	0.5	0.7
Turkey	-0.079	-0.122	-0.158
Portugal	-0.238	-0.371	-0.488
Spain	-0.192	-0.297	-0.388
Romania	-0.089	-0.139	-0.182
Hungary	-0.183	-0.290	-0.386
CSFR	-0.174	-0.277	-0.370
Poland	-0.132	-0.204	-0.268
Yugoslavia	-0.095	-0.149	-0.197

The optimal inflation rate if the marginal cost of taxation is:

MC = 0.3	f/y = 0	-0.02	-0.05	-0.1
Turkey	13.2	9.8	4.8	0.0
Portugal	8.4	7.7	6.6	4.8
Spain	9.8	8.8	7.2	4.6
Romania	26.0	19.9	11.0	4.6
Hungary	26.0	22.9	18.3	0.0
CSFR	26.0	22.7	17.9	11.1
Poland	26.0	21.8	15.6	10.4
Yugoslavia	26.0	20.3	11.9	5.9

MC = 0.5	f/y = 0	-0.02	-0.05	-0.1
Turkey	25.4	21.1	14.8	4.4
Portugal	16.2	15.3	13.9	11.6
Spain	18.9	17.6	15.6	12.3
Romania	50.0	42.2	30.9	13.1
Hungary	50.0	45.9	40.0	30.7
CSFR	50.0	45.8	39.6	29.9
Poland	50.0	44.5	36.6	23.9
Yugoslavia	50.0	42.7	32.2	15.4

(continues)

TABLE 3.1 (continued)

$MC = 0.7$	$f/y = 0$	-0.02	-0.05	-0.1
Turkey	40.4	35.0	27.1	14.3
Portugal	25.7	24.6	22.8	20.0
Spain	30.0	28.4	25.8	21.8
Romania	79.3	69.7	55.7	33.6
Hungary	79.3	74.2	66.8	55.1
CSFR	79.3	74.1	66.4	54.3
Poland	79.3	72.4	62.4	46.6
Yugoslavia	79.3	70.4	57.3	36.7

Note: If the optimal rate is less than zero, zero has been substituted. The assumed elasticity of money demand for the Eastern European economies is -3.0. Elasticities for Turkey, Portugal and Spain from Bahmani-Oskooee and Malixi (1991).

Table 3.2 provides some early estimated values of some of the relevant parameters for these calculations applied to the CIS countries. It is noteworthy that, in several of these economies, tax collections are very low. This is in spite of fairly high tax rates; in Georgia, for example, barely more than 11 percent of GDP was collected by the government in 1992 in spite of having a 28 percent VAT rate (since reduced to 14 percent) and an income tax with a top rate of 40 percent. These facts should make it clear that the tax administration system in Georgia and several other of these economies is highly inefficient. Most of these economies also have a fairly low degree of financial intermediation, as evidenced by the low velocity rates. Thus, there is a large amount of money in circulation that the authorities can extract if they so wish, and an inefficient tax system that induces them to do just that.

Conclusions

Truth in society is like strychnine in the individual body, medicinal in special conditions and minute doses; otherwise and in general, a deadly poison.

Frank Knight 1932

To suggest that inflation rates of 30 to 50 percent are acceptable for developing economies is unsound on two grounds. First, it may be far more difficult to justify a policy to reduce inflation from 50 percent to 30 percent than it is to justify a reduction from 5 percent to zero. If some inflation is good, one can argue, a little more cannot be all that bad. Yet the research provided here shows that the net effect of inflation can be harmful even at moderate rates. The thresholds demonstrated lie well below the levels often accepted as "moderate." Nor does the threshold rate imply that it helps an

Inflation and Optimal Seigniorage 75

TABLE 3.2 Factors in Optimal Inflation: CIS 1992

Country	GDP (bill Rb)	Tax/GDP	Velocity	Actual Inflation	Revenue Max Inflation	Optimal Inflation
Armenia	1125.9	17%	2.97	829%	63%	15%
Azerbaijan	2627.1	24%	2.07	1174%	63%	17%
Belarus	12593.4	15%	3.37	1116%	63%	14%
Estonia	1793.1	19%	1.12	19%	64%	19%
Kazakhstan	11967.9	19%	2.85	799%	63%	15%
Kyrgyzstan	1542.9	11%	2.90	1487%	63%	15%
Lativia	2126.7	19%	0.59	2655%	64%	20%
Lithuania	2043.3	12%	1.66	1850%	64%	18%
Moldova	2293.5	18%	2.59	1276%	63%	15%
Turkmenistan	2043.3	36%	2.89	1799%	61%	14%
Ukraine	36195.6	10%	3.36	1213%	63%	14%
Uzbekistan	7672.8	10%	2.47	698%	64%	16%
Russia	166049.4	21%	2.48	1314%	63%	16%

Notes: Data from OECD, *Short-Term Economic Indicators, Transition Economies*, except tax rates, from IMF courtesy of Marina Arbetman. Calculations are based on an interest elasticity of demand for money of -1.5, a marginal cost of taxation of 0.5, and an uncertainty cost of .05% GDP per 1% of inflation. Without uncertainty costs the revenue maximizing rate of inflation would be 66.7% and the optimal rate would be 22.2%.

economy to inflate up to that rate; we can only say that we cannot demonstrate harm before the threshold.

Second, as Buchanan and Wagner (1978) pointed out with regard to the effects of Keynesian theory on policymaking, policy advice is given to politicians who have clear revenue motives of their own to inflate to the threshold and beyond. As both sides realize this motive, there will be a tendency for the public to expect higher inflation rates, which both lower the expected revenue gains from money creation and induce lower output by the mechanisms we have discussed above. This would be a suboptimal result, and it could thus make some sense to use the inflation tax subject to a constitutional limit, as suggested by Brennan and Buchanan (1980). The analysis herein could provide an initial basis for laying out guidelines as what should be the constitutional limit.

This chapter has traced out the factors relevant for determining the optimal inflation rate in the transitional economies. Using some plausible estimates, inflation rates of about 1 percent per month could be viewed as an efficient tax on cash balances in economies with costly income tax systems, low degrees of financial intermediation and fairly inelastic demand for base money. Increasing the efficiency of the income tax system, or taxation of some other broad base, will increase the likelihood of success of policies for price stability. These calculations also demonstrate the value of repressing financial innovation in protecting a source of government revenue.

This chapter also emphasizes the importance of the uncertainty costs of inflation in the determination of its optimal and revenue-maximizing level. When anticipated inflation causes output losses, reliance on seigniorage diminishes the income base and decreases the revenue governments can receive. This suggests a natural restraint against excessive reliance on the inflation tax for governments that maximize revenue. But uncertainty costs also reduce the optimal rate of inflation, and it is this result that economic advisors should carry to developing economies.

Appendix
The Effect of Tax Rates, Elasticity of Money Demand, and Velocity on Optimal and Revenue Maximizing Inflation Rates

Using equation (1) for the revenue-maximizing rate, π_{RM}:

$$\partial \pi_{RM}/\partial t = -(f/y)(y/M)]/[\beta + \alpha(f/y)] < 0$$

$$\partial \pi_{RM}/\partial(f/y) = [\alpha - \beta t\,(y/M)]/[\beta + \alpha(f/y)]^2 > 0$$

$$\partial \pi_{RM}/\partial(y/M) = -t\,(f/y)/[\beta + \alpha(f/y)] < 0$$

$$\partial \pi_{RM}/\partial \beta = [1 + t\,(f/y)(y/M)]/[\beta + \alpha(f/y)]^2 > 0$$

$$\partial \pi_{RM}/\partial MC_\pi = 0$$

Using equation for (2) the optimal inflation rate, π^*_{RM}:

$$\partial \pi^*/\partial t = [-MC_\pi(f/y)(y/M)]/[\beta + \alpha\,(f/y)](1 + MC_\pi) < 0$$

$$\partial \pi^*/\partial(f/y) = \{(1 + MC_\pi)[\alpha MC_\pi - \beta(MC_\pi t + \phi)(y/M)]\} / \{[\beta + \alpha\,(f/y)](1 + MC_\pi)\}^2 > 0$$

$$\partial \pi^*/\partial(y/M) = [(-MC_\pi t + \phi)(f/y)]/[\beta + \alpha(f/y)](1 + MC_\pi) < 0$$

$$\partial \pi^*/\partial \beta = \pi^*/[\beta + \alpha(f/y)] < 0 \text{ if } \pi^* > 0$$

$$\partial \pi^*/\partial MC_\pi = -[1 + (t + \phi)(f/y)(y/M)]/[\beta + \alpha(f/y)](1 + MC_\pi)^2 > 0$$

Notes

1. This paper was developed from a panel discussion "Inflation and Fiscal Issues in the Former Communist Countries" at the 66th Annual Meetings of the Western Economics Association, Lake Tahoe, Nevada, June 21–24, 1993 and in a presentation to the Institute for World Economics, Budapest, Hungary. Helpful comments were received from Richard C. K. Burdekin, Pál Gáspár, Eduard Hochreiter, Suyono Salamun and Thomas D. Willett, none of whom are responsible for any errors or omissions.

2. Pazos (1990) suggests inflation of 40 to 50 percent annually is a reasonable target range, and Dornbusch and Fischer (1993) are sanguine about rates of 15 to 30 percent.

3. There is additionally a tax on nominal debt claims by citizens and foreign governments against the domestic government. When money creation is *unanticipated*, the resulting inflation reduces the real value of that debt. (Anticipated money creation will generate no gains as creditors will seek compensation in higher interest rates.) In a sense, unanticipated inflation could be seen as debt repudiation (Buiter 1985). However, the centrally planned economies historically have had little debt held by their citizens. What was held was often mandated by planners (a forced subscription equal to 10 percent of one's wages occurred in the Soviet Union until the 1950s), but this was a small fraction of GDP in these countries (Zwass 1979). In this chapter I discuss seigniorage more as an excise tax on money as a good than as debt repudiation.

4. Examples would include Bailey (1956), Tower (1971), Aurenheimer (1974), and Banaian, McClure and Willett (1994).

5. This statement assumes no production costs of money creation. See Goff and Toma (1993) for a relaxation of this assumption. One should note that this does not necessarily assume a zero real rate of interest; Gros (1989) points out that the revenue gain can be viewed alternatively as an interest savings from having the ability to issue zero interest securities—currency—rather than interest-bearing bonds.

6. Moldova was typical of several central banks in the Commonwealth of Independent States (CIS). The financing arrangements described here do not differ significantly between countries.

7. There is also seigniorage used in the "other items" category. This category includes an exchange rate adjustment account, gold reserves, float or interenterprise settlements in progress, and net worth. The float is likely a large source of changes to the monetary base in most of the CIS.

8. Moldova may gain from this loan if, for example, the loan were interest-free or made in perpetuity. However, Russia converted all loans to the rest of the CIS over time to sovereign debt at rates pegged to LIBOR. The value of this subsidy would appear in the national bank's net worth over time, information we can not know at present.

9. It may seem curious to outsiders why excess reserves would be so high in a country with such high inflation rates. Explanations could include uncertainty in lending to private enterprises or financial repression that makes it more difficult for banks to lend. Financial repression can be a significant source of seigniorage revenues. See Roubini and Sala-i-Martin (1992) and Giovannini and de Melo (1993).

10. Two of the Baltic states, Estonia and Latvia, have adopted currency boards, thus foreswearing use of seigniorage.

11. One could thus imagine that countries with corporatist wage structures would find these costs lower, since a bargaining system is already present and the frequency of strike activity low. However, most corporatist countries are found to have lower inflation rates; were the transaction costs lower, one would suspect that average rates would be higher. It appears that the amelioration of inflationary tendencies is one of the chief benefits of corporatist structures (Al-Marhubi and Willett 1994), though Havrilesky and Granato (1993) find no correlation once central bank structure is accounted for. Countries such as Austria and Germany have both fairly centralized wage-setting structures and independent central banks.

12. The following is adapted from the analysis in Banaian, McClure and Willett (1994).

13. It is not clear that negative inflation rates should be preferred, since these may incur the same contracting costs hypothesized as positive rates under Friedman's hypothesis. I assume hereafter that if I calculate an optimal rate of less than zero, the correct rate is zero.

References

Al-Marhubi, Fahim, and Thomas D. Willett. 1994. "The Anti-Inflationary Influence of Corporatist Structures and Central Bank Independence: The Importance of the Hump-Shaped Hypothesis." Mimeo, The Claremont Graduate School, August.

Aurenheimer, Leonardo. 1974. "The Honest Government's Guide to Revenue from Money Creation." *Journal of Political Economy* 82 (May/June): 598–606.

Bahmani-Oskooee, Moshen, and Margaret Malixi. 1991. "Exchange Rate Sensitivity of the Demand for Money in Developing Economies." *Applied Economics* 23: 1377–84.

Bailey, Martin. 1956. "The Welfare Cost of Inflationary Finance." *Journal of Political Economy* 64 (April): 93–110.

Banaian, King, J. Harold McClure and Thomas D. Willett. 1994. "The Inflation Tax is Likely Inefficient at Any Level." *Kredit und Kapital* 27, Heft 1: 30–42.

Bird, Richard M. 1991. "Tax Administration and Tax Reform: Reflections on Experience," in Javad Khalilzadeh-Shirazi and Anwar Shah, eds., *Tax Policy in Developing Countries*. Pp. 127–38. Washington, D.C.: The World Bank.

Brennan, James, and James M. Buchanan. 1980. *The Power to Tax*. Cambridge: Cambridge University Press.

Buchanan, James M., and Richard E. Wagner. 1978. *Democracy in Deficit: The Political Legacy of Lord Keynes*. New York: Academic Press.

Buiter, Willem H. 1985. "A Guide to Public Sector Debts and Deficits." *Economic Policy* 1 (November): 13–79.

Burdekin, Richard C. K., Suyono Salamun and Thomas D. Willett. 1995. "The Costs of Monetary Instability," in this volume.

Cagan, Phillip. 1956. "The Monetary Dynamics of Hyperinflation," in Milton Friedman, ed., *Studies in the Quantity Theory of Money*. Pp. 25–117. Chicago: University of Chicago Press.

Dornbusch, Rudiger, and Stanley Fischer. 1993. "Moderate Inflation." *World Bank Economic Review* 7(1): 1–44.

Edwards, Sebastian, and Guido Tabellini. 1991. "Explaining Inflation and Fiscal Deficits in Developing Countries." *Journal of International Money and Finance* 10 (March Supplement): 516–48.

Frenkel, Jacob A., and Mark P. Taylor. 1993. "Money Demand and Inflation in Yugoslavia, 1980–89." *Journal of Macroeconomics* 15(3): 455–81.

Friedman, Milton, 1971. "Government Revenue from Inflation." *Journal of Political Economy* 79 (July/August): 846–56.

―――――. 1977. "Nobel Lecture: Inflation and Unemployment." *Journal of Political Economy* 85 (June): 451–72.

Giovannini, Alberto, and Martha de Melo. 1993. "Government Revenue from Financial Repression." *American Economic Review* 83 (September): 953–63.

Goff, Brian, and Mark Toma. 1993. "Optimal Seigniorage, the Gold Standard, and Central Bank Financing." *Journal of Money, Credit and Banking* 25 (February): 79–95.

Gros, Daniel. 1989. "Seigniorage in the EC: The Implications of the EMS and Financial Market Integration." IMF Working Papers, Washington D.C., January.

Hansson, Ingemar, and Charles Stuart. 1992. "Sweden: Tax Reform in a High-Tax Environment," in Michael Boskin and Charles McLure, Jr., eds., *World Tax Reform: Case Studies of Developed and Developing Countries*. San Francisco: ICS Press.

Havrilesky, Thomas, and James Granato. 1993. "Determinants of Inflationary Performance: Corporatist Structures vs. Central Bank Independence." *Public Choice* 76 (July): 249–61.

Klein, Martin, and Manfred J. M. Neumann. 1990. "Seigniorage: What Is It and Who Gets It?" *Weltwirtschaftliches Archiv* 126: 205–21.

McClure, J. Harold, and Thomas D. Willett. 1988. "The Inflation Tax," in Thomas D. Willett, ed., *Political Business Cycles*. Pp. 177–85. Durham, N.C.: Duke University Press.

Neumann, Manfred J. M. 1992. "Seigniorage in the United States: How Much Does the U.S. Government Make from Money Production?" Federal Reserve Bank of St. Louis *Economic Review* (March/April): 29–40.

Paxos, Felipe. 1990. "Runaway Inflation: Experiences and Options." *Cepal Review* 42 (December): 115–30.

Phylaktis, Kate, and Mark P. Taylor. 1991. "Money Demand in High-Inflation Countries: A South American Perspective," in Mark Taylor, ed., *Money and Financial Markets*. Pp. 191–204. Cambridge, Mass.: Basil Blackwell.

Ramsey, Frank. 1927. "A Contribution to the Theory of Taxation." *Economic Journal* 37: 47–61.

Roubini, Nouriel, and Xavier Sala-i-Martin. 1992. "A Growth Model of Inflation, Tax Evasion, and Financial Repression." National Bureau of Economic Research Working Paper No. 4062, May.

Tower, Edward. 1971. "More on the Welfare Costs of Inflationary Finance." *Journal of Money, Credit and Banking* 3 (November): 850–60.

Zwass, Adam. 1979. *Money, Banking, and Credit in the Soviet Union and Eastern Europe*. White Plains, N.Y.: M. E. Sharpe.

4

The Politics of Inflation: An Empirical Assessment of the Emerging Market Economies

Marina Arbetman and Jacek Kugler

Introduction

This chapter deals with the connection between politics and inflation in central and eastern European nations that are attempting to make the transition from centrally planned to market-orientated economies. From a political perspective, inflation reflects the failure of a government to match the issue of money to the performance of the economy; inflation results when the growth of the money supply exceeds the growth of the economy. Indeed, the most direct way to trace the path from politics to inflation is to follow its footsteps: inflation is rising prices, and prices are closely linked to the money supply. Since issuing money is a government monopoly, inflation is driven to a large degree by government policies.

This work explores the potential relationship between the performance of governments and rates of inflation. We anticipate that governments of societies in transition from centrally planned to market economies will face very large inflationary pressures while they attempt to reduce governmental subsidies and transfers to state enterprises and limit the provision of housing, education and health to the population. We posit that strong governments under these circumstances will reduce government budget deficits, thereby making it feasible to control the issue of money and attract loans from international organizations by providing domestic and international investors with a stable economic outlook. Weak governments are expected to compensate for their lack of political support by continuing to subsidize government enterprises in order to minimize unemployment and maintaining subsidies for energy, housing and education. An exploration of inflation rates, therefore, provides us with a means of gauging the effectiveness with which governments will implement the transformation from planned to market economies.

The Link Between Politics and Inflation

From a political perspective high inflation is seldom a desirable outcome. In democracies, political support for the government is frequently linked to stable consumer prices concurrent with wage increases (Tufte 1978). In general, democratic governments anticipate reelection when wages rise and inflation is low or falling. They expect electoral defeat when inflation is not under control, and chances for re-election are further diminished when wages fail to keep up with inflation rates. The business community and international organizations similarly take a dim view of inflation. The credit rating of a country, and its attractiveness to foreign investors, are aided by low or declining inflation. High-risk investors can profit under double- or even triple-digit inflation, but few governments can tolerate sustained high inflation rates. Indeed, public trust in government and the buildup and retention of an effective, stable governing coalition in parliamentary governments are linked with low or sharply declining rates of inflation.

There are good reasons for the perception that rising inflation indicates governmental ineffectiveness. Weak governments, unable to extract resources from the population through conventional taxes, are prone to monetary expansion to cover budget deficits and maintain subsidies. This process is clearly seen in the last half decade in Russia and Central and Eastern Europe, including the former Soviet republics. The Russian central bank during 1992 and 1993 issued large amounts of money and credits to pay military salaries, continue subsidies to unprofitable public enterprises, minimize unemployment in industries that were undergoing conversion from military to civilian applications, maintain a semblance of the welfare functions previously provided by the Communist regime and, to a lesser degree, to provide housing, staples and energy at below-market costs. Analysis shows that the root of Yeltsin's political conflict with the Duma was disagreement over the degree to which public funds should be used to subsidize public services and support loss-generating public enterprises (Kugler and Bueno de Mesquita 1993). Hungary's unfinished transition can likewise be traced to the government's unwillingness to allow large public enterprises to face bankruptcy. In Poland the breakup of Solidarity was motivated in part by sharp disagreements among factions that wished to preserve large public enterprises and maintain full employment and those who wished to move rapidly to a competitive market economy. The partition of Czechoslovakia into the Czech and Slovak Republics was likewise motivated by the very dramatic disagreement between Mr. Klaus, the head of the Czech ethnic groups, and Mr. Merciar, the leader of the Movement of Democratic Slovakia, regarding the degree and speed of privatization of the economy. The resulting partition consolidated two approaches to the transition: the Czechs' pursuit of a rapid transition to a market economy, in which low inflation and privatization of state enterprises are key strategies, and the Slovaks' gradual approach that attempts to reduce the impact and lower the cost of the transition to individual citizens.

Surveys in Eastern Europe show the result of these conflicting perspectives: a majority of the population supports a market economy and simultaneously supports no reduction in the public sector. Without risk, markets do not work, a lesson not easily understood by the citizens of nations whose economies are in transition from a centralized to a market structure. This is not an isolated phenomenon. In Argentina, President Alfonsin was judged a failure, despite massive support for his government following the Falklands War and the removal of the military regime, because he failed to tame inflation. His successor, President Menem, is seen as a major success and will likely be re-elected simply because he succeeded in reducing inflation and pushed Argentina towards a market economy. His support does not come from supporters of privatization, rather it comes from a population yearning for monetary stability. In Brazil, Mr. Cardoso was elected because, under his tutelage, inflation has been reduced and not because there is overwhelming support for market reforms (*Economist*, October 1994). Illustrating the political importance of inflation in a country that endured an annual inflation rate of almost 4000 percent in 1994, Brazilian economist Portocarero reflected that "anybody that can make it so that when people go the grocery store, the prices are the same that month as they were the month before, could do anything in this country he wanted to" (*Los Angeles Times*, October 2, 1994, p. 1). Likewise, Chile's transition to democracy following Mr. Pinochet's rule was a success because the new democratic government maintained low inflation while expanding privatization. President Frei has, thus far, preserved low inflation and political stability.

From a political perspective then, we posit that governments attempting the transition from a centrally planned to a market economy have an incentive to maintain low levels of inflation. Popular support for their policies will come far more from monetary stability than from an inherent trust in market economies and privatization.

The failure to control inflation reflects the government's inability to control the issue of money. Inflation is a temporary escape from insolvency. In the emerging market economies under consideration, governments inherited a centralized economy and a bloated public sector where employment was valued above efficiency. To reconcile these inefficiencies with the demands of the market, transitional governments face grim political choices. To establish a market economy and re-induce economic growth, they must allow ineffective public sector enterprises to fail, permit a temporary rise in unemployment, refuse to subsidize consumer products whose prices were traditionally set by the government, and reduce employment in the institutions that previously implemented economic regulations. Each of these steps is difficult and politically costly. Success in controlling inflation can bring rewards, however; stable prices create an attractive climate for investment, decreased regulation reduces budget deficits and, more importantly, signals a willingness to restructure the economy and allow markets to decide the fate of business enterprises. The politics of inflation, therefore, are at the center of the transformation from centrally regulated to open market economies.

Inflation, in general, generates a short-term payoff to governments and private borrowers but steals from lenders, wage earners and particularly those on a fixed income (see, for example, Morley 1979 and Paarlberg 1993). It can be triggered by domestic decisions or by external shocks. For instance, increased international interest rates or oil prices create inflationary pressures not under the government's direct control. However, domestic decisions play a leading role in fueling and sustaining inflation. Governments that choose to finance development through borrowing frequently continue to subsidize state enterprises, do not impose wage restraint on trade unions, and rely on monetary expansion rather than taxation to finance national budgets. Such governmental policies are the most direct causes of inflation. Simplifying a far more complex process, governments generate inflation when they choose to borrow or print money instead of operating within the constraints imposed by revenues extracted from their populations.

To establish the political foundations of inflationary behavior we explore the transition to market economies underway in Eastern Europe and the former Soviet Union. This transformation of economic systems provides a unique opportunity to explore the interaction between inflation and politics because of the wide variations in both inflation rates and the policies observed in these countries. Governments possess several economic policy instruments to foster price stability, but also face constraints. When stabilization policies are implemented, some groups will gain and others will lose. Strong governments can tolerate the political repercussions of such tradeoffs, averting chronic inflation. Weak governments frequently cave in to avoid defections by key coalition members and their indecisiveness can easily generate an outburst of inflation that, if extended, can lead to hyperinflation. Stopping high inflation is difficult. Faced with such a situation, strong governments act, weak ones retreat. We argue, at the extreme, that inflation is a weak government's chosen policy and a strong government's menace.

Lord Keynes (1923) stated accurately our main contention that "[inflation] is that form of taxation which the public find hardest to evade and even the weakest government can enforce, when it can enforce nothing else." Strong governments are expected to pursue a stable monetary policy. We do not deny that inflation can be a useful policy tool. In the short term, for example, a strong government whose credibility has been established can use inflation as an inefficient tax, generating revenue through seigniorage, so long as rates remain relatively low (Phylaktis 1993; Easterly and Schmidt-Hebbel 1993). Further, Banaian, McClure and Willett (1994) show that in developed societies inflation is not a hidden tax, but that it still remains less visible than a direct tax. Thus, they surmise that in societies with high expenditures and relatively inefficient tax systems, "governments have political incentives to induce inflation as the politically optimal rate may lie above the politically optimal level" (p. 39). However, when governments are weak and induce high levels of inflation, individuals will adjust and inflation will become not only an ineffective tool to tax populations, but presumably also a politically costly one. Like Keynes, we assume that transitional governments in Eastern Europe, Russia and the former Soviet republics have failed to control inflation because they are weak and are unable to pay the high political costs of monetary restraint, even though they are aware that this policy jeopardizes the long-term goals of economic growth, privatization, and access to foreign capital and investment.

We test the relation between inflation and political strength by first defining the key political and economic variables. We then stipulate the model and present the preliminary results of our analysis.

Inflation

For political purposes inflation is a hidden tax. If populations do not recognize inflation as such, it is unlikely that changes in the political capability of governments would be connected to changes in inflation rates. Banaian, McClure and Willett (1994) suggest that while direct taxes and changes in income may be more obvious than the impact of inflation, populations exposed to inflation over time will come to see its effects as an indirect tax. For this reason inflation, measured by the Consumer Price Index (CPI), provides us with a good first approximation of the political impact of monetary growth. We chose this price index because it provides a gross measure of inflation that reflects its generalized and continuous effects in a society. While more sensitive measures of inflation can be gathered following individual commodities, and some—such as increases in gasoline prices or the removal of subsidies for basic commodities—have important political repercussions, we posit that price changes in a single commodity do not capture overall political trends until such changes ripple across the whole economy. For example, the exceptional rise in oil prices during 1973 generated lagged overall increases in the CPI in the economies of the West; yet, from a political perspective, its effects were felt not when oil prices increased but after the effects were generalized. We anticipate that the presence of generalized inflation, captured by the CPI, will produce political reactions far stronger than those generated by rises in the prices of individual commodities.

Political Capacity

We conceptualize political capacity as the ability of the government to carry out the tasks chosen by its political elite and other national actors (Organski and Kugler 1980, Organski et al. 1984, Arbetman 1990, Arbetman and Kugler 1995). From this perspective, one polity is more capable than another when the government can generate more human and material resources to accomplish the goals its elite has chosen. Organski and Kugler (1980:72) argue that highly capable political systems "need not be free, democratic, stable, orderly, representative, participatory or endowed with" any other characteristics frequently associated with normative conceptions of political capacity. Political capacity seen in this light captures the effectiveness of governments in achieving their goals. Political capacity does not imply legitimacy where populations accept and support the means and goals of the elite that constitute the government. Coercive governments may be effective and so may be participatory regimes. We adopt this conception of political capacity because a neutral position on means and goals allows us to provide a general gross benchmark that can be used to account for the performance of any political system. Two different but related components are used to estimate the concept of political capacity: (1) the ability of the government to effectively extract resources from the pool produced by a society, and (2) the ability of the government to reach and mobilize its population.[1]

Penetration and extraction behave autonomously, but are closely intertwined aspects that document changes in governmental capacity. The buildup of political structures takes place in a temporal sequence. Governments first increase political capacity by mobilizing populations and only then expand that capacity by extracting resources from the material pool produced by society. Penetration, therefore, precedes extraction because only after the government mobilizes human resources and creates a sense of a national whole can significant fiscal extraction be sustained. Political capacity starts with the penetration of populations by the governing elite, and political extraction consolidates and deepens that link.

Political Variables: Political Capacity

Changes in the political capacity of states are fueled by a government's capacity to achieve stated goals. To do so, governments must improve their ability to penetrate the human assets in their society and enhance their ability to extract resources from the pool of material assets produced by the society. We posit that, in the early stages, changes in penetration dictate changes in political capacity. But as governments become stronger, extraction adds to penetration and eventually dominates changes in political capacity. Organski et al. (1984) show that, over the modernization trajectory, the highest political costs of building up the political system are at two extremes: during the period of slow development and at the time when the society is fully developed. There is an intuitive explanation for these patterns. In the less developed, usually still very poor societies the organization of political structures is difficult because so few in the population are organized for political purposes and there is so little to give. Massive efforts are needed simply to access households. In developed societies governments have already achieved high levels of political penetration. Therefore, when they seek to improve extraction to enhance the effectiveness of established goals, the government must overcome organized opposition to new policy initiatives.[2] Concurrently improving extraction and penetration should further enhance overall political capacity. Below, we discuss the logic used to construct indices of penetration and extraction which are two aspects of the measure of political capacity.

Relative Political Penetration

Arbetman (1990) proposes that levels of governmental penetration can be inferred from the unofficial labor force, or those working in the black market economy (for earlier efforts to measure effective populations see Organski, Bueno de Mesquita and Lamborn 1972, Organski and Kugler 1980). Following the work of Pettenati (1979), the size of the informal sector is gauged by the difference between the average proportion of the economically active population in countries with similar levels of development and the actual active population in each country. (For alternative estimates see Fua 1976 and Contini et al. 1987.) Arbetman (1990) shows that this ratio can be used to approximate the level of illegal employment in societies with similar levels of development where an active population profile should be equivalent. The degree of political penetration is therefore the ratio between the average and the actual proportion of active population in countries at similar levels of socio-economic development:

$$RPP = Active\ Population_{jt}\ /\ Average\ Active\ Population_t$$

where

RPP = relative political penetration
j = nation
t = time.

When the relative political penetration index is larger than one, disguised labor activity is minimal because of the excess demand for labor compared to other countries with similar levels of development. When the index is less than one, the society has concealed labor and an excess supply exists. The relative political penetration index estimates relative penetration because the active population profiles used to characterize each nation are viable only within a narrow level of economic development. Meaningful comparisons based on deviations from such a moving base are useful only across countries that have similar levels of economic performance.

Relative Political Extraction

Organski and Kugler (1980) propose a measure of relative political extraction (RPE) rooted in the proposition that a government's ability to raise revenues is a critical indicator of effective performance because, after controlling for economic productivity, fiscal extraction measures the range and depth of governmental control. Indeed, few public operations, besides revenue collection, depend as heavily on popular support as on fear of punishment. Few are as carefully avoided.

A combination of political and economic factors determines government revenue levels. Thus, total tax revenues say very little about political extraction. We propose that if one specifies the economic preconditions correctly and separates them from government performance, revenue levels will accurately reflect political effectiveness. The problem is to obtain a tax ratio comparable across time and across countries.

Alternate means to tackle this issue have been advanced by a number of IMF fiscal economists who define the concept of tax "effort" as the ratio between actual tax collections (including tax revenues and excluding social security where the government is merely a conduit in the transfer of resources) and econometrically estimated tax collections which approximate average taxes in countries with similar economic structures. For developing nations, Lotz and Morse (1967), Chelliah (1971), Bahl (1971) and Chelliah et al. (1975) suggest that economic controls should include exports, imports, mining, agriculture, and per capita GDP. Each of these factors aids or obstructs the government in its efforts to extract resources from its population. For example, the government can easily collect taxes on foreign trade, oil, or diamond production. The availability of such resources is expected to boost revenues. Moreover, wealth reflected by higher levels of productivity provides a broader base from which to tax. The reverse is true for subsistence agricultural production because producers can effectively resist the attempts of the central elite to tax such production and avoid detection through barter. Organski and Kugler (1980) and Arbetman (1990) show that the alternate models proposed by the IMF fiscal group for estimating the tax base in developed societies produce consistent estimates. Agricultural controls are more effective in the less developed societies, while individual productivity controls are more appropriate in developing societies. Therefore, the estimation of predicted political extraction is obtained as follows:

Less Developed Countries:
$$Tax/GDP = \beta_0 + \beta_1(Time) + \beta_2(Mining/GDP) - \beta_3(Agr/GDP) + \beta_4(Exports/GDP)$$

Developing Countries:
$$Tax/GDP = \beta_0 + \beta_1(Time) + \beta_2(Mining/GDP) - \beta_3(GDP/Capita) + \beta_4(Exports/GDP)$$

Simple adjustments for inputs would not be applicable for governments of developed societies. In such societies the costs of the public sector are no longer driven simply by how much the government can extract from their economic structures, but are defined instead by the choice made between what is a private and a public sector. Governments' policy choices regarding the proportion of private and public goods reflect political values in a society, and this choice will in turn define, to a large extent, the levels of extraction. For example, Sweden chooses to provide public health services to the whole population whereas the United States still provides most health services privately. The lower level of taxation in the United States is due to societal preferences and not to the inability of the United States to draw revenues from its population. Thus, in developed societies, in addition to economic adjustments from the revenue side, compensations for expenditure choices must be included. Organski and Kugler (1979) and Tait et al. (1979) experiment with alternate controls to account for differences in the level of revenue extraction due to differences in the provision of public services for education, health, and defense. Recall that the objective of such controls is to insure that collected revenues reflect what the government is *able* to do and not what the government *chooses* to extract from the population. Estimates using expenditure controls for health produce consistent results and incorporate most of the effects added by controls for education and military expenditures in developed societies. The simplified equation used to estimate predicted political extraction for developed nations is[3]

$$Tax/GDP = \beta_0 + \beta_1(Time) + \beta_2(Mining/GDP) - \beta_3(GDP/Capita) + \beta_4(Exports/GDP) + \beta_5(Health\ Exp/GDP).$$

As with political penetration, extraction is assessed by a simple ratio:

$RPE = Actual\ Government\ Revenue_j/Predicted\ Government\ Revenue_j,$

where

RPE = relative political extraction
j = nation.

The ratio between actual and predicted revenues is used to estimate the relative effectiveness of extraction by governments in societies at given levels of economic development. Revenues which are already committed and government transfers are excluded. Relative political extraction is relative because absolute comparisons between countries at different levels of economic productivity are not meaningful. Sweden, for example, already collects over 50 percent of total resources produced to cover public services and cannot double its efforts, while Argentina, which in 1980 extracted less than 30 percent of the national product, could do so. Thus, relative political extraction levels provide effective comparisons of political performance among nations with similar economic structures and equivalent per capita productivity.

The limits on political extraction tell an important story about politics. Unlike economic performance which can grow without well-established limits, political performance is bound by the productivity of a society at a given point in time. For this reason, developed societies that enjoy high levels of extraction have a low potential "flexibility" to raise their effectiveness, while developing nations that still extract a relatively low amount of resources from the pool produced have a high potential "flexibility." Structural changes driven by political innovation should have far more dramatic effects on populations in developing nations than similar innovations in developed nations that already tap most sources of governmental resources.

Problems Associated with Estimates of Political Capacity in Emerging Market Economies

Data limitations seriously constrain this analysis. On the political side, the most reliable estimates are those of relative political penetration because in non-market economies it is possible to estimate the size of active black markets. Political penetration is apparent even under fixed prices and production quotas when shortages and bottlenecks develop, and the only escape from scarcity of goods is through participation in the black market. Thus, in politically repressed societies, black market participation is a reliable measure of governmental strength. Variations are important because in coercive environments the costs involved in defying the government are particularly high for individuals, and the presence and expansion of black markets is a particularly accurate measure of political compliance. Indeed, when black market activities are punishable by death, relative political penetration is very appropriate to show the presence or absence of a government's capacity. The shortcoming of relative political penetration indicators is that planners, prior to market reforms, tended to stockpile labor to meet the set targets, disregarded cost, and restricted mobility. Thus, often one finds concurrently underemployment and labor shortages. This situation is not different from that in developing societies where inflexible labor markets coexist with subsistence and informal economies. The relative political penetration indicator is therefore available but does not reflect exactly what is captured in competitive, open market economies.

The data used to calculate relative political extraction may not be totally reliable for theoretical and practical reasons. Theoretical reasons are related to the characteristics of centrally planned economies. Practical reasons stem from the statistical repercussions of predetermined relative values. In emerging economies the problems are due to the incipient know-how of the institutions that collect and analyze the data as well as the inexperience and mistrust of economic actors in reporting the information. Moreover, the dubious enforcement of the regulations and laws make defection quite inexpensive (World Bank 1993, chapter 2). Therefore the results should be taken as a first approach to finding indicators to monitor the performance of these emerging economies (Bird and Wallich 1993:4). Our work relies heavily on efforts by the World Bank to reconstruct estimates close to those available in market economies which are the best available approximations to the data we seek.

Tanzi (1993) is the source for the fiscal information. The data is available from 1985, when the formerly centrally planned economies started to show islands of liberalization such as Poland and Hungary and/or it was feasible to reconstruct the data. The fiscal system did not rely on direct taxes, such as personal income taxes, because they discouraged private activity by making the effective rates close to one hundred percent. Most of the tax revenue was collected from three sources: turnover taxes, profit and payroll taxes. "[T]urnover taxes can be thought as taxes charged on the sales from state enterprises to retailers, or as the difference between the prices charged to consumers (minus a small profit margin for retailers) and producers' costs" (Tanzi 1993:20). The rate of compliance of this tax was very high under centrally planned economies, since prices and volumes were set and the payments had to be made through state banks. In emerging economies, all enterprises and not just the state are included in the scheme. And, as prices are liberalized, the compliance rate depends more on the capacity of the government to levy taxes. Profit taxes were often negotiated between the state and state enterprises. These taxes were a way of recovering past investments—

through amortization—and dividends. Payroll taxes and social security contributions are very similar to those of market economies. Following the specification for market economies, social security contributions are discounted from tax revenues since the government can only marginally modify this entitlement. Moreover, there is evidence that emerging economies are raising social security and payroll taxes to institute social reform and to try to avoid popular discontent.

We control for exports for all economies after 1985. In market economies, exports are a source of economic growth and they reflect an area that is easily monitored by the government. In non-market economies, exports indicate the need for imports to obtain technology and capital goods unavailable domestically. The second goal of exports is to balance material resources. The economies in question favored trade with other members of the Council for Mutual Economic Assistance (CMEA) in the framework of bilateral clearing relations. Therefore, prices among CMEA members did not always reflect market values. Although the CMEA took international prices as an indicator, exchange rates were manipulated and market values distorted. Of course, in emerging economies exports should reflect market conditions and this variable will approach the conceptual significance of the traditional relative political extraction model. In spite of the difficulties mentioned above, the World Bank (1992, 1993) reconstructed the data to reflect market accounting methods as closely as possible.

Controls for productivity also present an obstacle in non-market economies. Too often, retail prices are lower than producer costs. In market economies this would result in widespread bankruptcies in the system. In centrally planned economies, deficits are covered by a web of transfers and subsidies. Work by the World Bank (1993:8) suggests that an effective picture of productivity emerges using purchasing power methods to estimate production. We adopt this procedure for all output-based controls (see World Bank 1992:39). In developing societies with subsistence economies, an alternative to controlling for productivity is to measure the degree to which the economy is dependent upon agriculture. The higher this dependency, the lower the expected resources that the government can collect. In the case of centrally planned economies, taxes and subsidies in agricultural sectors tend to distort their shares of production. Some sectors benefited from large subsidies, while others had to pay large taxes. However, most distortions tended to support industry over agriculture. Measures of relative political extraction using agricultural controls were constructed to provide a second estimate that avoids the problem of current to constant prices alluded to in the previous paragraph. Following the specification defined in the previous section, we developed a similar model below. The only variable that was not included is mineral production, which was unavailable.

The estimates reported in Table 4.1 are very tentative, based on a limited time frame, and are consistent with previous, more broadly based estimations for all economies' predicted government revenue ratios.[4] As we theoretically anticipated, in formerly planned economies agricultural production restricts revenue extraction while exports increase government revenues. These predicted values are used to construct relative political extraction values for emerging market economies and results for each nation as presented in the appendix.

Political penetration and extraction estimates provide us with a cross-temporal and cross-sectional glimpse of evolutionary political performance in emerging economies. Few of these governments show much strength. Indeed, indications are that prior to their collapse most of these governments had lost control over the human and material resources required to maintain high economic performance. Under these circumstances, one would anticipate that the emerging political groups will be fragile and they will not be in a position to take the tough steps necessary to control inflation. Let us test these insights.

Results

We propose that strong political structures are connected with low levels of inflation. Effective governments with high levels of relative political extraction (RPE), and governments that manage high levels of political penetration (RPP), are expected to implement macroeconomic policies that avoid sharp rises in inflation (CPI). We anticipate, therefore, that societies with relatively high political capacity will control inflation, while those with low political capacity will fail to implement effective inflation controls.

For the longer 1970–1990 period it is only possible to relate political penetration with inflation. These results for the formerly planned economies are presented in Table 4.2 below.

TABLE 4.1 Estimation of Predicted Political Extraction in Formerly Planned Economies after Controlling for Agriculture and Exports

tax rate	coeff.	stand.err.	t	P>t	95% conf. interval	
export/GDP[a]	.3710	.0982	3.775	.001	.1686	.5734
agric/GDP[b]	-.5580	.2886	-1.933	.065	-1.152	.0363
constant	29.817	4.9563	6.016	.000	19.609	40.0251

$N = 28$
$F(2,25) = 9.65$ Prob $>F = 0.0008$
$R^2 = 0.4355$ Adj. $R^2 = 0.3904$

[a] export/GDP = exports/gross domestic product
[b] agric/GDP = % agricultural production/gross domestic product

TABLE 4.2 Relationship Between Changes in Inflation and Political Penetration in Formerly Planned and Emerging Market Economies 1970–1990

CPI rate	coeff.	stand.err.	t	P>t	95% conf. interval	
RPP	-4.35	1.462	-2.97	0.003	-7.23	-1.46
constant	4.60	1.47	3.12	0.002	1.69	7.51

$N = 163$
$F(1,161) = 8.86$ Prob $> F = 0.0034$
$R^2 = 0.052$ Adj. $R^2 = 0.046$

Note: RPP = relative political penetration

The relationship between political penetration and inflation, while weak, shows the expected negative relation between penetration and inflation. These attenuated results should not be immediately discouraging, because during the period of centralized planning inflation was artificially controlled and these cases constitute the overwhelming majority of those considered. Nevertheless, at best, changes in relative political penetration only affect inflation at the margin.

Our investigation of the transition period centers on the effects of political extraction on inflation. Extraction deals with the utilization of material resources produced by a society and should be more directly related to changes in consumer prices. Table 4.3 shows the relationship between both political extraction indicators and inflation.

The figures in Table 4.3 show that political extraction allows us to better anticipate the level of inflation during the transition period. Note that relative political extraction, which measures resource extraction, affects inflation far more than did penetration despite the short period of analysis. We suspect that the reason for the stronger relationship is that governments of emerging economies are forced to extract resources to advance the market transformation. Tanzi (1993) may indeed be correct when he argues that governments are less inclined to mobilize and manipulate the population.[5] This is reinforced by the fact that we discover a continuing weak relation between penetration and inflation. Indeed, adding relative political penetration to the above equation marginally increases the variance explained but, due to multicollinearity, the coefficients are no longer significant.[6] The reason may be that as goods become scarce, populations acquire resources in the black market, and such activity is not reflected by market forces in emerging economies. Thus, levels of penetration do not directly affect inflation levels since these fluctuations reside in areas where market forces determine price.

Note in Table 4.3 that the inverse relationship between inflation and political extraction suggests that a .1 increase in extraction leads to

TABLE 4.3 Relationship Between Changes in Inflation and Political Extraction in Emerging Market Economics 1984–1990.

CPI rate	coeff.	stand.err.	t	P>t	95% conf. interval	
RPE	-9.15985	3.26142	-2.809	0.009	-15.8638	-2.4559
constant	9.95684	3.28755	3.029	0.005	3.1992	16.7145

$N = 28$
$F(1,26) = 7.89$ Prob $>F = 0.0093$
$R^2 = 0.2328$ Adj. $R^2 = 0.2033$

Note: RPE = relative political extraction

approximately a 1 percent decline in inflation. Since political extraction varies from .5 to 2.0 in peace time, inflation can be affected dramatically depending on the extractive capacity of the governing elite. The recent experience of Latin American nations strongly suggests an important impact of specific governments on inflation. The recent electoral changes in Poland and the Ukraine should provide opportunities for evaluating variations in capacity as well as policy to establish how political strength and policy interact in the area of inflation. We are aware that these results, based on only twenty-eight observations during the very early period of transformation, are only indicative of potential trends. Review of the regression residuals, however, suggests that the relationship is very strong and well patterned. Further exploration is needed to support this encouraging result.

Conclusions

We find a weak but stable relationship between inflation and political performance in emerging economies. Governments of emerging economies capable of extracting resources can install regulations that guide monetary behavior during the transition periods more efficiently than less extractive governments. On the other hand, governments that penetrate the fabric of their societies affect inflation rates only at the margin. These results suggests that aggregate indicators of political capacity do matter, but they matter less than we anticipated.

Governments that oversee the transformation from centralized to market economies face very serious political risks when they attempt to control inflation. Shrinking the flow of money reduces subsidies, expands unemployment in the public sector, restricts social security payments, reduces health coverage, removes housing allowances, and leads to bankruptcies in non-profitable public and recently privatized firms. The very stability of the government is at stake. This is rarely stressed by even the most distinguished economists. For example, when evaluating the collapse of the Russian ruble Jeffrey Sachs correctly points out that the former Central Bank chief, Mr. Garashchenko, did little to control inflation. "He has always been ready to run the bank's printing presses to benefit political patrons and has never been shy about confiscating the public's savings through inflation." He continues disapprovingly: "His most powerful backer has been Prime Minister Viktor Chernomyrdin," who "when President Boris Yeltsin exploded in fury at the collapse of the currency and called for Mr. Gerashchenko's head...rushed back and reportedly tried to protect the Central Bank chief." Sacks concludes, "Russia's monetary policy has been in the hands of a few powerful people who understand little and care little about normal monetary policy and instead view Central Bank credits as a resource to be manipulated at will for short-run advantage" (*New York Times*, October 15, 1994, p.15).

What Sachs overlooks is that had Chernomyrdin blocked payments to the military and, to a lesser degree, to public enterprises, President Yeltsin would not have survived the Duma's opposition led by Khasbulatov (Kugler and Bueno de Mesquita 1994). The balance between stable monetary policy and stable government is a tenuous one in economies that are undergoing the massive transformations that have followed the collapse of the Soviet Union. To achieve the twin goals of economic and political stability requires effective timing. Short-term adjustments are not necessarily driven by short-term advantages for those who care little about "normal monetary policy." Rather, they may result instead from a calculated attempt to maintain the political stability essential to economic reform. In the long run, inflation cannot be the source of governmental revenues. As experience in Latin America suggests, elected government officials that succeed in the fight against inflation also enhance long-term economic prospects and gain re-election. The inability to deal with relatively high inflation creates political instability.

In the emerging economies we have scrutinized, the reform task was so large that we anticipated very strong relations between aggregate indicators of political capacity and rates of inflation. Our work shows that this relation exists, but this link is far more attenuated than we anticipated. Controls for political competition suggest that the relationship with inflation in the short term may be more complex. In the longer run, as transitional societies move closer to a market economy, the impact of capable political governments should have stronger effects on inflation. Here we simply show that politics cannot be disregarded when one attempts to understand inflation patterns during the transition from a centralized to a market economy.

Appendix: Political Capacity in Non-market Economics
Relative Political Penetration

Year	Albania	Bulgaria	Czechoslovakia	E.Germany	Hungary
1970	.85	1.05	1.03	1.01	1.07
1971	.84	1.03	1.03	1.00	1.05
1972	.85	1.03	1.03	1.01	1.05
1973	.85	1.03	1.03	1.01	1.04
1974	.86	1.03	1.03	1.02	1.04
1975	.86	1.02	1.03	1.03	1.03
1976	.87	1.02	1.03	1.04	1.01
1977	.88	1.02	1.04	1.06	1.00
1978	.89	1.01	1.04	1.07	.99
1979	.90	1.01	1.04	1.08	.98
1980	.90	1.01	1.05	1.09	.97
1981	.91	1.00	1.05	1.09	.97
1982	.92	1.00	1.04	1.10	.97
1983	.92	1.00	1.04	1.11	.96
1984	.93	.99	1.04	1.12	.96
1985	.93	.99	1.04	1.13	.96
1986	.93	.99	1.04	1.13	.96
1987	.94	.99	1.04	1.13	.97
1988	.94	.99	1.04	1.13	.97
1989	.95	.99	1.04	1.13	.97
1990	.94	.98	1.03	1.22	.96

Year	Poland	Romania	U.S.S.R.	Yugoslavia
1970	.98	1.10	.97	.90
1971	1.06	1.07	.97	.90
1972	1.06	1.06	.97	.89
1973	1.06	1.06	.98	.89
1974	1.06	1.05	.98	.89
1975	1.06	1.04	.99	.89
1976	1.06	1.03	1.00	.89
1977	1.05	1.02	1.01	.89
1978	1.05	1.01	1.01	.89
1979	1.04	1.00	1.02	.89
1980	1.04	.99	1.03	.89
1981	1.03	.99	1.03	.89
1982	1.03	.99	1.02	.89
1983	1.02	.99	1.02	.89
1984	1.02	.99	1.02	.89
1985	1.02	.99	1.02	.89
1986	1.01	.99	1.01	.89

(continues)

Relative Political Penetration (continued)

Year	Poland	Romania	U.S.S.R.	Yugoslavia
1987	1.01	.99	1.00	.89
1988	1.01	.99	1.00	.89
1989	1.01	.99	.99	.89
1990	.99	.98	.98	.88

Relative Political Extraction

Year	Bulgaria	Czechoslovakia	Hungary	Poland	Romania	Yugoslavia
1984				1.14		
1985	.94	1.13	.93	1.15		.76
1986	1.06	1.08	1.01	1.15		.87
1987	.95	1.12	1.04	.99		.82
1988	.93	1.11	1.12	1.04	1.01	.68
1989	.97	1.04	.97	.94	1.12	.78

Notes

1. For extended treatment and applications see Organski and Kugler (1980), Organski et al. (1984), Arbetman (1992), and Arbetman and Kugler (1995). For an alternative treatment of political capacity, see Jackman (1994).

2. Support for these arguments is found in the analysis of war (Organski and Kugler 1980, chapter 2; Kugler and Domke 1986), the evaluation of exchange rates (Arbetman 1990), the debt crisis (Snider 1988), and the evaluation of black market fluctuations, inflation and economic growth (Arbetman and Kugler, forthcoming, 1995). Methodological evaluations are in Kugler (1983).

3. Arbetman and Kugler (1995) discuss other alternatives.

4. Estimates of predicted government revenue for developing countries have an R^2 of .36 to .44 for open developing economies. All coefficients have similar directions and patterns (Arbetman 1990, table 39).

5. The relative level of extraction shows how committed the government is to economic reform and how efficient it will be in pursuing such policy. For instance, an examination of the different policies pursued in Eastern Europe suggests that the shock privatization therapy implemented in Poland left the population without any frame of reference and one of the effects was rampant inflation. Czechoslovakia and Hungary have been more cautious and the results are more encouraging

6. The crosscorrelation between RPE and RPP = .8041.

References

Arbetman, Marina. 1990. *The Political Economy of Exchange Rate Fluctuations*. Ph.D. Dissertation, Vanderbilt University.

Arbetman, Marina, and Jacek Kugler. 1995. *Political Capacity and Economic Behavior*. Forthcoming.

Bahl, Roy W. 1971. "A Regression Approach to Tax Effort and Tax Ratio Analysis." *IMF Staff Papers* 18: 570–612.
Banaian, King, J. Harold McClure and Thomas D. Willett. 1994. "The Inflation Tax Is Likely to Be Inefficient at Any Level." *Kredit und Kapital* 1: 30–42.
Bird, Richard, and Christine Wallich. 1993. *Fiscal Decentralization and Intergovernmental Relations in Transition Economies.* World Bank, Policy Research Department, Working Paper No. 1122, March.
Brown, A. J. 1985. *World Inflation Since 1950.* Cambridge: University of Cambridge, Bath Press.
Cagan, P. 1956. "The Monetary Dynamics of Hyperinflation," in *Studies in the Quantity Theory of Money.* Chicago: Chicago University Press.
Chelliah, Raja. 1971. "Trends in Taxation in Developing Countries." *IMF Staff Papers* 18: 254–31.
Chelliah, Raja, Hassel Bass and Margaret Kelly. 1975. "Tax Ratios and Tax Effort in Developing Countries, 1969–1971." *IMF Staff Papers* 22: 1–22.
Contini, Bruno. 1979. *Lo Sviluppo di Un'Economia Parallela.* Milan: Edizioni di Comunita.
———. 1981a. "Labor Market Segmentation and the Development of the Parallel Economy—The Italian Experience." *Oxford Economic Papers* 33: 401–12.
———. 1981b. "The Second Economy of Italy." *Taxing and Spending* 3: 18–24.
Contini, Bruno, et al. 1987. "New Forms and New Areas of Employment Growth." Final Report, Program for Research and Actions on the Development of the Labour Market. Torino, Italy: Commission of the European Communities.
Easterly, William, and Klaus Schmidt-Hebbel. 1993. "Fiscal Accounts and Macroeconomic Performance." *World Bank Policy Research Bulletin* 4 (3), May.
Fua, Giorgio. 1976. *Occupazione e Capacita Produttive: La Realta Italiana.* Bologna: Il Mulino.
Gaetani-D'Aragona, Gabriele. 1981. "The Hidden Economy: Concealed Labor Markets in Italy." *Rivista Internazionale di Scienze Economiche e Commerciali* 28: 270–89.
Hirschman, Albert O. 1985. "Reflections on the Latin American Experience," in Leon Lindberg and Charles S. Mailer, eds., *The Politics of Inflation and Economic Stagnation.* Washington, D.C.: The Brookings Institution.
Keynes, John Maynard. 1923. *A Tract on Monetary Reform.* London: Macmillian.
Kugler, Jacek. 1983. "Use of Residuals: An Option to Measure Concepts Indirectly." *Political Methodology* 9(1): 103–20.
Kugler, Jacek, and Bueno de Mesquita. 1993. "The Political Dimensions of the Russian Economic Reform." Mimeo.
Lotz, Jorgen R., and Elliott R. Morse. 1967. "Measuring 'Tax Effort' in Developing Countries." *IMF Staff Papers* 14.
Mitchell, William. 1988. "Inflation and Politics: Six Theories in Search of Reality" in Leon Lindberg and Charles S. Maier, eds., *The Politics of Inflation and Economic Stagnation.* Washington: Brookings Institution.
Morley, Samuel. 1979. *Inflation and Unemployment.* Hinsdale, Illinois: The Dryden Press.
Organski, A. F. K., Bueno De Mesquita, and Alan Lamborn. 1972. "The Effective Population in International Politics," in R. Clinton, W. Flash, and R. K. Goodwin, eds., *Political Science in Population Studies.* Pp. 79–100. Lexington: D.C. Heath.

Organski, A. F. K., and Jacek Kugler. 1979. "Technical Report: A Program of Research of National Estimates." Defense Advanced Research Projects Agency, U.S. Department of Defense, #N00014-78-C-0247.

Organski, A.F.K., and Jacek Kugler. 1980. *The War Ledger*. Chicago: Chicago University Press.

Organski, A.F.K., Jacek Kugler, Timothy Johnson, and Youssef Cohen. 1984. *Births, Deaths and Taxes*. Chicago: University of Chicago Press.

Paarlberg, Don. 1993. *An Analysis and History of Inflation*. Westport, Connecticut: Praeger.

Pettenati, Paolo. 1979. "Illegal and Unrecorded Employment in Italy." *Economic Notes* 8(1): 14–30.

Phylaktis, Kate, and Mark P. Taylor. 1993. "Money Demand, the Cagan Model and the Inflation Tax: Some Latin American Evidence." *The Review of Economics and Statistics* 75(1): 32–38.

Portes, Alejandro, and Saskia Sassen-Koob. 1987. "Making It Underground: Comparative Material on the Informal Sector in Western Market Economies." *American Journal of Sociology* 93(1): 30–61.

Rouyer, Alwyn. 1987. "Political Capacity and the Decline of Fertility in India." *American Political Science Review* 81(2): 453–68.

Sachs, Jeffrey. 1994. "How to Keep the Ruble off the Rollercoaster." *New York Times*, October 15, p. 15.

Snider, Lewis W. 1988. "Political Strength, Economic Structure, and the Debt Servicing Potential of Developing Countries." *Comparative Political Studies* 20: 4.

Tait, Alan, W. Gratz and B. Eichengreen. 1979. "International Comparisons of Taxation for Selected Developing countries, 1972–76." *IMF Staff Papers*, 26 (1).

Tanzi, Vito. 1993. "Tax Reform and the Move to a Market Economy: Overview of the Issues" in *The Role of Tax Reform in Central and Eastern European Economies*. Paris: OECD.

Tilly, Charles. 1975. *The Formation of National States in Western Europe*. Princeton: Princeton University Press.

Tokman, Victor E. 1978. "Tecnologia para el Sector Informal Urbano." *Demografia y Economia* 7(2): 35.

———. 1985. *Beyond The Crisis*. PREALC. Geneva, Switzerland: International Labour Organization.

Tufte, E. 1978. *The Political Control of the Economy*. Princeton: Princeton University Press.

Webber, Carolyn, and Aaron Wildavsky. 1987. *History of Taxation and Expenditures in the Western World*. New York: Simon and Schuster.

Willett Thomas D., ed. 1988. *Political Business Cycles: The Political Economy of Money, Inflation and Unemployment*. Durham: Duke University Press.

World Bank. 1993. *Historically Planned Economies*. Washington D.C.: The World Bank.

World Bank. 1992. *Historically Planned Economies*. Washington D.C.: The World Bank.

PART TWO

Institutional Mechanisms for Promoting Economic Stability

5

Guidelines for Constructing Monetary Constitutions

Thomas D. Willett[1]

Introduction

One of the longest running debates in macroeconomics is the relative desirability of rules versus discretion for macroeconomic policymakers. The last two decades have witnessed major theoretical advances in the analysis that economists have brought to bear on this issue, but no clear consensus has emerged on what the answer should be.

This is easily explained. Analysis based on rational expectations, the dynamic inconsistency of optimal monetary policy, and other political economy pressures on policymakers has strengthened the case for well-functioning rules. But analysis of the most commonly proposed rules to guide monetary policy, such as adopting a fixed exchange rate, returning to a commodity standard, or following a monetary base or money supply growth rule, suggests that any of these rules would at times *increase* monetary instability in the domestic economy. This is because all of the simple rules rely on the assumption that one or more key parameters or economic variables such as velocity, the money multiplier, or the equilibrium real exchange rate display little variability.[2] An open-minded reading of the empirical evidence sharply contradicts these assumptions for the industrial countries, and one would expect this to be even more of a problem in the transitional economies.

This creates serious problems for the design of monetary institutions. The following section of this chapter discusses the dangers of adopting oversimplified analysis. We question whether any type of simple monetary policy rule will both constrain political manipulation of the macroeconomy and provide protection from destabilizing shocks. Section 3 briefly discusses the evolution of the optimal policy rule literature to deal with economies facing an array of shocks. Essentially, such complexity implies that simple, complete rules for monetary policy are not possible. Rather, multipart strategies which distinguish between intermediate and ultimate target variables are required to blend simplicity and lucidity of objectives with operational mechanisms for constraining behavior when designing monetary institutions. The superiority of a constraint approach over the traditional optimal policy rule approach is stressed in section 4. This distinction flows naturally from viewing monetary institutions from a constitutional perspective. "Constitutional" in this sense refers to the basic ground rules and institutional framework for policymaking, whether actually specified in a constitution or in basic legislation. Thus the gold standard or the Bretton Woods international monetary system are constitutional arrangements. In section 5 the criteria for the design of monetary constitutions are discussed. Section 6 reviews the case for central bank independence and argues that greater attention needs to be given to the question of just what the bank is being made independent from. We argue that the objective should be to isolate the bank from political pressures to destabilize the macroeconomy for short-term political gain. However, the central bank should still be held to account for its policy actions: central bank officials ought not be given unlimited discretion. These issues are considered further in the following chapter by Burdekin and Willett. Section 7 summarizes the key points and discusses other reforms which would help promote monetary stability.

The Dangers of One-Dimensional Analysis

One sees a wide array of conflicting proposals offered for monetary reform in the emerging market economies (and elsewhere). A major reason for this is the tendency for advocates of a particular policy to present highly oversimplified analyses in which economies face one specific type of monetary problem or disturbance and other shocks are implicitly assumed to be absent. Thus, for example, many of the recent analyses advocating the adoption of currency boards are based on the implicit assumption that equilibrium real exchange rates remain constant so that the country adopting a currency board will import the rate of inflation of the country to which it has fixed its exchange rate.[3] However, with shocks to the equilibrium exchange rate, the currency-board country would run an initial balance of payments surplus or deficit that would generate inflationary or deflationary policies domestically.

It is now well understood from the theory of economic policy that the relative desirability of alternative short-run policy strategies such as interest rate versus money growth targeting or fixed exchange rate versus fixed reserves (i.e. flexible exchange rate) rules will depend on the pattern of disturbances hitting the economy.[4] Thus, for example, if the predominant shocks are to the demand for money, constant interest rate and exchange rate policies are desirable, whereas if the disturbance is an investment boom, a constant money supply strategy is preferable.[5] Economists should be careful not to present correct ceteris paribus analysis as if it were the only relevant case without carefully justifying the relevance of its assumptions.

Consider, for example, the argument that because demand for money functions are likely to be quite unstable in the initial stages of transition, countries in this situation should adopt fixed exchange rates.[6] While based on an analytically valid analysis of the effects of instability in the demand for money, in our judgement this policy advice is highly dangerous. It would be correct if the equilibrium real exchange rate were constant, but this is highly unlikely to be the case. For reasons analogous to why a transitional economy is likely to have instability in the demand for money, it is also likely that its equilibrium real exchange rate will be particularly hard to discern at any given point in time and will vary considerably as the transition advances. This presents a powerful argument, ceteris paribus, for promoting substantial domestic wage and price flexibility and, failing this, it argues against the adoption of fixed exchange rates. There has not yet been enough empirical research on the economies in transition to reach informed judgements on the relative strength of these considerations. There will probably be a good bit of variation from one economy to another. A priori, however, there is no strong reason to suppose that one effect will be more important than the other.[7] At best, we can say that formulating monetary policy will be particularly difficult for economies in transition, but not that one policy strategy is superior to another in this context.

Dealing with Complex Economies

If an economy were subject to only one major type of private sector disturbance, the adoption of an optimal policy rule would serve the dual purpose of stabilizing the macroeconomy as much as possible in response to shocks and constraining the government from following policies that provide short-run political gains but destabilize the economy over the longer run. In a more complex world with a competent, far-sighted, and benign government, contingent discretionary policy would be the ideal, albeit with the degree of government activism being tempered by uncertainty about the nature of shocks and effects of policy. Leaving out political considerations, the ideal answer to the rules versus discretion debate turns out to be a contingent set of policy rules which specify macroeconomic policy reactions under different types of circumstances.[8]

Where the number of relevant situations is small, actual contingent policy rules could be developed. This is the view of policymaking most congenial to rational expectations theorists, and reasonably complex policy rules have been often simulated in macroeconomic policies. To many economists, however, the number of possible relevant situations appears to be far too large to develop a complete operational set of policy rules. Such complexity suggests the need for discretionary policymaking. Discretionary policymaking should be based on a coherent strategy, but not be subject to a complete policy reaction function, i.e., a set of contingent policy rules. Even with the ability of modern computers to handle large equation systems, the need to operationally identify situations virtually assures that optimal policy would involve leaving at least some, and possibly considerable, discretionary authority to monetary policymakers.

The Constraint Approach to Monetary Institutions

The most important argument against giving policymakers wide discretionary authority is not that hubris would cause them to engage in excessive fine tuning (which would prevent their reducing macroeconomic instability to the minimum technically feasible level), but rather that political pressures to place excessive weight on short-run considerations would generate an inflationary bias.[9] A reading of the relevant theory and empirical evidence suggests there is a strong political case for constraining the scope of the government's discretionary economic policymaking. Unfortunately, it is not easy to devise a set of constraints for a complex economy which will control undesirable capitulation to short-term political pressures but not force policy responses that may destabilize the economy in the face of various types of economic shocks.

Viewed as an optimal policy rule, a constraint system is likely to have undesirable features. For example, if the constraints are ignored until they are hit, the resulting system is likely to be dynamically unstable. However, the approach of a constraint should lead the monetary authorities to modify their behavior well before constraints bind.[10] The major concern with the design of a constraint system, in addition to its effectiveness in securing the long-run objective, is to minimize the likelihood that it would impose monetary instability on the economy.

Viewing the design of monetary institutions from a constitutional rather than an optimal policy perspective—i.e., as a system of constraints rather than as a set of optimal policy rules—is a major step forward conceptually.[11] It recognizes that some degree of discretionary policymaking is both inevitable and desirable and focuses on how the scope of this discretion should be limited. The constitutional approach can benefit from the insights derived from the optimal policy approach, because these can be used to analyze the costs of various constraint systems. Thus, if there are likely to be substantial changes in the equilibrium real exchange rate, then fixed exchange rates would be an extremely costly form of monetary constraint system to adopt, at least in the absence of substantial domestic wage and price flexibility and/or factor mobility.

There is, of course, an inherent tradeoff between flexibility and the constraint imposed by a system. Different institutional designs can vary the terms of this tradeoff, however. An ideal system would give considerable scope for "good" stabilizing discretionary policy responses while limiting the scope for "bad" destabilizing policy responses. In the past, the major costs of short-run-oriented macroeconomic policymaking have come from its role in initiating and sustaining higher rates of inflation over the medium and longer term.[12] The major benefits from policy discretion come from the ability to cushion the short-run effects of shocks. This suggests a basic design strategy which focuses on giving more weight to flexibility in delineating the scope for short-run discretionary policy while constraining policy over the longer term. In other words, the emphasis in institutional design should be on avoiding the persistent cumulation of discretionary policy actions over time. Thus, the monetary authorities might be given a modestly broad range for changes in the money supply or inflation rate or the price level over, say, a one-year time frame, but this zone would not be rebased each period.[13] Thus, if money growth or inflation was above target in period one, it would have to be cut enough in following periods to bring it back on target. This can be achieved either by specifying the allowable bounds in terms of high and low values for multiperiod averages, or by allowing a band of permissible levels of some monetary aggregate or price variable to change only slowly (say to reflect real growth) if at all over time. Bernholz (1983) points out that in practice the gold standard tended to have this property. Contrary to the textbook rules of the game, the effects of gold flows on national monetary supplies were frequently at least partially sterilized in the short run, but the need to avoid persistent balance-of-payments surpluses or deficits assured that the gold standard did operate as a constraint system over the longer run.

Criteria for a Monetary Constitution

There is a general agreement about several desirable features for the design of a monetary constitution.

1. *Simplicity*. Rules should be simple enough to be easily understood by the general public.
2. *Accountability and Enforceability*. The behavior of the monetary authority should be easily monitored and mechanisms should be in place to enforce compliance with the rules.
3. *Credibility and Durability*. To stabilize long-run expectations, the rules must be credible; i.e., the public must believe that the rules will be followed while the regime is in force and that the probability of a change in regime is relatively low.

The application of these criteria is not always easy, for the criteria often conflict. Perhaps the simplest, most easily understood rule is that the monetary authority provide price stability. The price level is not, however, under the direct control of the monetary authority. Thus the authority can meet this objective only with a considerable degree of leeway, and the specification of operational rules for monetary policy in order to meet the objective could be quite complex.

Specifying the degree of permissible discretion or flexibility can also be quite tricky. The same is true with respect to provisions for overriding the normal rules in special circumstances. Ceteris paribus, the narrower is the range of discretion and the more difficult it is to override the rules or change the regime, the more stable should be the expectations generated. If the rules are too rigid, however, then in the face of adverse shocks the credibility of the whole regime may come into question. As a practical matter there is no way to guarantee that a regime will never be abandoned. It is possible that explicit provisions for overrides in particular circumstances could help to stabilize expectations. But the provisions for overrides need to be handled cautiously. The danger that every year will be seen as a new special case is all too great.

The 1989 Reserve Bank Act of New Zealand provides a model with considerable virtues.[14] It specifies price stability as the general objective, but relies upon negotiations between the central bank and finance ministry to define operational targets for a specific measure of inflation for one year ahead. The governor of the central bank is responsible for meeting the agreed inflation target, but its range may be renegotiated in the face of supply shocks. Failure to meet the goals can result in dismissal of the governor. The new law took effect in 1990. By mid-1992 inflation had fallen to near zero.

It is unlikely that any set of institutional provisions will be immune to abuse, and the New Zealand law is no exception to this rule. A cooperative central bank governor could certainly help a finance minister engage in some degree of politically motivated manipulation of macroeconomic policy and a mild long-term inflationary bias could easily be introduced through the choice of price indices. Nor is it clear that dismissal of the central bank governor is necessarily the best mechanism for enforcing compliance. The transparency of targeting required by the New Zealand law is an important virtue, and overall the law appears to have worked quite well so far. Its basic structure is certainly worth serious consideration by other countries.

The Misspecified Issue of Central Bank Independence

In recent years there has been substantially increased interest in the possible benefits of central bank independence as an institutional mechanism to help control inflationary biases. However, because it attempts to curb the influence of elected officials on monetary policy, central bank independence has been criticized, with some justification, of being antidemocratic. The resolution to this conflict rests upon considering "independent from what?"

From a constitutional perspective, it is perfectly legitimate to argue that in some areas certain actions should not be prohibited. The U.S. Bill of Rights provides examples. In other areas it is likewise legitimate to argue that some decisions be made only with super majorities of the legislature or that they be delegated to decision makers outside of the political process. Thus, there is nothing inherently antidemocratic about seeking to shield monetary policymaking from short-term political pressures.

There is a legitimate basis for concern, however, about the accountability of such decision makers. Advocates of central bank independence do not mean that central bankers should be free to follow capricious policy whims. Rather, they favor attempting to reduce the influence of short-run political pressures on decision makers so that long-term efficiency can better be pursued.

What is necessary is to carefully distinguish between what Debelle and Fisher (1994) have termed goal independence and instrument independence.[15] The objectives of monetary policy should be determined through the political process in a constitutional or quasi-constitutional manner. Recent theoretical and empirical research has presented a strong case that, in the long run, price stability promotes employment growth despite the fact that these objectives often conflict in the short run.[16] Thus, there is a strong case for making price stability the sole goal for monetary policy over the long term. This should be specified in the basic central bank legislation or constitution.

The central bank should then be given autonomy to determine the best way to meet this objective. It should be free to formulate monetary policy as it sees fit subject to the constraint that it succeed in meeting the objective of price stability. The monetary authorities' accountability should be specified in terms of their obligations to meet their policy objective in an operationally specified manner. The New Zealand Bank Law follows this formulation. Thus, while specific operational provisions remain appropriate areas for policy debate, we have in the New Zealand example an institutional framework for monetary policy which is superior to the variety of traditional specifications which have been practiced throughout the world.[17]

Concluding Remarks

Underlying the discussion in this paper has been the assumption that institutions matter. This has been coupled with the recognition that laws are frequently not enforced effectively. There is strong evidence that it is not enough simply to legislate good intentions. There is likely to be some slippage in the effectiveness of even the most carefully developed institutional design, and in some cases the amount of slippage is severe. However, this does not justify the conclusion sometimes drawn that efforts to develop institutional mechanisms to help achieve economic goals are a waste of time.

Institutional arrangements can influence the costs and benefits of following alternative strategies within a regime; they can also influence the costs and benefits of changing regimes. What is needed when designing institutions is to pay careful attention not only to how the system would work if it operated as the designers would like, but also to how the incentives of relevant actors are influenced and how this might influence the operation of the system in practice.

On both these counts it is not enough to decide that price stability is the appropriate long-run goal. The institutional mechanism to achieve this goal needs to be carefully analyzed and debated. In such analysis, it is important to consider the specific situation of the country in question. For example, for a small open economy with a large stable primary trading partner, the adoption of a currency board or some other type of fixed exchange rate system may make considerable sense. Both Austria and the Netherlands provide examples of how such hard currency policies can work well. But the theory of optimum currency areas shows that exchange rate arrangements that work well for one type of economy may be costly for another.[18] Thus fixed exchange rates are unlikely to be desirable as a universal mechanism of inflation control.

Likewise, political structures and cultural norms may vary greatly from one country to another. Historical experience often plays a significant role in shaping the actual relationship between central banks and governments. The traditions of the German Bundesbank cannot be instantly created in economies in transition. Expectations that legislation will be respected also vary a great deal from country to country. This may be one reason why the creation of various forms of central bank independence appears to have been much more effective in reducing inflation in the industrial countries than in the developing countries (see Cukierman 1992). Given that the political institutions of the former centrally planned economies are still young, it would be wise to pay particular attention to ways in which new institutional arrangements could be circumvented and how the actual incentive structures facing relevant actors are likely to change.

While this analysis has not attempted to judge specific proposals for monetary constitutions, we have attempted to illustrate the dangers of adopting excessively simple approaches to this issue and to discuss how the complexity of the patterns of shocks which hit an economy complicates the choice of optimal policy rules.

We wish to emphasize the importance of viewing monetary institutions as a constraint system. We argue that the objectives of monetary constitutions should be specified in terms of long-term price stability. There are nontrivial issues involved in formulating operational measures for the achievement of this goal, however. This is a particularly serious problem in the initial stages of economic transition where patterns of consumption and production are changing rapidly. Thus, merely adopting a vaguely defined price stability objective is not enough.

Fortunately, the extensive policy research of the last several decades does suggest a basis for developing the basic framework of an operational monetary constitution. In general, such a framework consists of a multipart structure involving the adoption of a goal such as price stability or constant nominal income growth, which is not under direct control of the monetary authorities, combined with operational provisions concerning how the monetary authorities should pursue that goal and/or how they may be penalized if the goal is not met.

This approach allows the criteria of simplicity to be met in the specification of the goal, yet permits greater complexity in the formulation of implementation criteria. At this stage, transparency and a reasonable degree of comprehensibility remain important, however. The recently introduced Reserve Bank Law of New Zealand provides a useful practical example of this approach.

A final word concerns complementary institutional reforms. Well-designed monetary institutions can provide a valuable cushion against inflationary pressures, but if these pressures are too strong even the best-designed monetary constitution must yield. Thus it is still important to keep the size of budget deficits to manageable proportions and to promote flexibility in factor mobility and wages and prices in the domestic economy. Such measures should be viewed as complements rather than substitutes for monetary policies.

It is also true that the establishment of credible monetary institutions can help provide incentives for greater discipline in private sector wage and price decisions and public sector budget decisions. The evidence suggests, however, that it commonly takes some time to establish the credibility of new monetary institutions or regimes.[19] Hence it would not be wise to place too much hope that the discipline effects of new monetary constitutions would greatly reduce the costs of disinflationary policies. Monetary reform should be viewed as part of a more comprehensive institutional package designed to promote monetary stability and improve the operation of the economy.

Notes

1. I am indebted to Richard Burdekin, Arthur Denzau, Eduard Hochreiter, Tamara Mast, Pamela Martin and Thomas Mayer for helpful comments on earlier drafts of this paper.

2. See Mayer and Willett (1988) for an analysis of these monetary policy proposals.

3. For recent analyses of currency boards see Hanke, Jonung, and Schuler (1994) and Schwartz (1993).

4. See, for example, Argy (1994) and Byrant (1980,1983).

5. The optimal exchange rate response would vary depending on the model used and the weights attached to different macroeconomic objectives.

6. See, for example, Bofinger (1991) and Bofinger, Svindland and Thanner (1993).

7. We should note that if purchasing power parity (PPP) holds fairly well, then changes in equilibrium real exchange rates will be of limited importance. While PPP is often assumed in monetary models, the empirical evidence sharply contradicts strong versions of PPP. The evidence on weaker versions is mixed. For a review of the theoretical issues and empirical evidence on PPP in the context of exchange rate policies for the economies in transition see Sweeney, Wihlborg, and Willett (1995).

8. See, for example, Byrant (1980,1983), Byrant, Hooper, and Mann (1993), Christ (1983), and McCallum (1988). Typically simulation studies find that targeting a nominal income variable is associated with less macroeconomic variability than targeting simple price, exchange rate or money supply variables.

9. See Alesina (1988) and Willett (1988b) for discussions of the interaction between economic policymaking and political considerations.

10. See Willett (1987).

11. For discussion of taking a constitutional approach to such issues and how it differs from the traditional optimal policy approach see Bernholz (1983), Buchanan (1983), Leijonhufvud (1984), Masciandaro and Spinelli (1993), Willett (1987, 1988a, 1989), and Yeager (1962).

12. The ever-increasing price levels of the industrial countries since World War II contrast with a period of virtually no long-run trend in the price level of countries like the U.K. over the preceding 300 years. See Bordo and Schwartz (1984).

13. An example to avoid is the famous Federal Reserve's "base drift" under implementation of money supply targeting during the 1970s.

14. For a discussion of the details of the New Zealand Bank law and an evaluation of its conformity with the recent literature on optimal contracts for central banks see Walsh (1994) and the discussion and references in the following chapter by Burdekin and Willett.

15. This is a variant of Grilli, Masciandaro, and Tabellini's (1991) concept of economic versus political independence.

16. See the analysis and references in the accompanying paper in this volume by Burdekin et al.

17. See the next chapter by Burdekin and Willett for further discussion of the institutional arrangements of central banks.

18. See, for example, Wihlborg and Willett (1991). For applications to economies in transition see Willett and Al-Marhubi (forthcoming) and the accompanying volume edited by Sweeney, Wihlborg and Willett (1995).

19. On the New Zealand and Canadian cases of the adoption of price stability objectives see Ammer and Freeman (1994) and Fischer (1994). On the Austrian hard currency policy see Hochreiter and Winckler (1994) and on the effects of the European Monetary System see Burdekin, Westbrook, and Willett (1994). For a differing view with respect to the credibility effects of the Estonian currency board see Hansson and Sachs (1994).

References

Alesina, Alberto. 1988. "Macroeconomics and Politics," in Stanley Fischer, ed., *NBER Macroeconomics Annual 1988*. Pp. 13–52. Cambridge, Mass.: The MIT Press.

Ammer, John, and Richard T. Freeman. 1994. "Inflation Targeting in the 1990s: The Experiences of New Zealand, Canada, and the United Kingdom." Federal Reserve Bank International Finance Discussion Papers No. 473.

Argy, Victor. 1994. *International Macroeconomics*. New York: Routledge.

Bernholz, Peter. 1983. "Inflation and Monetary Constitutions in Historical Perspective." *Kyklos* 36: 397–419.

Bofinger, Peter. 1991. "The Transition to Convertibility in Eastern Europe: A Monetary View," in John Williamson, ed., *Currency Convertibility in Eastern Europe*. Pp. 116–38. Washington, D.C.: Institute for International Economics.

Bofinger, Peter, Eirik Svindland, and Benedikt Thanner. 1993. "Prospects of the Monetary Order in the Republics of the FSU," in Peter Bofinger et al., *The Economics of New Currencies*. Pp. 9–33. London: Centre for Economic Policy Research.

Bordo, M. D., and A. J. Schwartz, eds. 1984. *A Retrospective on the Classical Gold Standard, 1821–1931*. Chicago: University of Chicago Press for the NBER.

Byrant, Ralph C. 1980. *Money and Monetary Policy in Interdependent Nations*. Washington, D.C.: The Brookings Institution.

———. 1983. *Controlling Money: The Federal Reserve and Its Critics*. Washington, D.C.: The Brookings Institution.

Bryant, Ralph C., Peter Hooper, and Catherine L. Mann. 1993. *Evaluating Policy Regimes*. Washington, D.C.: The Brookings Institution

Buchanan, J. M. 1983. "Monetary Research, Monetary Rules, and Monetary Regimes." *Cato Journal* 3: 143–46.

Burdekin, Richard C. K., Jilleen R. Westbrook and Thomas D. Willett. 1994. "Exchange Rate Pegging as a Disinflation Strategy: Evidence from the European Monetary System" in *Varieties of Monetary Reform*. Pp. 45–72. Boston: Kluwer Academic Publishers.

Christ, C. 1983. "Rules vs. Discretion in Monetary Policy." *Cato Journal* 3: 121–41.

Cukierman, Alex. 1992. *Central Bank Strategy, Credibility, and Independence: Theory and Evidence*. Cambridge, Mass.: MIT Press.

Debelle, Guy, and Stanley Fischer. 1994. "How Independent Should a Central Bank Be?" Paper presented at Federal Reserve Bank of San Francisco Monetary Conference, Stanford University.

Fischer, Andreas. 1994. "Inflation Targeting: The New Zealand and Canadian Cases." *Cato Journal* 13(1):1–27.

Grilli, Vittorio, Donato Masciandaro, and Guido Tabellini. 1991. "Political and Monetary Institutions and Public Financial Policies in the Industrial Countries." *Economic Policy* 6(2): 341–92.

Hanke, Steve H., Lars Jonung and Kurt Schuler. 1993. *Russian Currency and Finance*. New York: Routledge.

Hansson, Ardo, and Jeffrey Sachs. 1994. "Monetary Institutions and Credible Stabilization: A Comparison of Experience in the Baltics." Paper presented at the conference on Central Banks in Eastern Europe and the Newly Independent States, University of Chicago Law School.

Hochreiter, Eduard, and Georg Winckler. 1994. "Signaling a Hard Currency Strategy: The Case of Austria." *Kredit und Kapital* 27, in press.

Leijonhufvud, A. 1984. "Constitutional Constraints on the Monetary Powers of Governments," in R. B. McKenzie, ed., *Constitutional Economics*. Lexington, Mass.: Lexington Books.

Masciandaro, Donato, and Franco Spinelli. 1993. "Monetary Constitutionalism Once Again: Theory, Institutions and Central Banks' View." Mimeo, Centre for Monetary and Financial Economics, Universita Commerciale Luigi Bocconi. Milan, Italy, February.

Mayer, Thomas, and Thomas D. Willett. 1988. "Evaluating Proposals for Fundamental Monetary Reform," in Thomas D. Willett, ed. *Political Business Cycles*. Pp. 398–423. Durham, N.C.: Duke University Press.

McCallum, Bennett T. 1988. "Robustness Properties of a Rule for Monetary Policy." *Carnegie-Rochester Conference Series on Public Policy* 29 (August): 173–203.

Schwartz, Anna J. 1993. "Currency Boards." *Carnegie-Rochester Conference Series on Public Policy* 39: 147–87.

Sweeney, Richard J., Clas Wihlborg and Thomas D. Willett, eds. 1995. *Currency Policies for Emerging Market Economies*. Boulder, Colo.: Westview Press.

Walsh, Carl E. 1994. "Is New Zealand's Reserve Bank Act of 1989 an Optimal Central Bank Contract?" Mimeo, University of California at Santa Cruz.

Wihlborg, Clas G., and Thomas D. Willett. 1991. "Optimal Currency Areas Revisited," in Clas G. Wihlborg, Michele Fratianni, and Thomas D. Willett, eds., *Financial Regulation and Monetary Arrangements After 1992*. Pp. 279–297. Amsterdam: North Holland.

Willett, Thomas D. 1987. "A New Monetary Constitution? An Evaluation of the Need and Major Alternatives," in James Dorn and Anna Schwartz, eds., *The Search for Stable Money*. Pp. 145–60. Chicago: University of Chicago Press.

———. 1988a. "Key Exchange-Rate Regimes: A Constitutional Perspective." *Cato Journal*, Fall: 1–17.

———, ed. 1988b. *Political Business Cycles: The Political Economy of Money, Inflation, and Unemployment*. Durham, N.C.: Duke University Press.

———. 1989. "A Public Choice Analysis of Strategies for Restoring International Economic Stability," in Hans-Jurgen Vosgerau, ed., *New Institutional Arrangements for the World Economy*. Pp. 9–30. New York: Springer-Verlag.

Willett, Thomas D., and Fahim Al-Marhubi. Forthcoming. "Currency Policies for Inflation Control in the Formerly Centrally Planned Economies." *World Economy*.

Yeager, Leland, ed. 1962. *In Search of a Monetary Constitution*. Cambridge, Mass.: Harvard University Press.

6

Designing Central Bank Arrangements to Promote Monetary Stability

Richard C. K. Burdekin and Thomas D. Willett[1]

Introduction

Recent research suggests that "independent" central banks in the industrial countries have delivered average rates of inflation in the postwar period that are some 2 to 4 percent a year lower than for dependent central banks whose monetary policy decisions are controlled directly by the government.[2] Specific estimates vary reflecting differences in the rankings of central bank independence that have been proposed and the specifications of the inflation equations. The general finding that the most independent central banks are associated with the lowest average rates of inflation has proven to be quite robust, however. Some of this statistical correlation probably stems from basic societal attitudes and institutional structures that, while not captured by our statistical equations, can account for *both* the adoption of independent central banks *and* lower levels of inflationary pressures. Yet there are solid theoretical reasons for believing that institutional design can influence whether conflicting pressures are resolved in favor of higher or lower inflation. New Zealand's success in substantially lowering its rate of inflation relative to the world average since 1990, when its new central bank law took effect, suggests that central bank institutions *do* matter. Given that mounting evidence suggests that, over the longer term, price stability actually helps to increase employment and growth, we believe that there is a strong case for adopting central banking institutions designed to promote long-run price stability.

In surveying current central banking institutions across the world, one discovers a substantial variety of arrangements and numerous mechanisms through which supposedly independent central banks are subject to political pressures. Drawing on our own work and other recent research in this area, we present in this chapter a brief summary of findings about the effects of different types of central bank institutional structures and discuss some implications for the design of effective monetary institutions.

Objectives

Given the preponderance of evidence that, over the long term, price stability promotes growth, the case for choosing long-run price stability as the goal for monetary policy is quite strong.[3] In the short run, there is likely some scope for occasionally using monetary policy to cushion the adverse effects of certain shocks without this posing a threat to long-run price stability. The pursuit of short-run employment and growth objectives, however, will very likely generate inflationary biases in the operation of monetary policy.

In general, we would expect central banks that have price stability as their primary mandated goal to perform better than those that have been given multiple objectives. The Swiss National Bank and the Bank of Canada are examples of central banks whose mandatory objectives combine price stability with a potentially conflicting full-employment objective. In practice, however, the *implementation* of monetary policy in Switzerland has been consistent with the preeminent importance of price and exchange rate stability (Burdekin 1987). The Bank of Canada's recent voluntary focus on inflation targets also reminds us that a mandated single price-stability goal is not a prerequisite for anti-inflationary policy.

One attractive specification of central bank law is to provide limited scope for responding to shocks by specifying as a secondary objective that the central bank is obligated to support the general economic policies of the government, as long as this does not conflict with its primary objective of pursuing price stability. Examples of this type of formulation are found in the central bank laws of Germany and Austria.

An alternative approach, that will be discussed further below, is taken by the Reserve Bank of New Zealand Act 1989. The specific inflation targets in New Zealand are negotiated on a yearly basis and provision is made for their revision in the face of supply shocks.[4] As pointed out by Walsh (1994), this approximates the recommendation—stemming from the recent literature on optimal contracts for central banks—that provisions be made for adjusting short-run inflation targets in the face of supply shocks but not demand shocks.[5] Persson and Tabellini (1993) also emphasize that the policy targets agreements provide a performance-based contract for the central bank in New Zealand, yielding a degree of accountability that is generally lacking elsewhere.

A number of central bank laws express concern with maintaining the external as well as the internal value of the currency. Examples are Austria and the Netherlands. There is currently considerable debate over the role of exchange rate policies in the pursuit of monetary stability. From the theory of optimal currency areas (OCA), we know that the case for fixing the exchange rate (or more generally specifying the weight which should be given to exchange rate considerations in the formulation of monetary policy) will vary substantially from one country to another depending upon such factors as their size and openness, the patterns of shocks that they face, and the availability of a large, stable trading partner.[6] Thus, while granting that there is a strong case for exchange-rate-based "hard currency" policies in some countries, such as Austria with its peg to the Deutsche mark (DM), we do not believe that exchange rate objectives should standardly be included in the objectives of central bank legislation.

While some have argued against the current relevance of optimum currency area theory because of its Keynesian basis, such critics have overlooked a minority strand of the theory that focuses on the objective of price stability and discusses how, even with perfect wage and price flexibility, there is a case for some countries using exchange rate adjustments to protect themselves from imported inflation.[7] Even small open economies can find exchange rate adjustments helpful in offering partial protection against high rates of inflation in major trading partners. The appreciation of the currencies of the Baltic states against the Russian ruble provides an important example. Less dramatically, the recent balance of payments surplus in the Czech Republic has begun to pose a dilemma for the monetary authorities. To maintain their hard currency peg to the Deutsche mark and the dollar they may have to reduce the degree to which they have been sterilizing the effects of their growing international reserves by reducing the domestic component of the monetary base.

We certainly believe that in most cases it is wisest to specify the objectives of monetary policy in terms of general price stability (which of course includes prices in the external sector) rather than including the stability of the external value of the currency as a separate additional objective.

Implementation

Just specifying an objective does not, by any means, assure that it will be achieved. Most governments profess to seek long-term price stability as an objective, but only a few have made it a high priority and fewer still have been successful in accomplishing it. Moreover, while having a price stability goal "on the books" may help, much depends on the interpretation of "price stability." In Germany and Switzerland, success in achieving this goal would require near zero inflation. In Brazil, anything less than hyperinflation could suffice. Particularly in countries that do not share the strong proclivity towards, and history of, price stability recently enjoyed by Germany and Switzerland, an enforcement mechanism of the New Zealand type may be sorely needed. There must also be a clear standard to which the central bank is held accountable.

The traditional approach to central bank independence has assumed that governments will tend to display an inflationary bias in their discretionary policy activities. This implies that by providing institutional arrangements to shield monetary policymakers from some of these pressures (i.e., by giving them some degree of independence), decisions will be made that will correspond better to the long-run interests of the economy and the public. This approach raises two key issues. One is how to most effectively shield monetary policymakers from political pressures while allowing some room to respond to shocks in the short run. The second is how to provide an appropriate degree of accountability for such decision makers.

In economies with only one particular type of shock it is easy to design simple monetary rules that would perform close to optimally. However, as was stressed in the preceding chapter by Willett, real world economies are hit by a wide variety of shocks, and attempts to follow simple rules could be quite costly. Thus, one needs to either specify complex rules or allow some range of discretion for monetary authorities. Obviously, the greater the amount of discretion given to monetary authorities the more important become issues of accountability and the scope for destabilizing political pressures. Where economies are too complex to reach broad agreement on optimal policy rules, the trade-offs among accountability, flexibility, and commitment to long-term price stability come to the fore. There is likely no way to eliminate these trade-offs, but some types of institutional designs can provide more attractive trade-offs than others.

The search for institutional designs which will provide favorable trade-offs is one of the most important issues in the political economy of monetary policy.[8] The thrust of recent research has been to put much greater emphasis on accountability than did the earlier literature on central bank arrangements. As we have argued elsewhere (Banaian, Burdekin, and Willett 1995), the goals of those advocating central bank "independence" should be explicitly formulated in terms of independence from short-run political pressures that can induce destabilizing policy actions. This does not imply independence to do whatever the monetary authorities might wish. As pointed out by Chant and Acheson (1972) and Acheson and Chant (1973), if central bankers are given carte blanche to design central bank institutions, their self interest is likely to lead them to emphasize autonomy and secrecy over accountability. Havrilesky (1994) discusses how this is reflected in the design of the central bank law to accompany European Monetary Union, where the emphasis is on autonomy with minimal transparency and accountability.

While at this stage of our knowledge the optimal structure of central bank arrangements is far from obvious, a number of points do seem clear. It is important to clearly specify the goals for monetary policy and to develop mechanisms for holding the monetary authorities responsible for meeting these objectives. For this approach to work, goals must be feasible and operationally specified. Monetary officials need to be given the policy instruments and authority necessary to achieve these goals, and there should be clear provisions for dealing with failures to meet the objectives through some combination of rewards and penalties.[9]

Feasibility requires that monetary policymakers not be given conflicting goals to pursue, such as short-run maximization of growth and employment as well as price stability. Meanwhile, targets for rates of money growth, much less price level or inflation targets, would have to be specified in terms of a range rather than a precise number. In making operational the goals on which the monetary authorities will be monitored, a wide variety of variables such as nominal income growth, the price level, inflation rates, and measures of the monetary base and other monetary aggregates have all been advocated at one time or another. A detailed discussion of the comparative advantages and disadvantages of each measure and the alternative mechanisms for feedback rules is beyond the scope of this paper.[10] It is important to recognize, however, that definitions of precise acceptable ranges for many of these variables are likely to become obsolete over time. Thus, ways to change operational definitions over time must be devised, but with an eye to minimizing the possibility of manipulating definitions for short-run purposes.

In general, the need for revision of price-level indicators should tend to be less than for monetary aggregates where financial innovations can lead to substantial changes in trend rates of velocity. For the formerly centrally planned economies in the initial stages of transition, the use of specific price targets can present substantial problems. Even after price liberalization and the imposition of consumption or value-added taxes has been completed, changing patterns of consumption and production can present major problems both for data collection and for the construction of composite indices. As is illustrated in the charts in the following chapter by Eduard Hochreiter, in some of the transition economies the differences in the movements of consumer and producer price indices and monetary variables increase the relative attractiveness of using the exchange rate as a nominal anchor or target. In terms of ease of monitoring, it is by far the most attractive type of variable. On this score, a single-currency peg such as has been adopted by Argentina, Austria and Estonia would be superior to composite pegs that can involve changing weights (as with the Czech Republic, Hungary, and Poland in the post-1989 period). Still, even a composite peg is much easier to monitor than the other major possible target variables.

The problem with this exchange-rate based approach, which is discussed in the preceding chapter, is that changes in equilibrium real exchange rates can turn a nominal exchange rate target into a source of domestic monetary instability. It would be a major mistake to choose a bad target variable just because it was the easiest to monitor. The general point, however, is that some way must be found to deal with changing economic conditions over time.

The traditional approach to this problem has been to keep the objective rather vaguely defined and provide some degree of independence to the central bank authorities in judging how the basic objective should be pursued over time. While this approach is not entirely unreasonable, it suffers in our view from at least two major difficulties. First, even where the central bank is given formal decision-making independence, there are a number of channels through which political pressures may be brought to bear. Prospects for non-reappointment, or even forced resignations or firings, are cases in point. Thus, the longer are central bankers' terms and the greater the difficulty of removal, the greater will be the effective independence of monetary decision makers. Having a number of the members of policy-making boards appointed through mechanisms outside of the political process, such as the regional bank presidents in the Federal Reserve System in the United States, can also increase the effective degree of independence of central banks.[11] Likewise, prohibitions or limits on the financing of budget deficits, and provision for the central bank having its own sources of finance, may help strengthen the hand of central bankers in resisting political pressures.

It should be noted that, while discussions of central bank independence have most often focused on independence from the executive branch, independence from the legislative branch is also of key importance. This helps to explain why the so-called "independent" central bank of Russia presided over inflation rates exceeding 1000 percent per year in the early 1990s. At that time it was free of executive control but not from the legislative branch. Consequently, it was highly susceptible to the inflationary pressures emanating from the Russian Parliament. (For further discussion, see Lewarne's chapter in this volume).

Even if sufficient institutional safeguards can be provided to achieve true independence from short-run political pressures, the accountability of the monetary authorities remains an issue. One approach is to downplay the weight given to this consideration. While it is difficult to justify the complete absence of reporting requirements contained in the German central bank legislation, it can be argued that the systematic provision of ex post explanations for monetary policy decisions should be sufficient. This would mirror the transparency requirements placed on high court judges through the publication of opinions justifying their decisions.

An alternative approach is to follow the general lines of the Reserve Bank of New Zealand Act 1989, which focuses not on central bank independence from the government but on making both the central bank and parliament accountable for achieving the price stability goal laid down in the Act. Prior to the 1989 Act, the Reserve Bank of New Zealand had price stability as a vaguely specified goal (along with other objectives such as full employment), but this did not stop New Zealand from having one of the worst inflation records among the OECD countries over the 1970s and 1980s. The 1989 Act leaves the numerical inflation targets to be set jointly by the governor of the Reserve Bank and the minister of finance. If these targets are not in accordance with price stability, however, the government would be vulnerable to public scrutiny and its deviation from the terms of the Act—while not impossible—would certainly be costly politically.

The Reserve Bank of New Zealand is given an essentially free hand with regard to the *methods* used to meet the inflation targets. This allows the Reserve Bank to, for example, move away from money supply targeting in the face of velocity shocks and prevents the "locking in" of a strategy that subsequent conditions render inappropriate. Yet, if the targets fail to be met, the governor's job is explicitly put on the line. Only if the higher inflation is due to such prespecified conditions as supply shocks, higher indirect taxes, and so forth that lie outside the Reserve Bank's control, would over-shooting of the targets be acceptable.

New Zealand's inflation was reduced from double-digit levels in the pre-1989 period to less than one percent by mid-1992. The lengthening duration of labor market contracts is one indication of the credibility of the anti-inflationary policy (Fischer 1993). The New Zealand government has also taken steps to bring its budget deficit under control. The government achieved budget balance in the 1993/94 fiscal year and has now committed itself—under the 1994 Fiscal Responsibility Act—to running future surpluses to pay off debt built up in the past (see the Honorable Ruth Richardson's "Foreword" in Burdekin and Langdana 1995). Thus, the New Zealand government appears to be aware of the long-run infeasibility of pursuing anti-inflationary monetary policy in the presence of large budget deficits (see the earlier chapter by Burdekin in this volume).[12]

The weakness of the New Zealand legislation, however, appears to lie in the absence of any definite constraint on the numerical targets that can be set by the bank's governor and the minister of finance. While near-zero inflation was maintained into 1994, the Reserve Bank has warned that some increase in inflation may occur in 1995–1997 (Reserve Bank of New Zealand 1994). The projected increase is very mild, and yet it reminds us that the definition of price stability, like that of beauty, remains firmly in the eye of the beholder. The problem in defining "price stability" in the 1989 Act itself is, of course, that the validity of the chosen price index—or alternative guidepost, such as the value of the currency defined in terms of foreign exchange or in terms of a commodity such as gold—may not hold up over extended periods of time. It is certainly easier to pinpoint the possible weakness in the 1989 Act than it is to suggest a remedy, much less a "final solution," to this problem.

Another issue concerns the status of the legal provisions spelling out the central bank arrangements. Economists tend to treat such arrangements as constitutional issues in the sense that they provide the basic institutional framework within which short-term decision making takes place. In most countries, however, central bank arrangements have been provided through ordinary legislation rather than constitutional provision (Switzerland is an exception among the industrial countries). In some developing countries, such as Mexico, central bank independence has, in fact, been provided through constitutional amendment. While non-constitutional legislation often takes on a special status over time, and hence becomes more difficult to change than the average piece of legislation, a strong case can be made that the existing arrangements should require at least some type of high majority vote of the legislature for revisions. At a minimum, specific central bank legislation should be required for revisions.

The postwar history of the U.S. debt limit legislation and gold backing requirements for note issue shows that such requirements for legislative actions may have little restraining effect, however. In these cases, each time the public debt and note issue limits were approached, new legislation was passed. Still, the need for explicit legislation would be superior to cases where revisions to the central bank laws can be passed as provisions or riders to other legislative actions. An example of an undesirable status for central bank legislation is the current case in Hungary where provisions in budget laws take precedence over the central bank legislation, thereby potentially compromising the limitations on deficit financing contained in the original central bank law.

Concluding Remarks

It is important to point out that the emerging market economies lack the tradition of, and apparent consensus on, price stability enjoyed in countries like Germany and Switzerland. As recent events in Hungary and elsewhere suggest, nominal independence does not ensure legitimacy for the central bank nor does it automatically confer any real degree of protection from political influence. The New Zealand "model" may be more attractive than the attempt to use the Bundesbank as a basis for the new institutions in Central and Eastern Europe. The New Zealand Act makes accountable not only the central bank but also the parliament. Moreover, the Act has enjoyed at least initial success in a country that, like the emerging market economies, has had a poor inflation record in the past.

Much as we favor independence in the *implementation* of monetary policy, it is highly unlikely that one could legislate into existence overnight a central bank equipped to effectively resist the demands of the government. In any event, if the government runs sufficiently large deficits, no central bank will be able to resist the pressures to monetize these deficits—particularly when alternative methods of finance are limited by the absence of developed financial markets to absorb the government's bond issues. Why not make the government explicitly responsible for insuring that the price stability goal is met? While this may not prevent the government from demanding new credits from the central bank, contradictions with the price stability objective should be made obvious and potentially costly politically.

Notes

1. The authors have benefited from helpful comments from King Banaian, Pamela Martin, Tamara Mast, Thomas Mayer, and Pierre Siklos.

2. See, for example, Grilli, Masciandaro and Tabellini (1991), Cukierman (1992), Havrilesky and Granato (1993), and Banaian, Burdekin and Willett (1995).

3. See the earlier chapter by Burdekin, Salamun and Willett.

4. For more detail on the New Zealand institutional arrangements, see Archer (1992), Fischer (1993), and Walsh (1994).

5. On the optimal contracting approach see Fratianni, von Hagen, and Waller (1993), Persson and Tabellini (1993), Debelle and Fischer (1994), and Walsh (1994 and 1995).

6. See, for example, Wihlborg and Willett (1991). These issues are considered in detail in a companion volume, Sweeney, Wihlborg and Willett (1995). On the problems generated by high inflation in a country's major trading partner see the discussion of the breakdown of the ruble zone in chapter 11 by Banaian and Zhukov in this volume. For an analysis of strategy for small open economies without a single major trading partner see Grimes and Wong (1994). This latter situation poses an obvious problem for the Baltic states.

7. See Tower and Willett (1976) and Sweeney, Wihlborg and Willett (1995). For analysis of the use of exchange rate policies as anti-inflation devices in the formerly centrally planned economies, see also Willett and Al-Marhubi (forthcoming).

8. For recent work on this problem in addition to the literature discussed in the preceding chapter by Willett (1995) and the papers on central bank contracts referenced in footnote 5, see also the work by Bernanke and Mishkin (1992) and Lohmann (1992).

9. For an early contribution presenting the case for developing a penalty-reward structure, see Havrilesky (1972).

10. For discussions of these issues see, for example, Barro (1986); Meltzer (1987), Sibert and Weiner (1988), McCallum (1989), Gavin and Stockman (1991), Phelps (1991), Fischer (1993), and Judd and Motley (1993).

11. On these issues see Burdekin and Willett (1991), Havrilesky (1993), and Banaian, Burdekin and Willett (1995).

12. At the same time, it is possible that the lesser empirical support for the credibility of the Canadian inflation targets (Fischer 1993; Svensson 1993) reflects, in part, the continuing large budget deficits in Canada.

References

Acheson, Keith, and John F. Chant. 1973. "Bureaucratic Theory and the Choice of Central Bank Goals: The Case of the Bank of Canada." *Journal of Money, Credit, and Banking* 5: 637–55.

Archer, David J. 1992. "Organizing a Central Bank to Control Inflation: The Case of New Zealand." Paper presented at the meetings of the Western Economic Association in San Francisco, California, July 9–13.

Banaian, King, Richard C. K. Burdekin and Thomas D. Willett. 1995. "On the Political Economy of Central Bank Independence," in Kevin D. Hoover and Steven M. Sheffrin, eds., *Monetarism and the Methodology of Economics: Essays in Honor of Thomas Mayer*. Brookfield, Vt.: Edward Elgar.

Banaian, King, and Eugene Zhukov. 1995. "Currency Policies and Central Banking Arrangements in Former Soviet Republics," this volume.

Barro, Robert J. 1986. "Recent Developments in the Theory of Rules versus Discretion." *Economic Journal* 96 (Supplement): 23–37.

Bernanke, Ben, and Frederic Mishkin. 1992. "Central Bank Behavior and the Strategy of Monetary Policy: Observations from Six Industrialized Countries," in Jean Blanchard Olivier and Stanley Fischer, eds., *NBER Macroeconomics Annual 1992*. Cambridge, Mass: MIT Press.

Burdekin, Richard C. K. 1987. "Swiss Monetary Policy: Central Bank Independence and Stabilization Goals." *Kredit und Kapital* 20: 454–66.

———. 1995. "Budget Deficits and Inflation: The Importance of Budget Controls for Monetary Stability," this volume.

Burdekin, Richard C. K., and Farrokh K. Langdana. 1995. *Confidence, Credibility, and Macroeconomic Policy: Past, Present, Future*. London: Routledge.

Burdekin, Richard C. K., Suyono Salamun, and Thomas D. Willett. 1995. "The High Costs of Monetary Instability," this volume.

Burdekin, Richard C. K., and Thomas D. Willett. 1991. "Central Bank Reform: The Federal Reserve in International Perspective." *Public Budgeting and Financial Management* 3: 619–49.

Chant, John F., and Keith Acheson. 1972. "The Choice of Monetary Instruments and the Theory of Bureaucracy." *Public Choice* 12: 13–33.

Cukierman, Alex. 1992. *Central Bank Strategy, Credibility, and Independence: Theory and Evidence*. Cambridge, Mass: MIT Press.

Debelle, Guy, and Stanley Fischer. 1994. "How Independent Should a Central Bank

Be?" Publication No. 392, Center for Economic Policy Research, Stanford University.
Fischer, Andreas M. 1993. "Inflation Targeting: The New Zealand and Canadian Cases." *Cato Journal* 13: 1–27.
Fratianni, Michele, Jürgen von Hagen, and Christopher Waller. 1993. "Central Banking as a Political Principal-Agent Problem." Mimeo, Indiana University.
Gavin, William T., and Alan C. Stockman. 1991. "Why a Rule for Stable Prices May Dominate a Rule for Zero Inflation." Federal Reserve Bank of Cleveland, *Economic Review* 24(1): 2–8.
Grilli, Vittorio, Donato Masciandaro and Guido Tabellini. 1991. "Political and Monetary Institutions and Public Financial Policies in the Industrial Countries." *Economic Policy* 18: 341–92.
Grimes, Arthur, and Jason Wong. 1994. "The Role of the Exchange Rate in New Zealand Monetary Policy," in Reuven Glick and Michael M. Hutchison, eds., *Exchange Rate Policy and Interdependence*. Cambridge: Cambridge University Press.
Havrilesky, Thomas. 1972. "A New Program for More Monetary Stability." *Journal of Political Economy* 30: 171–75.
_____. 1993. *The Pressures on American Monetary Policy*. Boston, Mass.: Kluwer Academic Publishers.
_____. 1994. "A Model of Optimal European Central Bank Restructuring." Mimeo, Duke University.
Havrilesky, Thomas, and James Granato. 1993. "Determinants of Inflationary Performance: Corporatist Structures vs. Central Bank Autonomy." *Public Choice* 76: 249–61.
Hochreiter, Eduard. 1995. "Central Banking in Economies in Transition," this volume.
Judd, John P., and Brian Motley. 1993. "Using a Nominal GDP Rule to Guide Discretionary Monetary Policy." Federal Reserve Bank of San Francisco, *Economic Review* 3: 3–11.
Lewarne, Stephen. 1995. "The Russian Central Bank and the Conduct of Monetary Policy," this volume.
Lohmann, Susanne. 1992. "Optimal Commitment in Monetary Policy: Credibility versus Flexibility." *American Economic Review* 82: 273–86.
McCallum, Bennett T. 1989. "Targets, Indicators, and Instruments of Monetary Policy." *NBER Working Paper* No. 3047.
Meltzer, Allan H. 1987. "Limits of Short-run Stabilization Policy: Presidential Address to the Western Economic Association, July 3, 1986." *Economic Inquiry* 25: 1–14.
Persson, Torsten, and Guido Tabellini. 1993. "Designing Institutions for Monetary Stability." *Carnegie-Rochester Conference Series on Public Policy* 39: 53–84.
Phelps, Edmund S. 1991. "Precommitment to Rules in Monetary Policy," in Michael T. Belongia, ed., *Monetary Policy on the 75th Anniversary of the Federal Reserve System: Proceedings of the Fourteenth Annual Economic Policy Conference of the Federal Reserve Bank of St. Louis*. Boston, Mass: Kluwer Academic Publishers.
Reserve Bank of New Zealand. 1994. *Monetary Policy Statement, June 1994*. Wellington, New Zealand.
Sibert, Anne, and Stuart E. Weiner. 1988. "Maintaining Central Bank Credibility." Federal Reserve Bank of Kansas City, *Economic Review* (September/October):

3–15.

Svensson, Lars E. O. 1993. "The Simplest Test of Inflation Target Credibility." *NBER Working Paper* No. 4604.

Sweeney, Richard J., Clas Wihlborg, and Thomas D. Willett, eds. 1995. *Currency Policies for Emerging Market Economies*. Boulder, Colo: Westview Press, forthcoming.

Tower, Edward, and Thomas D. Willett. 1976. *The Theory of Optimum Currency Areas*. Princeton, N.J.: Princeton Studies in International Finance.

Walsh, Carl E. 1994. "Is New Zealand's Reserve Bank Act of 1989 an Optimal Central Bank Contract?" Mimeo, University of California at Santa Cruz.

_____. 1995. "Optimal Contracts for Central Bankers." *American Economic Review*, forthcoming.

Wihlborg, Clas, and Thomas D. Willett. 1991. "Optimum Currency Areas Revisited on the Transition Path to a Currency Union," in Clas Wihlborg, Michele Fratianni and Thomas D. Willett, eds., *Financial Regulation and Monetary Arrangements After 1992*. Pp. 279–297. Amsterdam: Elsevier.

Willett, Thomas D. 1995. "Guidelines for Constructing Monetary Constitutions," this volume.

Willett, Thomas D., and Fahim Al-Marhubi. "Currency Policies for Inflation Control in the Formerly Centrally Planned Economies." *World Economy*, forthcoming.

7

Central Banking in Economies in Transition

Eduard Hochreiter[1]

Introduction

Five years ago the political and economic integration of Central and Eastern Europe under the Warsaw Pact and the CMEA arrangements collapsed. Since then the former members of these pacts have striven for rapid reintegration into the world economy. They face formidable obstacles. On the real economy side, a more or less complete reallocation of resources and, over the longer term, production is required. In the short to medium term, adequate access to Western markets is indispensable to stimulate growth and to sustain the reform process. On the monetary side, financial markets have to be established and a convertible and stable currency secured. On the political level, institutions have to be devised that facilitate market operations and minimize adjustment costs and frictions.

These daunting challenges have been taken up on a very broad scale and—what is often overlooked—with considerable success. In fact, changes are happening so fast—and so much has been accomplished—that it is next to impossible to keep track.

This chapter examines attempts to build central banking institutions in Bulgaria, the Czech Republic, Hungary, Poland, Slovakia and Slovenia.[2] It attempts to strike a balance between analysis and factual information by concentrating on issues and facts which, it is hoped, will be of longer-term interest. In particular, it asks whether the establishment of social-partnership type institutions might help to ease the reform process and contribute to the sustainability of stability-oriented monetary policies. In the final section some conclusions are drawn.

Institutional Issues

A functioning market economy requires institutions that lay down and enforce the "rules of the game." Properly designed institutions may also speed up the transition from a command to a market economy by reducing friction. As far as the financial sphere is concerned, the establishment of a two-tier banking system with an independent central bank whose main tasks are clearly specified is of paramount importance. The central bank also needs to possess the appropriate instruments to design and implement monetary policy. We argue that social-partnership institutions, e.g., of the Austrian type, may be helpful in implementing stability-oriented (monetary) policies. Such institutions may be even more important in sustaining the monetary standard adopted.[3]

The overriding importance of rapid financial reform for the transition from command to market economies was not foreseen at the outset. The typical sequencing of reforms did not give top priority to financial market reform, and in hindsight this has been identified as the single most important sequencing error.[4] Nonetheless, much has been accomplished in the last five years. The monobank system was dismantled, competing commercial banks were set up, new central bank legislation based on Western models was passed and financial markets are developing.

The New Central Banks

There is widespread agreement that the stabilization of the macroeconomy is a necessary but not sufficient condition for successful systemic change. Monetary policy, i.e., the central bank, also has an important role to play; and the experience of Western European countries after the Second World War would seem to confirm this view.[5] Since monetary policy had no economic relevance in the old system (see appendix 1), the necessary institutions, policy instruments and markets have had to be developed from scratch. Moreover, central banks have had to earn credibility for their monetary policy and the reputation of the central banks has had to be established.

The design of a credible monetary policy depends on the institutional set-up of the central bank. New central bank laws have already been adopted in most of the transitional economies. A notable exception is Poland, where the national bank still operates under a "prerevolutionary" act, passed in 1989, which, however, has now been revised more than fifteen times.[6] A new act along the lines of the central bank legislation in other reforming countries (establishing central bank independence, price stability as the prime objective of monetary policy and the explicit prohibition of fiscal financing) has been in preparation for some time. It is unclear when the new law will be ready for parliamentary approval.

The widely held view that the Bundesbank Act served as a blueprint for the new central bank legislation in the transitional economies has been contested by Siklos (1993) and other authors. Indeed, a case can be made that with regard to the prime goal of the central bank—price stability—and its independence, certain provisions of the new central bank laws resemble the Austrian National Bank Act rather than the Bundesbank Act.[7]

The legal status of the central bank, while not sufficient by itself to guarantee a stability-oriented monetary policy, is especially relevant for countries in transition. A number of papers have argued that there is a statistically significant negative correlation between the legal status of the central bank and the rate of inflation.[8] If, in addition, the rate of inflation is also negatively correlated with the rate of real growth, then an independent central bank becomes even more important.[9] Finally, legislated independence becomes critical in countries such as the transitional economies where there is no tradition of a stability-oriented monetary policy.

There is almost universal agreement in the West that the maintenance of price stability should be the key task of the central bank. There is also broad consensus that the bank should be politically and technically independent and that it should not directly finance public expenditures.[10]

Looking at the new central bank laws in Central and Eastern Europe, the following tentative picture emerges:[11]

1. The top representatives are—in most cases—appointed by the parliament, and the bank's governor is usually appointed by the president of the republic. Their term of office is at least five years (except in Hungary). Thus, the central banks are legally no longer subservient to the politicians. In fact, today they are equipped with a high degree of formal independence.
2. Price stability (except in Poland) has been identified as the prime objective.
3. Given this constraint, the central bank is to support the economic policy of the government (except in the Czech Republic and Slovenia).
4. Fiscal financing generally is limited. There are, however, significant differences from country to country.

These laws were passed within the last few years, so we have limited evidence of how well they will work. Prima facie evidence suggests that the fiscal financing provisions remain the weakest point in practice. This weakness is in large part a legacy of past financial practices.

Let us now look at the provisions of the new central bank laws in more detail.[12]

The Prime Objective of Monetary Policy: Price Stability

In all but one (Poland) of the countries considered in this study, the central bank laws specify price stability as the bank's prime objective. In Bulgaria and Hungary—in analogy to the Austrian National Bank Act—the central bank is called upon to safeguard both the internal and external value of the currency. The Polish National Bank Act, which, as has already been noted, dates back to the pre-reform period, requires the central bank to "strengthen" the currency (*National Bank of Poland Act*, article 5 (1)). It is, however, very difficult to interpret the meaning of this legal requirement in terms of operational exchange rate policy.

Prohibition of Fiscal Financing

As in the Bundesbank Act[13] and the Austrian National Bank Act, the extension of (temporary) direct credit to the government by the central bank is severely restricted by law in most of the transitional economies (Bulgaria, Hungary, the Czech Republic and Slovakia), being limited to 3 to 5 percent of budget revenues for the current or previous year.[14] Nonetheless, the fiscal financing restrictions are in most of the countries in question definitely the weak spot in the legislation. The Polish National Bank Act contains conflicting provisions with regard to limitations on fiscal financing. According to article 14 (1) of the Polish National Bank Act, limitations on fiscal financing are subject to negotiation between the President of the Polish National Bank and the Minister of Finance. At the same time, article 34 states that the "PNB may buy in any given fiscal year debt securities issued by the Treasury to the total amount not exceeding 2 percent of planned expenditures of the state budget" (Gronkiewicz-Waltz 1994). Up till now the parliament has suspended the provisions of article 34. Thus, article 14 (1) has been the relevant provision. In Bulgaria the permissible amount of fiscal financing is not to exceed the central bank's paid-in capital and reserve funds. In Slovenia fiscal financing is restricted to one-fifth of the total expected budget deficit. In view of the difficult and in some cases deteriorating public deficit position in many of the countries and their nascent capital markets, pressure on the central banks to increase direct financing of the public authorities has risen substantially.[15]

In addition to the problems even mature industrialized countries may face in securing sound fiscal policies, there are serious problems specific to the transitional economies resulting from the past practices of the communist regimes. As Siklos and Ábel (1993) point out, central banks have been forced to continue lending to loss-making state enterprises, a practice which constitutes a form of fiscal financing. Such lending has continued because the financial systems remain underdeveloped. Consequently, the central bank, through the monetization of public deficits, acts as a shock absorber.

As a consequence of both these factors—the fiscal deficit and continued credit to unprofitable enterprises—legislated restrictions on fiscal financing are being overruled by parliaments (e.g., Bulgaria and Hungary) or the negotiated amount of fiscal financing is higher than prudent central banking would warrant (Poland[16]). In this way formal central bank independence is being seriously undermined. In fact, one may, at least in the less advanced transitional economies, at present question the relevance of the concept of central bank independence altogether.

A High Degree of Political and Policy Independence

Political Independence. All the central bank laws under consideration (with the exception of those of the Czech Republic and Slovenia) contain provisions regarding the relationship between the central bank and the government. Generally, the central bank is committed to support the government's economic policy. While Western central bank acts contain similar clauses (notably, the Austrian and German laws), how these provisions will be interpreted in Central and Eastern Europe is as yet unclear. The evidence to date, however, points to the conclusion that in practice central bank independence is less than a reading of the statutes suggests.

The usual term of service of the top bank management ranges from five to eight years and thus is longer than the electoral cycle. In Hungary, the only exception, the term of office of the top management is three years with the exception of the bank governor who serves six years. Board members cannot be removed from office unless they are convicted of a crime, they become unable to perform their duties (e.g., extended illness) and, in most cases, if they resign. In the Hungarian central bank act a rather vague clause —unworthiness of office—has been added, possibly encroaching on the de facto independence of the top management. No specific provisions exist in the Polish law regarding removal from office.

Policy Independence. In most Western countries the choice of exchange rate regime rests with the government, although the central bank has, to varying degrees, a role in the decision-making process. The situation appears to be different in the transitional economies under consideration. In the Czech Republic the central bank "proclaims" the exchange rate of the Czech currency vis-à-vis foreign currencies (article 35 lit. a) and sets monetary policy (article 2 lit. a). Similarly, the National Bank of Slovakia "establishes" the exchange rate in relation to foreign currencies (§ 28 lit. a) and "defines" monetary policy

(§ 2 lit. a). In Poland "the principle of establishing the exchange rate of the Zloty against foreign currencies is determined by the council of ministers. It decides at a motion of the President of the Central Bank in consultation with the Ministry of Finance and the Ministry of Economic Co-operation with Abroad" (Kicinsky and Golic 1994). In Hungary the central bank has "the right to change the exchange rate with regard to the basket of foreign currencies within a +/- 5% range centered at the level established by the government. Any correction beyond +/- 5% is for the government to decide upon" (Pasztor and Baar 1994).[17] In Slovenia the central bank has the right to set the exchange rate. Article 20 of the Bank of Slovenia Act says that "in materializing its competencies the Bank of Slovenia shall determine the monetary policy and take measures for its implementation." Article 3 of the Bulgarian National Bank Act states that "in defining the general directions of the monetary and credit policy, the Bulgarian National Bank and the council of ministers shall inform each other of their intentions and actions." Article 3 by itself is ambiguous about how much influence the council of ministers is to exert on monetary policy. In article 2 (1) the Bulgarian National Bank is called upon to "formulate and implement the national monetary and credit policy." Therefore, it appears that the choice of exchange rate regime rests with, or at least is significantly influenced by, the Bulgarian National Bank. In all countries the central bank has control over the use of policy instruments in day-to-day business.

Legitimacy and Accountability

The central banks covered in this study derive their democratic legitimacy from their national parliaments and are governed by parliamentary statutes. The banks are therefore directly accountable to the law or the parliament. In order to facilitate the exchange of information between the government and the bank, the central bank governors in these countries have the right to attend meetings of the executive branch in an advisory capacity and to state the bank's position in relevant policy matters. (The governor of the National Bank of Hungary may only attend meetings dealing with matters affecting the tasks of the central bank.) In Poland the bank governor may attend parliamentary sessions as well.[18] Finally, the central banks of Bulgaria, the Czech Republic and Slovakia have an obligation to (at least) twice a year inform parliament about monetary policy, and in Hungary it must report once a year. In the Czech Republic and Slovakia a report to the general public must be issued every three months. The most elaborate reporting requirements exist in Poland. There are no explicit reporting requirements in Slovenia. These provisions are designed to facilitate monitoring of central bank policies by the government and society at large.

Supporting Social-Partnership Institutions

Holzmann and Winckler (1993) have rightly pointed to the important role social institutions can play in transitional economies by backing sound economic policies, particularly stability-oriented monetary policy (for instance in the form of a hard-currency peg). The example of Austria shows that such informal institutions do in fact facilitate consensus building among social groups. These groups typically attempt to reach a consensus on economic aims and, importantly, also on ways in which to achieve them.[19]

What we have in mind are informal and voluntary institutional fora which bring together the main social groups, e.g., industry, entrepreneurial organizations, agriculture, trade and employees' organizations, trade unions, etc., to discuss economic and social policy issues and to devise ways to achieve the aims agreed upon. These meetings may be useful in building a consensus to support structural change.[20] In essence, this is what Austrians understand by social partnership. It is very important to understand that social partnership, while comprising wage restraint (that is, incomes policy in the Anglo-Saxon sense), is much more. Taking this into account one can also understand why incomes policy in the Anglo-Saxon sense has failed repeatedly, whereas the Austrian version has been successful for over thirty years.

We believe that establishing some kind of social-partnership institution in the transitional economies could significantly reduce the economic cost of transition (i.e., less unemployment) by raising real wage flexibility (generating more employment) and backing supply-oriented, productivity-enhancing policies (which raise the equilibrium real wage). Thus, social-partnership institutions may help to "generate growth in economies in transition" (Holzmann and Winckler 1993:2) and may also help to sustain a currency peg.

The economics underlying social-partnership actions is very simple and transparent. As shown below, "social-partnership economics" is nothing more than basic economics reduced to its first principles. Its main ingredients are:

1. Social partners base highly centralized wage negotiations on the assumption that the real wage depends on productivity advances and not so much on the nominal wage. At the same time it is realized that unproductive work can only lead to low incomes and is therefore undesirable. Knowing that productivity advances are the key to success, the trade unions will support innovation and rationalization by enterprises. Note that in this context the unions can also accept temporary subsidies to employers as long as they are used to enhance the productivity of the enterprise and hence ultimately raise the equilibrium real wage.
2. It is understood that no sizeable long-term economic growth can occur without price stability. This view is based on the assumption that a

lower rate of inflation reduces the risk of price level volatility and hence lengthens the time horizon of investors. If this is so, it is also in the union's interest to support an independent central bank pursuing price stability as its prime objective because this will, in the longer term, lead to higher employment.[21]

3. In the end there is no free lunch; thus the scope for running large fiscal deficits is limited. All parties recognize that "excessive" fiscal deficits may endanger macroeconomic stability which—as has been pointed out above—is not in the trade union's interest.

In order to work efficiently, such an institution needs players (employer and employee organizations) that trust each other, that are of roughly equal political strength and that can exert their power. In addition, an arbitrator (the government) is needed, offering, if necessary, short-term sweeteners (temporary support) for those sectors which are most hurt by structural change.

What are the prospects for social-partnership institutions in the countries of our study? Three important problems immediately spring to mind: First, the old trade union movement has been discredited in most cases; second, employers' organizations are just beginning to be formed, are badly organized and not yet effective; third, the population at large is highly skeptical of such institutions and the possible role of the state as arbitrator because of its experiences with them under communism.

Despite these difficulties we are convinced that the potential benefits of such institutions backing economic policies could be so great for (at least the smaller) transitional countries that an attempt to institute them is warranted.[22] Indeed, all of the countries under consideration have established on an informal basis institutions to facilitate dialogue among social groups. Unfortunately, reports of these discussions indicate that they may be more concerned with incomes policy in the Anglo-Saxon sense (i.e., wage controls) than in the Austrian social-partnership sense (i.e., economic decision making *including* wages).[23]

In Hungary, a "National Council for Conciliation," representing employers, employees and the government, was established to promote co-operation in wage policy and to provide advice on (and influence) the budget process.[24] The social partners are also called upon for their opinion about budgetary aspects of changes in the tax system. More recently, Mr. Gyula Horn, chairman of the Hungarian Socialist Party, has explicitly referred to Austria and Spain as models for Hungarian social-partnership agreements. This view, according to newspaper reports, is held by most of the other major parties in Hungary.[25] Similar institutions exist in the Czech Republic and Slovakia. It must be added that their existence in the Czech Republic seems to be more a matter of political pragmatism than of economic ideology, which does not provide for such institutions. Only in Poland has a form of social partnership been established by law.[26] Bulgaria has established a trilateral commission, but its functioning has been hampered by poor organization in the unions and the de facto nonexistence of an employer's organization. The situation is somewhat different in Slovenia, which has traditionally had a management system in which labor performed functions that are normally divided between management (or owners) and labor. As a consequence, labor enjoyed disproportionate power. Thus contracts among the social partners were generally restricted to wage-restraint agreements.[27] All considered, it appears that social-partnership institutions, as described above, do not as yet exist in the countries under consideration.

Summary and Conclusions

The new central bank acts of Bulgaria, the Czech Republic, Hungary, Poland, Slovenia and Slovakia closely resemble those regulating Western central banks, in particular the Austrian National Bank Act. They endow the central banks with a high degree of political and policy independence. Price stability has been singled out as the prime task of the central bank. Fiscal financing is legally restricted (Poland, in practice, being the exception). The most important difference from the typical Western central bank act concerns the decisive (formal) say the central banks of transitional economies have in the selection of the monetary regime. The main weakness relates to limitations on fiscal financing: because financial markets remain underdeveloped the central banks may be forced to subsidize state enterprises regardless of the legislated limitations.

While a high degree of independence is an important prerequisite for stability-oriented monetary policy, social-partnership institutions might help reduce the cost of transition and so increase the sustainability of stability-oriented policies. Although some attempts have been made to establish a forum for discussion among major social groups in all these countries, we must conclude that institutions of an Austrian type do not as yet exist.

Appendix 1
Stylized Facts of a Centrally Planned Economy

A centrally planned economy typically concentrates on producing physical output as envisaged by an elaborate plan. Such an economy has no place for Western-style financial services or for monetary policy as we know it. The planned output is financed through the central bank and a number of specialized banks that are either directly or indirectly controlled by the central bank. The central bank itself is state owned and also fulfills commercial bank functions. This setup is called a monobank system.

A centrally planned economy has two financial circuits. One serves the enterprise sector. Enterprises receive credits from banks and make their payments through bank accounts, while employees are paid in cash. The second circuit serves households, which can place deposits in the specialized savings bank. This bank also extends credit to individuals. Private individuals are not allowed to invest in or lend to enterprises. In this system the markets for funds are completely segmented; e.g., the savings bank, which serves the households, is not allowed to engage in business with an (investment) bank serving enterprises and vice versa.

Monetary policy is executed by extending credit to enterprises and to budget entities as well as by providing the cash to pay households. Foreign exchange transactions are executed by another specialized bank (the Foreign Trade Bank). Its transactions do not influence the money supply.

Prices in a centrally planned economy do not reflect scarcities. Output prices are determined by planners, frequently without any relation to input prices. Interest rates on credit and deposits are often low and fixed. The exchange rate only serves as a unit of account to convert foreign into domestic prices. The proliferation of conversion factors (in some cases even for different products) implies that there are, in fact, a myriad of different exchange rates at any given time.

Central planning has resulted in economies with massively distorted prices, low household savings and a preference by entrepreneurs to accumulate real assets in the form of inventories, plants, etc. The typical centrally planned economy suffers from unproductive overinvestment.

Enterprises operate under a soft budget constraint. A firm which cannot generate enough funds through its operations to meet its contractual obligations simply receives a government subsidy to close the gap between the outlays and the revenues. Bankruptcies cannot occur. Earned profits—with minor exceptions—cannot be retained but instead have to be transferred to the budget of the branch ministry. Thus there is no incentive to use resources in a productive way.

A centrally planned economy does not require a monetary system nor a central bank of the Western type. "The role of money is predetermined by the central plan, with cash flows merely its passive reflection" (Zahradnik 1991: 217). Financial services are rudimentary, and the banking system is employed to fulfill the physical plan.

A centrally planned economy is not integrated into the world economy.

Appendix 2
National Bank Laws in Central and Eastern Europe[a]
Institutional Features[b]

Country	Statutory Policy Independence	Legislated Prime Objectives
Bulgaria	yes[c]	internal and external currency stability
Czech Republic	yes[d]	currency stability
Hungary	yes[e]	internal and external currency stability
Poland	no reference[f]	strengthening the national currency
Slovenia	yes[g]	currency stability
Slovak Republic	yes[h]	currency stability

Country	Management	Appointed by	Term of Service (Years)
Bulgaria	Managing Board		
	- Governor	Parliament	5
	- 3 Vice-governors	Parliament	5
	- 5 Directors	President[i]	5
	Plenary Council		
	- Managing Board		
	- 6 experts	Governor	3
Czech Republic	Bank Board		
	- Governor	President	6
	- 2 Vice-governors	President	6
	- 4 Senior national bank officers	President	6
Hungary	Central Bank Council		
	- Governor	President	6
	- up to 5 Vice-governors	President	3
	- up to 5 members	President	3
	Board of Directors		
	- Chairman	General Assembly	not specified
	- Vice-chairmen	General Assembly	not specified
	- Board members	General Assembly	not specified
	Supervisory Commission		
	- Chairman	Parliament	term of parliament[j]
	- 3 members	Parliament	term of parliament
	- representative of the Minister of Finance	Minister of Finance	term of parliament
	- expert General Assembly	Minister of Finance	term of parliament

Poland	Managing Board		
	- Governor	Parliament	6
	- Vice-governors	President	term not specified
	- Board members	Governor	by law
Slovenia	Governing Board		
	- Governor	Parliament	6
	- Deputy Governor	Parliament	6
	- 3 Vice-governors	Parliament	6
	- 6 independent experts	Parliament	6
Slovak Republic	Bank Board		
	- Governor	President	6
	- 2 Vice-governors	President	6
	- 2 Executive directors	Government	6
	- 3 other members	Government	4
	Directorate		
	- Vice-governor	Governor	6
	- Executive directors	Governor	6

Suspension of Governor

Country	Conditions
Bulgaria	- at sentencing for crimes of general nature - inability to perform functions for more than a year
Czech Republic	- at sentencing for crimes - board decision stating loss of ability to perform functions - upon own request submitted to bank board - simultaneous membership in parliament, government, or boards of banks and commercial companies
Hungary	- upon resignation - loss of ability to perform functions - at sentencing for crimes - unworthiness of the office held
Poland	- upon resignation - at sentencing for crimes - terminal illness
Slovenia	- upon recall by parliament
Slovak Republic	- upon recall by the president upon a proposal of government - upon resignation - upon sentencing for crimes - board decision stating loss of ability to perform functions - simultaneous membership in parliament, government, or boards of banks, commercial companies and other entrepreneurial groups

Lending to Government

Country	Limit	Repayment	Days to maturity
Bulgaria	5% of planned budget revenues in current year not exceeding the paid-in capital and reserve funds	end of calendar year	maximum 3 months[k]
Czech Republic	5% of budget revenues in previous year	-	maximum 3 months
Hungary	3% of budget revenues[l]	-	shorter and/or longer than 1 year
Poland	in principle 2 % of budget expenditures	-	-
Slovenia	5 % of planned budget of current year and shall not exceed 1/5 of expected total budget deficit	end of fiscal year	short-term loans[m]
Slovak Republic	5 % of budget revenues in previous year	-	maximum 3 months

[a]Information from the National Bank Acts of Poland-January 31, 1989, and various amendments; Slovenia-June 25, 1991; Bulgaria-June 28, 1991; Hungary-October 21, 1991; Slovakia-November 18, 1992; the Czech Republic-December 17, 1992.

[b]Positions not explicitly specified in the corresponding laws are indicated with "-".

[c]"In performing its functions the Bank shall be independent from instructions from the Council of Ministers and other state bodies" (article 47). "The BNB [Bulgarian National Bank] and the government shall inform each other of their intentions and actions in defining the general directions of the monetary and credit policy" (article 3).

[d]"In providing for its primary objective the CNB [Czech National Bank] shall be independent of any instructions given by the government" (article 9.1). There is no reference in the Czech National Bank Act concerning the relationship between the national bank and the government as far as economic policy is concerned.

[e]The National Bank of Hungary develops its monetary policy "in an autonomous way in the framework of this (National Bank) Act" (article 6). "The NBH supports the implementation of the economic policy programme of the government with monetary policy means available to it" (article 3).

[f]"The NBP [National Bank of Poland] co-operates with the state authorities in determining and realizing the state economic policy, in particular taking into consideration the strengthening of the Polish currency" (articles 5.2 and 16.1).

[g]"The Bank of Slovenia shall be independent in materializing its assignment and empowerment" (article 2). As in the Czech case there is no specification of the relationship between the bank and the government with regard to economic policy.

[h]"In fulfilling the primary objective...the National Bank of Slovakia shall be independent of instructions given by the government" (article 12.2). "The National Bank of Slovakia within the limits defined by this law supports (the) economic policy of the Slovak Republic" (article 12.1).

[i]Presidents of state are hereafter referred to as "President" and central bank governors as "Governor."

[j]The members of the Supervisory Commission are elected for the term of the

parliament, i.e., four years.

ᵏPursuant to the State Budget Law a ten-year credit to the government was sanctioned by the board in September 1992.

ˡRevenues from privatization which are used to reduce the state debt are not to be taken into account. Credit granted to the government shall be considered for the first time when the budget objectives for 1995 are drawn up. Such credit was unlimited in 1992. The ratios in 1993 and 1994 are 5 percent and 4 percent respectively. The interest charged on credit granted before the enactment of the law was 40 percent of the prevailing basic interest rate.

ᵐBridging loans to the budget are allowed.

Notes

1. Prepared for the Annual Meeting of the Western Economic Association, Vancouver, June 29–July 4, 1994. Parts of earlier versions were presented at the conferences on "Central Bank Independence and Accountability," Bocconi University, March 4, 1994 and on "Central Bank Independence in Eastern Europe and the NIS," the University of Chicago, the Law School, April 21–23, 1994. Helpful comments by seminar participants, notably Alfred Steinherr and Robert Z. Aliber as well as Richard Burdekin, Wayne Camard, Peter Dittus, Hans Genberg, George Neshev, Miroslav Hrnčíř, Elena Kohutikova, Ryszard Kokoszczynski, Kurt Mauler, Olga Radzyner, Sandra Riesinger, Pierre Siklos, Petr Vojtisek and Tom Willett, are kindly acknowledged. Efficient research assistance was provided by Peter Backé and Ekaterina Angelova. The views expressed in this paper are those of the author and do not necessarily represent the opinions of the Austrian National Bank.

2. Other reforming countries will be analyzed in a future study.

3. An excellent analysis of (potential) institutional arrangements for periods of transition, including Austrian-style social-partnership institutions, can be found in Holzmann and Winckler (1993).

4. See Nuti and Portes (1993:16).

5. For a discussion of the Austrian experience after the Second World War, see Klier (1990).

6. In the main text we will stick to the original 1989 Act but will add the most important changes in brackets.

7. For a rough comparative analysis of the Austrian National Bank Act, see Hochreiter (1990).

8. See, e.g., Cukierman et al. (1992:370) or Willett (1993). For a discussion see Swinburne and Castello-Branco (1991:420). Note, however, that no such relationship has been found for developing countries.

9. A recent study by Burdekin et al. (1993) does arrive at such a conclusion. The study also points to the importance of this link for countries in transition.

10. There is less agreement as to the central banks' role in banking supervision and in the clearing and payment systems. An excellent analysis of the evolution of prudential regulation and supervision in Czechoslovakia (the Czech Republic), Hungary and Poland can be found in Dittus (1994).

11. Detailed information is presented in appendix 2.

12. To facilitate comparison with the Austrian National Bank Act, the discussion follows the structure of Hochreiter (1994b).

13. In view of the prohibition on granting direct credit to the government in the Maastricht Treaty (article 104), the Bundesbank Act was changed as of January 1, 1994.

14. Bod (1994:55) explicitly makes the point that monetary policy autonomy is being limited by the budget deficit.

15. Hungary may serve as evidence that such a threat really exists. When deciding on the 1994 budget deficit in December 1993, parliament raised the maximum legally permissible public debt ratio from 4 percent of projected revenues (some 50 billion forint) to 80 billion forint. In Bulgaria, the Law on Updating the 1991 State Budget (July 18, 1991) provided that up to 50 percent of the 1991 budget deficit be financed through national bank credit in violation of the National Bank Law provisions. The Bulgarian National Bank's compromise was to grant the credit through short-term advances extended every three months. At the end of 1991 the total amount of credit received was transformed into a credit with a ten-year term (*Bulgarian National Bank News Bulletin* No. 3). Maciejewski (1994) points to this danger for Poland. The suspension of article 34 and its successive redefinition documents it.

16. See *Neue Zürcher Zeitung*, February 15, 1994, p. 10.

17. Section 13 (2) of the Hungarian National Bank Act states: "The order of fixing and/or influencing the exchange rate is determined by the government in agreement with the NBH."

18. The right of the governor to attend government meetings is not unproblematic. It could well be that the governor is thereby seen as being party to government decisions by the public. If so, the independence of the central bank could be compromised.

19. For a succinct discussion of Austria's social partnership, see Hochreiter and Schubert (1991:133–68).

20. If such a consensus cannot be arrived at, social partnership may be detrimental to structural adjustment.

21. In Austria there is also a strong political reason for the trade union to support price stability. It is generally accepted that the hyperinflation after the end of the First World War destroyed the middle class and thereby laid the groundwork for the rise of fascism in Austria.

22. In a survey undertaken in the Czech Republic, Hungary, Poland and Slovakia during the summer of 1992 and the winter of 1993, between 50 percent (Slovakia) and 57 percent (Czech Republic) were in favor of (an Austrian type of) social partnership, while between 13 percent (Poland) and 22 percent (Czech Republic) opted for a liberal market economy (Austria Presse Agentur, September 24, 1993).

23. A very useful analysis of the unions' structures and politics in Bulgaria, Hungary and Poland is contained in Schienstock and Traxler (1993).

24. Its predecessor, the National Council for the Reconciliation of Interests, was established in 1988.

25. Austria Presse Agentur, April 5, 1994 and Magyar Tavirati Iroda, April 26, 1994.

26. Representatives of employers, employees and the government reached an agreement in 1993, with the enactment of the "Pact Concerning State Enterprises" planned for later that year. The new government has—for the time being—shelved the law. It did establish a trilateral Socio-Economic Commission on February 15, 1994. Moreover, the following laws were passed: Law on Trade Unions (May 23, 1991), Law on Employers' Organizations (May 23, 1991), and Law on Solving of Collective Disputes (May 23, 1991).

27. Note that a hardening of the budget constraint for enterprises reduced wage pressure despite the fact that the self-management system remains intact.

References

Austria Presse Agentur. September 24, 1993.

Banaian, King, Richard C. K. Burdekin, and Thomas D. Willett. 1993. "On the Political Economy of Central Bank Independence," in Kevin Hoover and Steven Sheffrin, eds., *Monetarism and the Methodology of Economics: Essays in Honor of Thomas Mayer*. Brookfield, Vt.: Edward Elgar, forthcoming.

Bod, Peter A. 1994. "Monetary Policy and Exchange Rate Policy in Hungary During the Years of Transition," in Dieter Duwendag, ed., *Geld—und Währungspolitik in Kleinen, Offenen Volkswirtschaften: Österreich, Schweiz, Osteuropa*. Schriftenreihe des Vereins für Socialpolitik, Neue Folge Band 230. Pp. 55–70. Berlin: Duncker und Humblot.

Bonin, John P., and István P. Székely, eds. 1994. *The Development and Reform of Financial Systems in Central and Eastern Europe*. Brookfield, Vt.: Edward Elgar, forthcoming.

Burdekin, Richard C. K., Thomas Goodwin, Suyono Salamun and Thomas D. Willett. 1993. "When Does Inflation Hurt Economic Growth?" Mimeo, Claremont Graduate School.

Cottarelli, Carlo. 1993. *Limiting Central Bank Credit to the Government: Theory and Practice*. International Monetary Fund Occasional Paper No. 110.

Cukierman, Alex, Sidney Webb, and Bilin Neyapti. 1992. "Measuring the Independence of Central Banks and Its Effects on Policy Outcomes." *The World Bank Economic Review* 6 (3): 353–98.

Czech National Bank Act. December 17, 1992.

Dittus, Peter. 1994. "Corporate Governance in Central Europe: The Role of Banks." Mimeo, Bank for International Settlements.

Dobrinsky, Rumen. 1994. "Reform of the Financial System in Bulgaria," in John P. Bonin and István P. Székely, eds. *The Development and Reform of Financial Systems in Central and Eastern Europe*. Pp. 311–343. Brookfield, Vt.: Edward Elgar.

Downes, Patrick, and Reza Vaez-Zadeh, eds. 1991. *The Evolving Role of Central Banks*. Washington D.C.: International Monetary Fund.

Gronkiewicz-Waltz, Hanna. 1994. "The Central Bank's Role as Lender to the Government." Mimeo, National Bank of Poland.

Hochreiter, Eduard. 1994a. "Comment on Reform of the Financial System in Bulgaria," in John P. Bonin and István P. Székely, eds., *The Development and Reform of*

Financial Systems in Central and Eastern Europe. Pp. 343–45. Brookfield, Vt.: Edward Elgar.

———. 1994b. "Reflections on Central Bank Independence and Monetary Policy—The Case of Austria," in Bernhard Böhm and Lionello F. Punzo, eds., *Economic Performance.* Berlin: Physica-Verlag, in press.

———. 1990. "The Austrian National Bank Act: What Does It Say About Monetary Policy ?" *Konjunkturpolitik* 36 (4). Berlin: Duncker & Humbold: 245–56.

Hochreiter, Eduard, and Aurel Schubert. 1991. "National Economic Policies in Other Major OECD-Countries: Austria, Australia, Canada and Sweden," in Dominik Salvatore, ed., *Handbook of Comparative National Economic Policies*, Vol. 1. Pp. 133–68. New York: Greenwood Press.

Holzmann, Robert, and Georg Winckler. 1993. "Fiscal, Monetary and Social Institutions Needed for Restructuring." Mimeo, University of Saarbrücken and University of Vienna.

Hrnčíř, Miroslav. 1993b. "Reform of the Banking Sector in the Czech Republic." Mimeo, Czech National Bank.

Kicinsky, W., and M. Golik. 1994. "Exchange Rate Policy and Exchange Reserves." Mimeo, National Bank of Poland.

Klier, Rudolf, ed. 1990. "From Control to Market—Austria's Experiences in the Post-War Period." *Internationale Schriftenreihe der Oesterreichischen Nationalbank* 4, Vienna.

Kohutikova, Elena. 1993. "Some Issues Concerning Monetary Developments and Banking System Progress in the Slovak Republic." Mimeo, National Bank of Slovakia.

Kokoszczynski, Ryszard. 1993. "Money and Capital Market Reform in Poland." Mimeo, National Bank of Poland.

Law on the Bank of Slovenia. June 25, 1991.

Law on the Bulgarian National Bank. June 28, 1991.

Maciejewski, Wojciech. 1994. "Current State of the Polish Economy and the Problem with the Reforms." Mimeo, Wojoiech: Warsaw University.

National Council of the Slovak Republic. *Law of the National Bank of Slovakia.* November 18, 1992.

National Bank of Hungary Act. October 21, 1991.

National Bank of Poland Act. January 31, 1989.

Neue Zürcher Zeitung. "Die Frau, die den Zloty Hütet." February 15, 1994.

Nuti, Mario D., and Richard Portes, eds. 1993. *Economic Transformation in Central Europe: A Program Report.* London: CEPR and European Communities.

Pasztor, Csapa, and Ilona Baar. 1994. "Hungarian Exchange Rate Policy and Foreign Exchange Reserves." Mimeo, National Bank of Hungary.

Pönisch, Herbert. 1992. "The Central Banks of Eastern Europe," in A. Prindl, ed., *Banking and Finance in Eastern Europe.* New York: Woodhead-Faulkner.

Schaffer, Mark. 1993. "Polish Economic Transformation: From Recession to Recovery and the Challenges Ahead." *Business Strategy Review* 3(3): 53–69.

Schienstock, Gerhard, and Fritz Traxler. 1993. "Economic Transformation and Institutional Change—A Cross-national Study in the Conversion of Union Structures and Politics in Eastern Europe." Research Memorandum No. 314. Vienna: Institute for Advanced Studies, February.

Siklos, Pierre. 1993. "Central Bank Independence in Central Europe: A Preliminary Investigation." Mimeo, Wilfred Laurier University.

Siklos, Pierre, and István Ábel. 1995. "Fiscal and Monetary Policies in the Transition: Searching for the Credit Crunch," this volume.

Swinburne, Mark, and Martha Castello-Branco. 1991. "Central Bank Independence and Central Bank Functions," in Patrick Downes and Reza Vaez-Zadeh, eds., *The Evolving Role of Central Banks*. Pp. 414–44. Washington D.C.: International Monetary Fund.

Tanzi, Vito. 1993. "The Budget Deficit in Transition—A Cautionary Note." *International Monetary Fund Staff Papers* 40(3): 697–707.

Willett, Thomas D. 1993. "Some Often Neglected Aspects of the Political Economy of European Monetary Integration." Mimeo, Claremont Graduate School.

Zahradnik, Jaromir. 1991. "Czechoslovakia," in John Williamson, ed., *Currency Convertibility in Eastern Europe*. Pp. 217–25. Washington, D.C.: Institute for International Economics.

8

Alternative Approaches to Monetary Reform in the Formerly Communist Countries: A Parallel Strategy

Annelise Anderson[1]

Introduction

The literature on the transition of ex-Communist economies to the market system frequently recommends the transformation of institutions in these societies into their Western, market-oriented counterparts. It is proposed, for example, to convert defense enterprises producing armaments into enterprises producing consumer goods. From the sale of flats in government-built housing is to come a competitive housing sector. State-owned monopolies, converted to joint stock companies with managers compensated on the basis of profits, are to behave like competitive private corporations. Organizations that mediated disputes among state enterprises using the criterion of meeting the objectives of the Communist state are supposed to become Western-style courts enforcing contracts and hearing commercial disputes.

This is no less the case in the banking sector, where the old state bank (Gosbank) is expected to spin off its commercial activities, thereby creating commercial banks, and to limit its own functions to those of an independent central bank. Thus the 1991 report on the Soviet economy prepared by four major international financial organizations—the International Monetary Fund, the World Bank, the Organization for Economic Cooperation and Development, and the new European Bank for Reconstruction and

Development—recommends further efforts toward a two-tier banking system, that is, a central bank and a network of independent commercial banks (IMF 1991, 2:107–35).

The report further envisions the banking system playing the same role it plays in developed Western market economies: providing the basic payments system and acting as the principal source of credit to enterprises and households (IMF 1991, 2:115). To this end it recommends "some form of deposit insurance" (p. 120), the commercialization and privatization of spinoffs from the old state bank, a regulatory and supervisory structure similar to that in many Western countries, the development of securities markets, and (implicitly) a fiat currency with the continued monopoly of the central bank on its issue—all structures and arrangements that have evolved in the West since the Bank of England acquired the powers of a central bank in British legislation of 1844 and 1845.

Another widely publicized reform plan, which became known as the "Grand Bargain" because of the substantial amounts of Western aid proposed, was developed by a working group chaired by economist Grigory Yavlinsky of the (then) Soviet Union and Graham Allison of Harvard University. This plan emphasized as an early step the implementation of "a single currency and a single monetary policy pursued by an independent Central Bank."[2] In 1992 "the independence of the Central Bank is established and it is reorganized along the lines of the Federal Reserve System" (FSIB 1991:49). Other elements of the reform package identified in *Izvestia* and in testimony presented to the U.S. Senate Foreign Relations Committee by Yavlinsky and Allison on June 19, 1991, include, for 1992, the completion of "the legal and economic framework of the market economy," as well as "improved enforcement of contract law and commercial codes." The year 1993 was to see, among other things, the development of financial markets and intensification of defense conversion[3] (Allison and Yavlinsky 1991: Table 1 and p. 5). The Yavlinsky-Allison plan also envisions "active implementation of antimonopoly policies" (Table 1, Stage 3), "large-scale investment plans . . . for the development of the market infrastructure—a banking system, transport, communications, telecommunications," and "retooling of industry" (FSIB 1991: 50–51).

The work done by Western economists on the problems of transition has been extremely beneficial in explicating the fundamental features of a market economy. These are well recognized and developed in the IMF report, the Yavlinsky-Allison plan, and the many other reform programs or proposals developed in general or specifically for particular governments in Eastern Europe or the former Soviet Union.

The fundamental features include first and foremost market prices and private property. "Market prices" includes not only the prices of retail goods and services, but, in more comprehensive plans, the prices of producer goods, land, wages and salaries, and interest rates.[4] Given private ownership of enterprises and financial institutions and developed capital markets, investment decisions can be based on expected rates of return on alternative investments and the willingness of private individuals or organizations to supply debt or equity capital.

Also recognized as critical is the legal environment—especially property rights, contract law, and a commercial code—and the ability and willingness of the government to enforce such law. Most plans also note the need for social legislation to address problems of unemployment during the transition and to reform existing social legislation such as pensions.

Fiscal and monetary policies that restrain government spending and limit inflation are considered critical, and most approaches put them first under the rubric of macroeconomic stabilization. Finally, openness to international trade and currency convertibility is important to joining the world economy, attracting foreign investment, and providing competition for the monopolies typical of centrally managed economies.

These fundamental features or prerequisites for a market economy appear in one form or another in nearly all analyses of the problems of transition or proposals for reform. Economist Charles Wolf, Jr. of RAND (1991) provides an excellent summary of the changes required to transform a centrally controlled economy to a market economy, describing the links among the major components of transformation and emphasizing the importance of proceeding on all fronts simultaneously. The issue is not the basic understanding of the market economy but the assumption that its critical features—such as a reasonably stable currency and private financial markets—can be replicated by converting institutions developed under Communism into their Western counterparts.

The institutions of Communist countries have at times developed in peculiar ways. By 1991, when the IMF report was published, the Soviet Union had established central banks in each of its republics, all of them issuing (through bank credit to enterprises and governmental units) the same currency. Although the printing presses were in Russia, control of the presses did not effectively restrain the creation of money. After the breakup of the Soviet Union into fifteen independent republics these central banks continued in operation for some time. Several republics made plans to issue their own currencies, always central bank fiat issues.

During 1992 this common currency was differentiated into Russian rubles, Ukrainian rubles, and so forth, to limit the transmission of inflation from one republic to another. Payment by the Ukraine to Russia, for example, had to be made in Russian rubles. Enforcing such a differentiation of a common monetary unit would seem to require centralized approval of transactions and funds transfers and, possibly, allocation by the central government in each republic of such rubles as happened to be scarce. This development runs counter to the objective of a market-based commercial banking sector.

In mid-1993 the Central Bank of Russia invalidated all rubles printed before 1993 in an effort to end the export of inflation by other republics. By 1994 most of the republics had issued their own currencies. Two of them, Tajikistan and Belarus, rejoined the ruble zone—the new ruble zone—agreeing in principle to let the Central Bank of Russia determine monetary policy. Kahzakstan also remained in the ruble zone.

Inflation, as measured by the ruble/dollar exchange rate (see Table 8.1) at the Moscow Interbank Currency Exchange auctions, was high in 1992 but lessened considerably in 1993 and 1994. In the last seven months of 1992 the increase in the ruble/dollar exchange rate averaged 25 percent a month. In the following six-month periods it dropped to 14 percent, 6.5 percent, and, in the first six months of 1994, to about 5 percent a month. Inflation, as measured by a retail price index, was considerably higher but also declined, from 25 percent a month in early 1993 to under 10 percent in the early months of 1994 (RFE/RL Daily Report).

These were years of considerable political turmoil. The Russian Central Bank started as an institution under the formal control of the Russian parliament, came under the control of the president (by decree), and now possesses a limited constitutional independence that can be overridden by the president.

Problems of Transformation of Communist Institutions to Their Western Counterparts and the Alternative Parallel Strategy

There are three basic problems with the approach of transforming institutions created under Communism to what appear to be their Western counterparts. First, these institutions may be very difficult to change. The

TABLE 8.1 Ruble/Dollar Exchange Rate: Moscow Interbank Currency Exchange

Date	Rubles/Dollar
June 9, 1992	112
September 2, 1992	211
December 15, 1992	418
March 23, 1993	684
June 24, 1993	1066
September 23, 1993	1299
December 20, 1993	1205
March 18, 1994	1722
July 8, 1994	2012

literature on organizational change and adaptability suggests that change will be difficult even when managers are highly motivated; the public choice theory of economics addresses the difficulty of changing the established distribution of benefits. Second, the original purpose of the institutions in question may differ from that of the apparent Western counterpart, and perhaps even contradict it. Third, it may be that the full institutional framework existing in the West is no longer appropriate. The Western institutions may have developed to serve purposes that are now being taken over by other institutions. Thus following a transformation strategy may result in the establishment in reforming economies of institutions that have passed their prime.[5] One notes, for example, that in the United States banks have been losing market share and are a less important source of credit to households and businesses than they once were. Furthermore, other needs may need to be met—needs that were met in the West in the eighteenth, nineteenth, and early twentieth centuries in ways that all but economic historians have forgotten. The transformation approach may inhibit the spontaneous development of businesses or organizations needed in economies attempting to make the transition to the market. It is not clear that the services required must, in these changing economies, be performed by the same institutions that now perform them in the West.

The alternative to the transformation of formerly Communist institutions is the creation of new institutions, or more precisely, legislation that permits new institutions to be created. The benefits of this parallel strategy are several. Old institutions would have competition, thus providing a spur to their own transformation and a demonstration of ways in which they might change. If transformation of the old institutions were to fail, new institutions would exist to take over and provide the goods or services the old institutions failed to provide. The new institutions are also likely to be more suited and adaptable to the current needs of these economies than either the old institutions or even their Western counterparts.

The Difficulty of Change

The Western literature on organization change usually assumes that organizations are rationally designed and managed. They are also assumed to be capable of adapting to changes in their external environments and buffering themselves against external change through a variety of methods or tactics (Scott 1987:209). Even given the capability to adapt, survival through organizational change is not assured; the organization may fail to perceive or observe its external environment or may not change rapidly enough to survive.

A second approach to organizations argues that the variety of observable organizational forms is not the result of adaptation, even though organizations do change, but is primarily the result of selection. This ecological view holds that organizational change is not necessarily purposeful and rational, and that surviving organizations are those most suited to the environment as it has changed over time. Michael T. Hannan and John Freeman, major proponents of this view, note a variety of internal and external constraints leading to inertia (Hannan and Freeman 1977:931-32).

Among the internal constraints are prior capital investment and specialized personnel, limitations on the information received by managers about both internal activities and external matters, internal political constraints arising from resistance to the reallocation of resources within the organization (some subunits are likely to be hurt), and the organization's own history, through which it has arrived at internally accepted standards and distribution of authority. Externally the organization may be limited by legal or financial constraints, by the availability of information about the external environment and the cost of obtaining it, and by the external view of the organization's legitimate role.

According to Hannan and Freeman, adaptability comes at a cost: organizations that are more adaptable may perform less well in a stable environment (Hannan and Freeman 1977:93). They further argue that the process of selection in fact favors organizations that are resistant to change (Hannan and Freeman 1984:149). This is so, the hypothesis goes, because the reliability of an organization's output and its accountability are valued. Reliability of performance increases with the stability of the organization and its ability to maintain or reproduce its structures of roles, authority, and communication (Hannan and Freeman 1977:154). But with increased reliability come inertial pressures. Reliability, and with it structural inertia, is assumed to increase with age and size (1977:158). Both the rational adaptations approach to organizations and the population ecology approach are considered useful in understanding modern organizations (Scott 1987:202).

Public choice theory in economics also addresses problems of change, specifically the problem of changing policies that have given rents—non-productive transfers—to some groups in the society. A change in policy may be especially difficult if one group stands to lose from the change. James Buchanan sums up the problem this way: "Those persons and groups who have established what they consider to be entitlements in the positive gains that have been artificially created will not agree to change, and those persons and groups who suffer losses will not willingly pay off what they consider to be immoral gainers" (1980:365). Buchanan's hope is that widespread efficiency-reducing institutions will lead to a situation where many groups will agree to give up their gains since all will benefit; thus, constitutional change can occur where piece-meal change is impossible (p. 366).[6]

The question is what insights modern organization theory and public choice theory provide about the problems and prospects of what is now the Russian Central Bank and used to be the State Bank of the Soviet Union. As the IMF report explains, the role of the Soviet state bank (Gosbank) was not to conduct monetary policy, but to extend credit to enterprises and make transfers among enterprises in accordance with the central plan. It was the central plan that gave enterprises access to resources, not the existence of money on deposit at the bank (IMF 1991, 2:107–8). In fact, the accounts of enterprises were usually jointly owned with their controlling ministries, who could reallocate resources among the enterprises under their control. Surplus funds on deposit—funds not designated for a particular purpose such as payment of wages or for supplies, or funds for social purposes of the enterprises such as employee housing and education—belonged to the government.

From this perspective the function of the state bank was not that of a central bank, but rather that of a bookkeeper and a monitoring agency, enforcing the allocation of resources and the distribution of output directed by the central planners and ensuring that no funds in enterprise accounts were spent except for approved purposes.[7] The state bank can also be viewed as the government's tax collector and the manager of its funds: all deposits of enterprises were receipts of the government transferable only in accordance with government directives. Finally, the state bank has been the government's own supplier of credit.

As an enforcer and monitor of the government's central economic plan and the manager of the government's funds, the State Bank of the Soviet Union, now the Central Bank of Russia, developed the characteristics of an organization with substantial structural inertia. It had a long history of established standards and procedures and has presumably acted with considerable reliability and accountability—as a bookkeeper, economic enforcement agency, tax collector, manager of the government's funds, and extender of credit. Among its enforcement tools was the prohibition against the use of currency by enterprises for virtually any purposes except the payment of wages, a prohibition that continues to this day.

Not only is the state bank a large, old, established organization, it was also established for purposes other than those of a central bank operating in a market economy and exhibits characteristics contradictory to those considered the norm for central banks. Specifically:

1. The current Central Bank of Russia is not independent of political forces, but is in fact heavily embroiled in them. The question of extension of credit to state-owned enterprises—and new, private enterprises—is a major issue in economic reform. In this debate the bank has sided with the military-industrial complex, and it continues to

be an important player in the struggle for power over policies for economic reform.

No central bank is, of course, entirely free from legislative and executive pressures relating to monetary policy, and every central bank is necessarily the creature of alterable provisions, whether they be constitutional, legislative, or executive. The Central Bank of Russia has exhibited, however, the exact opposite of independence.

2. The Central Bank of Russia is not independent of the government's need for deficit financing, but is in fact the primary domestic source of that financing.
3. The Central Bank of Russia continues to participate actively not only in decisions on the stringency or ease of the availability of bank credit (in 1992 it resisted the restraint sought by President Boris Yeltsin's chief economic reform strategist, Egor Gaidar), but also on the allocation of credit to the commercial banks and cooperative banks established in the last few years. Many of the newly established commercial banks are owned by some combination of state-owned enterprises, government ministries, and the central bank itself. The imposition of credit ceilings as a device to control the creation of money keeps the Central Bank of Russia in the center of resource allocation, where it may favor credit to state-owned enterprises over credit to privately owned enterprises.
4. The Central Bank of Russia has failed to provide a payments mechanism that allows funds to be transferred among enterprises, individuals, and other organizations; fund transfers may take a month or more. Providing an efficient mechanism may deprive the bank of a role it played in the Communist system. Some Russian bankers think the bank is blocking efforts to create such a system (Ignatius and Banerjee 1994:A8).
5. The Central Bank of Russia has achieved some apparent control of inflation by not delivering cash rubles for wage payments and not transferring funds due to enterprises from other enterprises or the government. Whether this has resulted in repressed inflation that will surface as these problems are unwound remains to be seen. Russian officials expected inflation to increase in late 1994. The chairman of the Russian Central Bank, Viktor Gerashenko, announced that in August and September of 1994 "money should and will be disbursed through the budget" (*Economist* 1994:40). Nominal interest rates have increased (RFE/RL June 13, 1994:1) but at 185 percent a year are still below the rate of inflation as measured by retail prices; the central bank lends at 150 percent a year. Pursuing a market interest rate policy would place the leadership of the bank in conflict with its political allies in the military/industrial establishment.

Given its historical purposes and functions, its explicit interest in the continuation of its historical power relationships, and the conflict with pursuing the objectives of a modern, independent central bank, one might well conclude that the transformation of the old state bank to a modern central bank is not a reasonable expectation. Nor is its historical role consistent with the encouragement of a competitive banking sector with new banks under private or cooperative ownership rather than state ownership of one form or another.

One option that arises from this analysis is that of establishing a new central bank while finding other functions—tax collection or monitoring state-owned enterprises, for example—for the old state bank organization to perform to which it might be more suited than central banking. Creating new organizations to compete with old ones and take over some of the functions of the old is a possible approach, but concurrent responsibility is less appropriate when dealing with the government monopoly on the issue of currency than it is with, say, legal jurisdiction, where civil litigants may choose one or another court or court system.

The Parallel Strategy in Banking and Financial Institutions

The objectives of a reform of monetary and financial arrangements in the former Soviet Union are to provide sound money—one or more monetary standards useful as a medium of exchange, a store of value, and a unit of account—and to ensure that financial institutions serving the savings and credit needs of businesses and households (including the need for an effective payments mechanism) are able to develop and make their decisions on the basis of market opportunities rather than political expediency. The attempt to transform existing institutions into their institutional counterparts that do, in the West, meet these objectives may well fail. Thus, a parallel strategy should be sought.

In its application to money and banking, the parallel strategy in Russia would call for the national government to permit competition in providing a monetary standard. The national government would allow lesser political jurisdictions to arrange for alternative currencies that would circulate along with the ruble. Two different but related ways to do this exist in the historical record of the industrialized free world.

Currency Boards

The most successful rapid establishment of reliable currencies has historically taken place through currency boards, an arrangement whereby the currency board issues a new currency backed on a one-to-one basis by commodity money or by a foreign hard currency (or a basket thereof). Such a board cannot engage in discretionary monetary policy but stands ready at all times to convert its currency issues into the reserve currency. (Some currency boards are set up to operate with greater discretion than this implies, but are still limited in the extent of their discretion by available resources.) Commercial banks are able to create deposits denominated in the currency issued by the board in the process of making loans, but they must be able to meet the demands of depositors for withdrawals.

Currency boards exist today in Hong Kong and Singapore and were used extensively by Great Britain to establish local sound money in its various colonies. Great Britain's currency boards were owned by the British government, which controlled and protected the boards' assets. A currency board can be established with any amount of foreign hard currency a government, its citizens, and international financial organizations choose to provide; if the existing currency is not replaced, both the national government's currency and the notes issued by currency boards circulate. Establishing trust in the issue of the currency board is a critical problem, and enabling legislation should permit local governments to contract with outside agencies for the establishment of currency boards.

Several economists, including Milton Friedman (1991), Alan Walters (1992), Steve Hanke (Hanke and Schuler 1992), and George Selgin (1992), have proposed a currency board as a quick and effective way to provide the countries of Eastern Europe and the former Soviet Union with convertible currencies. Hanke, Jonung and Schuler provide a book-length treatment (1993). Robert L. Hetzel, an economist with the Federal Reserve Bank of Richmond, sees the disadvantage of currency boards in the absence of a binding way to prevent the government from forcing the board to devalue. Peter Boettke (1992:8–9, 88–105, 123–25) also questions the currency board as a credible way for the government to make a binding commitment. Hetzel's solution is the straightforward adoption of a foreign hard currency as the monetary standard in spite of the seigniorage that would go to the originating country: "Governments desiring to establish a market economy can limit government intervention in the economy by limiting the ability of their central banks to produce unpredictable changes in the price level, to allocate capital, and to allocate foreign exchange. The most direct way to limit intervention of the central bank in the economy is to eliminate the central bank" (Hetzel 1990:18).

Free Banking

The second approach is for the national government to permit local political jurisdictions to adopt legislation allowing the establishment of private banks able to issue their own currencies, backed by a reserve currency (including, possibly, the currency issued by a currency board) or commodity of each bank's own choice.

Creating a local option for provinces, cities, and other defined political units allows for competition among these units to provide monetary and financial institutions conducive to economic growth, trade, and foreign investment. At the same time it leaves the national government responsible for the ruble.

The characteristics of a free-banking system are freedom of entry and freedom of note issue with minimal government regulation. The role of the government (beyond enabling legislation) is the enforcement of contracts and laws against fraud and other criminal activity. A free-banking system has no central bank and no lender of last resort.

Since F. A. Hayek's publications on competitive currencies in 1976 and 1978, the history and record, as well as the theory, of competitive private currency issue has received renewed attention from Western economists. Historical examples continue to come to light. In most of these cases the monetary standard—the reserve money into which the notes were convertible—was the same for all the banks in the system. What Hayek proposed was competition among currencies denominated in different units. He foresaw the possibility that such competition would lead to a monetary standard kept constant in terms of the value of a group of commodities. The essential point he and others have made is that government monopoly of currency issue and the monetary standard has been so pervasive that the market has never had the opportunity to experiment with providing the kinds of money consumers might want.

Whatever the characteristics of the ultimate competitive monetary system, the historical record demonstrates what can be expected of competitive private currency issue, whether or not all banks use the same monetary standard. That record in a number of countries over periods of time exceeding, in the case of Scotland, a century, and in the states of the United States between 1838 and 1860, is far better than is commonly believed (Anderson 1992).[8] The theory of free banking, which has developed side-by-side with the historical re-examination, addresses the significant free-banking issues, generally concluding that a free-banking system is not inflationary (leading to systematic over-issue of currency) and would not lead to an infinite or indeterminate price level, does not lead to monetary disequilibrium or fluctuations in the value of money, would not be unstable (subject to runs and panics) and would use resources efficiently.[9]

Both the historical record and theory support the market as an efficient and effective supplier of money. The historical record also demonstrates that when governments decide to end a free-banking regime, they (unfortunately) have no problems doing so, and they do so for their own purposes—in order to obtain the benefits for themselves of monopoly issue and the ability to inflate the currency.

Under a free-banking system each local jurisdiction would adopt at its own option a model statute permitting private banks to accept deposits of hard currency, gold, or other valuables and to issue notes and establish deposits convertible into a hard currency or a basket of currencies, gold, or the current market value of one or more internationally traded commodities such as oil.

The statute would further specify that no restrictions would be placed on the use of the deposits or notes of these banks in transactions or contracts, and that the national and lesser governments would provide specific-performance enforcement of these contracts in the same manner and with the same care they enforce contracts in the ruble or any currency issued by or under the auspices of the government; and that they would also enforce laws concerning fraud, counterfeiting, and the like as they do for their own currency issues.

A license or charter to create such a bank would be based on meeting certain specific and minimal requirements—the names, addresses, and character of the owners (people with a criminal record under current law could be excluded), a copy of the by-laws of the bank representing its contractual commitments and relationships to shareholders, depositors, and note holders, and the names and addresses of its auditors. Each bank could be required to include in its name a standard phrase, such as "non-state," indicating that the bank was not government-owned or backed and its deposits and notes were not insured by the government. Individual jurisdictions might choose to make foreign individuals and enterprises eligible for bank licenses, either as sole or partial owners of a bank.

The model enabling legislation would require that contractual commitments to note holders and deposit holders be met; in the event they were not, the government would close down the bank according to pre-established rules on the bankruptcy of private banks and the bank's own by-laws on priority of claims.

The model statute could require that every bank provide frequent (perhaps even daily) audited public information on the condition of the bank in accordance with a defined format, posted in all public offices of the bank and made available to the financial press for publication. A further public-information requirement would be that the banks post and inform the government of the quantity of all bank notes printed and that all enterprises printing bank notes for such banks also inform the government and the public of the printing of such notes. The provision of public information would probably evolve even if it were not required by regulation. The assumption here is that a specific requirement can eliminate the trial period over which market participants generate the demand for the kind of information they need to evaluate private banks. (Some portion of the public needs to be both informed and concerned enough to monitor these institutions in order to set in motion the processes that prevent overissue.)

Beyond the initial licensing and public information requirements, neither the national nor the local government would regulate these banks. No restrictions would be placed on branching or other geographical activity or the financial services that could be provided (including clearing house activities). No reserve requirements would be established and no limits placed on interest rates on deposits or loans, the amount of reserves a bank must hold, or the kinds of loans (or even equity participation) a bank could make.

No limitations other than minimal licensing requirements would be placed on entry into the industry (with the possible exception of minimum capital), since competition is the essential regulator of a free-banking system. No restrictions would be placed on the conversion of deposits to currency or the use of devices such as checks, electronic transfers, teller machines, and the like. Nor would restrictions be placed on the nature of the bank's contractual commitments to deposit and note holders, including whether or not it was created as a limited or unlimited liability joint stock company. A bank might or might not choose to issue currency with a delayed redemption clause—one that permits the bank to redeem within six months, for example, rather than immediately. A bank might or might not choose to honor currencies issued by other banks at one time or another; clearing houses would also be free to make judgments about the banks they would accept as members. Currencies issued by banks would trade freely against each other and the ruble.

The Banking System: Policy Options

With either approach (or the local option to adopt either or both) should go legislation allowing the establishment of privately owned banks doing business in the new currencies and not subject to regulation by the Central Bank of Russia. The provision of sound money is only the first step; the second essential ingredient for successful economic development is financial institutions that do business in the sound money, accepting deposits and making loans without the credit allocations, interest rate controls, and limitations on the conversion of deposits to currency to which ruble banks are subject.

As an approach that requires a new banking law, the free banking approach has advantages over the currency board. It also has the potential for creating one or more new monetary standards based, unlike issues of currency boards, on something other than another country's fiat money.

Banks are not, however, the only source of funds for small or even large enterprises. Venture capital firms can also gather the savings of individuals and make them available as equity investment or debt to a variety of enterprises. Other financial institutions may also develop if basic legislation is sufficiently permissive.

Given the size of Russia, its great variety, and the disagreements within and between the legislative and executive branches on economic reform, it would seem easier and more acceptable for the national government to delegate the decision to adopt alternative monetary and banking arrangements to lesser governments rather than to attempt to adopt them for the nation at large.

The widespread acceptance of the standard two-tiered banking system suggests that consideration as a policy option of a currency board (or a local currency board option) or free banking is unlikely and its adoption even less likely. If, however, inflation in Russia again accelerates and becomes hyperinflation, radical policy change will be forced upon the government. History shows that hyperinflations end rather quickly when the government establishes a credible commitment to balance its budget and forswear borrowing from the central bank.[10] In Russia's case credibility would also require the end of central bank credit to state-owned enterprises, either directly or through central-bank loans to commercial banks. Such a program is far more rigorous than the conditions generally imposed by the IMF or the credit restraint sought by economic reformers in the Yeltsin government in 1992. Faced with this alternative the government may find currency boards or free banking attractive alternatives. A ten-year contract with an international agency to operate a currency board could give Russia ten years of a stable and convertible currency, allow it to disband its so-called central bank or alter its functions, and leave the country free to return to backing its own currency at the end of the contract period.

The major disadvantage of free banking in Russia today is the widespread corruption of government institutions and the weakness of legislation and the court system for enforcing contractual arrangements. If inflation continues at 10–25 percent a month, Russia is likely to continue struggling to turn its old state bank into a modern central bank. Within this context, the most practical approach for establishing a monetary system that can contribute to economic growth would be for Russia to expand the legal use of foreign currencies, permitting foreign currencies to be used in trade, as savings in banks, and in contracts without restraint. In fact the dollar is already used by some businesses in parts of Russia not as a medium of exchange, but as a unit of account: agreements are stated in dollars, but payments are made in rubles at the going rate of exchange. The countries providing foreign hard currencies would benefit—as they do now—from currency held in Russia not returned to the issuing country in exchange for goods or services (seigniorage). Compensation for this benefit to the issuing countries could be taken into account in the continual rescheduling of Russia's foreign hard currency obligations.

An Overview of the Parallel Strategy

One general assumption of the parallel strategy is that organizations are hard to change, especially long-established, specialized organizations. It is especially difficult to have Communist-era organizations act like what appear to be their Western counterparts when they were in fact established for different purposes and fulfill different functions. Furthermore, modelling change on existing Western institutions may introduce into formerly Communist countries institutions that have passed their prime. It is a reasonable assumption, also, that the most important organizations and institutions in the reforming economies will in ten or twenty years be organizations that are now in their infancy or do not even exist. With respect to Russia, a further assumption is that the size and diversity of the country will make it difficult to reform from the center, and that the future lies in competition among cities and regions for effective reform policies. If these assumptions are correct, an alternative strategy to that of attempting to transform existing institutions (which should continue) is to allow the parallel development of competing institutions. In the area of money and banking it has been suggested that allowing a local option may be the most effective way to do this. In general:

1. Legislation should make a wide variety of organizational arrangements possible, with different forms of ownership, liability, and so forth, and appropriate tax provisions. In the financial sector this would mean legislation that clearly makes possible venture capital from the small scale to the large as an alternative to the banking system as a means of concentrating savings for both debt and equity investments in privately owned enterprises.
2. The government should permit competition with its own enterprises and agencies in all fields, thus giving up its monopoly privileges. Competition from new enterprises should be possible in energy, telecommunications, transportation, and mail delivery, among others. Specific legislation would be required in some areas, such as requiring the state-owned railroad to allow private railroads to use its track, requiring the state-owned telephone company to permit private suppliers of telecommunications services to connect to its system, and so forth. If the government finds it impossible to privatize state-owned enterprises, it should limit investment in them to ensure the greater availability of funds to new private enterprises.
3. Where the national government cannot agree on allowing open competition, it can delegate to lesser governments such as provinces the option to adopt permissive legislation. At the same time, the national government can forbid the adoption by lesser jurisdictions of restrictive

legislation, such as legislation that discriminates against products produced elsewhere (tariffs, duties) and legislation that excludes the operation of enterprises legitimately established elsewhere.
4. The central government can and should treat state-owned enterprises differently from new enterprises and enterprises that have been privatized and are no longer dependent on the state or state-provided and subsidized credit. Government oversight of borrowing, wage payments, new investment, and so forth in the state sector alone should be directed toward restraining the state-owned sector sufficiently to make privatization and new private enterprises an attractive alternative for both managers and employees and to ensure that the state sector leaves some resources available for the private sector.

Notes

1. Earlier versions of this paper were delivered at the Annual Meeting of the Atlantic Economic Society, Session on Monetary Reform in Russia, Anaheim, California, January 5, 1993 and at the Conference on Monetary Reform in the Former Soviet Union, Claremont Institute for Economic Policy Studies, April 2, 1993. I wish to thank Professor Peter Boettke of New York University and Professor Samantha Carrington of the University of California-Santa Barbara, as well as the editors, for helpful comments.

2. This is from a summary appearing in *Izvestia* and published in translation by the Foreign Service Information Bulletin.

3. Proposals to convert defense establishments to producers of consumer goods or other commercial products fly in the face of even Western experience: recent research on defense conversion in the United States and Europe finds no example of a successful commercial product developed in this way. Products tend to be over-engineered; enterprises undertaking such conversions lack the skills of their competitors in assessing markets, mass producing at low cost, and marketing. Western corporations have been successful in diversifying product lines to reduce dependency on defense procurement, and individual communities have developed effective programs to attract new investment through a hospitable business environment and the marketing of existing resources such as factory space or facilities on closed military bases. Efforts of corporations and the government to provide job placement services and some retraining have also shown some success. See Lynch (1987) for specific articles and a bibliography. That even Western defense industries have been unable to convert defense production lines to commercial production suggests that following this strategy in formerly Communist countries, especially Russia, is likely to fail at the cost of substantial waste of resources. Defense conversion efforts were undertaken in the Soviet Union during the Gorbachev era and continue. In addition to direct production-line conversion, approaches included placing priority industries under the direction of the defense industry ministry and increasing production of nondefense products already produced by defense industries. One of the priority industries was food-processing

equipment. The new defense managers found out-dated equipment and the need for substantial investment. Other problems included access to materials and supplies, which were provided on a priority basis only to the defense sector. Unlike their defense customers who knew exactly what they wanted, the ministries ordering food-processing equipment did not seem to know what it was they wanted built. See Alexander (1991).

4. For one such plan to which the author contributed, see Bernstam and Leksin (1992), available only in Russian.

5. In the summer of 1992 American contractors to the Polish Ministry of Finance were developing a deposit insurance program for Poland along the lines of the U.S. deposit insurance system. According to people working on the project, the World Bank required the development of deposit insurance. The contractors were trying to limit the adverse incentives created by such a system but were not changing its basic structure.

6. See also Tullock (1980) for the problem of undoing government preferences.

7. The *Great Soviet Encyclopedia* (8:626) quotes Lenin: "Banking policy, without being limited to the nationalization of the banks, should gradually but constantly be directed toward converting the banks to a unified apparatus of accounting and regulating the socialistically organized economic life of the entire nation as a whole." See Moore (1981) for an interpretation of many Soviet institutions and attempted reforms as efforts to monitor the behavior of agents (enterprise managers) by the state. Such institutions and efforts to reduce agency costs are carried out by these means in the absence of Western institutions that help control agency costs—the capital market, the market for corporate control, and the market for managers.

8. On the history of free banking in a number of countries, see Rockoff (1975), Rolnick and Weber (1984), Sandberg (1978), Vaubel (1984), Weber (1988), and White (1984).

9. On the theory of free banking and related issues, see Glasner (1989), Greenfield and Yeager (1987), Klein (1983), Selgin (1988), Vaubel (1987) and White (1984, 1989a, 1989b).

10. See Sargent (1982:41-97).

References

Alexander, Arthur J. 1991. *The Conversion of the Soviet Defense Industry*. The RAND Corporation Working Paper P-7620. Santa Monica, Calif., January.

Allison, Graham, and Grigory Yavlinsky. 1991. "Window of Opportunity: Transforming the Soviet Union into a Democracy with a Market Economy." John F. Kennedy School of Government, Harvard University, mimeo, June 19, 1991. Testimony presented at Hearing on "The Soviet Crisis and the U.S. Interest: Future of the Soviet Economy," June 19, 1991, Senate Foreign Relations Committee, Subcommittee on European Affairs, Washington, D.C.

Anderson, Annelise. 1992. *The Ruble Problem: A Competitive Solution*. Essays in Public Policy No. 31. Stanford, Calif.: The Hoover Institution.

Bernstam, Mikhail, and Vladimir N. Leksin. 1992. *Reform Without Shock (Reforma Bez Shoka)*. Moscow: The Supreme Economic Council of the Presidium of the Russian Supreme Soviet.

Boettke, Peter. 1992. *Why Perestroika Failed: The Politics and Economics of Socialist Transformation*. London: Routledge.
Buchanan, James M. 1980. "Reform in the Rent-Seeking Society," in James M. Buchanan, Robert D. Tollison, and Gordon Tullock, eds. *Toward a Theory of the Rent-Seeking Society*. Pp. 359–67. College Station, Texas: A&M University Press.
Economist. 1994. "It's Inflation, Stupid." August 20: 40–41.
Foreign Service Information Bulletin. 1991. "Yavlinsky Economic Program Summarized," translated from *Izvestia*, June 25, 1991, Union Edition, p. 2, unattributed. FSIB-SOV-91-123, 26 June: 47–51.
Friedman, Milton. 1991. Statement at conference on the Economic Transition in Central and Eastern Europe held at the Hoover Institution, Stanford, Calif., May 8–10.
Glasner, David. 1989. *Free Banking and Monetary Reform*. Cambridge: Cambridge University Press.
Great Soviet Encyclopedia: A Translation of the Third Edition. 1975. Vol. 8. New York: Macmillan, Inc.
Greenfield, Robert L., and Leland B. Yeager. 1987. "A Laissez-Faire Approach to Monetary Stability." *Journal of Money, Credit, and Banking* 19 (November): 457–68.
Hanke, Steve H., Lars Jonung, and Kurt Schuler. 1993. *Russian Currency and Finance: A Currency Board Approach to Reform*. New York: Routledge.
Hanke, Steve H., and Kurt Schuler. 1992. "Clearing the Ruble." *Reason*, March: 44–46.
Hannan, Michael T., and John Freeman. 1984. "Structural Inertia and Organizational Change." *American Sociological Review* 49 (April): 149–64.
_____. 1977. "The Population Ecology of Organizations." *American Journal of Sociology* 82: 929–64.
Hayek, F. A. 1976. *Denationalisation of Money: An Analysis of the Theory and Practice of Concurrent Currencies*. London: Institute of Economic Affairs.
Hetzel, Robert H. 1990. "Free Enterprise and Central Banking in Formerly Communist Countries." Federal Reserve Bank of Richmond *Economic Review* (May/June): 13–19.
Ignatius, Adi, and Neela Banerjee. 1994. "Russian Bankers Bring Tricks of the Trade Home After U.S. Visit." *Wall Street Journal*, May 23: A1, A8.
International Monetary Fund, World Bank, Organization for Economic Co-operation and Development, and European Bank for Reconstruction and Development. 1991. *A Study of the Soviet Economy*, Vol. 1–3. Paris, France.
Klein, Benjamin. 1983. "The Competitive Supply of Money." *Journal of Monetary Economics* 12 (May): 127–58.
Lynch, John E., ed. 1987. *Economic Adjustment and Conversion of Defense Industries*. Boulder, Colo.: Westview Press.
Moore, John H. 1981. "Agency Costs, Technological Change, and Soviet Central Planning." *The Journal of Law & Economics* XXIV(2) October: 189–214.
Radio Free Europe/Radio Liberty Research Institute. "RFE/RL Daily Report." Munich, Germany, various issues.
Rockoff, Hugh. 1975. *The Free Banking Era: A Re-Examination*. New York: Arno Press.
Rolnick, Arthur J., and Warren E. Weber. 1984. "The Causes of Free Bank Failures: A Detailed Examination." *Journal of Monetary Economics* 14: 267–92.

Sandberg, Lars G. 1978. "Banking and Economic Growth in Sweden Before World War I." *Journal of Economic History* 38(3) September: 650–80.

Sargent, Thomas J. 1982. "The Ends of Four Big Inflations," in Robert Hall, ed., *Inflation*. Chicago: National Bureau of Economic Research.

Scott, W. Richard. 1987. *Organizations: Rational, Natural, and Open Systems*, 2nd ed. Englewood Cliffs, N. J.: Prentice-Hall, Inc.

Selgin, George. 1992. "The ECU Could Stabilize CIS Currencies." *The Wall Street Journal Europe*, January 9.

———. 1988. *The Theory of Free Banking*. Totowa, N.J.: Rowman & Littlefield.

Tullock, Gordon. 1980. "The Transitional Gains Trap," in James M. Buchanan, Robert D. Tollison, and Gordon Tullock, eds., *Toward a Theory of the Rent-Seeking Society*. Pp. 211–21. College Station, Texas: Texas A&M University Press.

Vaubel, Roland. 1987. "Competing Currencies: The Case for Free Entry," in James A. Dorn and Anna J. Schwartz, eds., *The Search for Stable Money: Essays on Monetary Reform*. Pp. 281–96. Chicago: University of Chicago Press.

———. 1984. "Private Competitive Note Issue in Monetary History," in P. Salin, ed. *Currency Competition and Monetary Union*. Pp. 59–73. The Hague: Martinus Nijhoff Publishers.

Walters, Alan. 1992. "A Hard Ruble for the New Republics." *National Review*, February 3: 34–36.

Weber, Ernst Juerg. 1988. "Currency Competition in Switzerland, 1826–1850." *Kyklos* 4: 459–78.

White, Lawrence H. 1984. *Free Banking in Britain: Theory, Experience, and Debate, 1800–45*. Cambridge: Cambridge University Press.

———. 1989a. *Competition and Currency*. New York: New York University Press.

———. 1989b. "What Kinds of Monetary Institutions Would a Free Market Deliver?" *Cato Journal* 9(2) Fall: 367–90.

Wolf, Jr., Charles. 1991. "Getting to Market." *The National Interest*, Spring: 43–50.

PART THREE

Case Studies

9

The Russian Central Bank and the Conduct of Monetary Policy

Stephen Lewarne[1]

Introduction

Since becoming an independent state, Russia has adopted many of the types of banking laws we associate with western banking institutions—particularly those stressing independence of the monetary authority. However, much of this legislation has been altered in significant ways, particularly regarding the crucial role of the governor of the central bank. This raises the question addressed in this paper: Is the Central Bank of Russia, as it now stands, appropriately constructed to fight inflation?

I begin with a brief discussion of the background to the establishment of the Central Bank of Russia. This is followed by an analysis of the current Russian banking legislation, which is considered in light of the conflict that is currently underway between the fiscal and monetary authorities in Russia. I close with some thoughts on the nature of central bank independence.

Some Background

The Central Bank of Russia was created during one of the most tumultuous periods in the modern history of Russia. The Soviet Union, finally, had begun to unravel. With the government burdened with debts and nearly completely delegitimized, the time was ripe for the political opposition represented by Boris Yeltsin to act. One of the more important actions he took was to create the Central Bank of Russia (CBR), an institution distinct from the State Bank of the Soviet Union (GOSBANK USSR), and one which was to be a crucial actor in the transition to a market economy.

One of the characteristics of the old Soviet regime was the subservience of the financial sector to the real sector. The planning authorities were unwilling to tolerate any kind of independent monetary policy decision-making body that could disrupt their plan objectives. This meant that the state bank (GOSBANK) was in essence an arm of the finance ministry and issued extra credits to enterprises or increased the issue of money to support the government's specified production goals.

As central planning was relaxed over the 1989 to 1991 period, increased reliance was placed on macroeconomic stabilization through monetary means, and that meant controlling the credit markets and currency issue. Of particular importance became the impact of central bank policies on inflation. While there are several sources of inflation in any economy, the central bank can go a long way toward easing or aggravating inflation via its control of the money supply. In addition, expected inflation plays a crucial role in the dynamics of the inflation process, and the formation of price expectations is based in part on how the monetary authority is perceived by the public. If it is seen as a responsible steward of the money supply, then one source of expected inflation can be eliminated. If it is seen as irresponsible, then the public's expectation of loose money adds to the inflationary pressure. With the fall of central planning and the advent of monetary policy, the degree of independence of the new monetary authority, *and* how that new independence is used, becomes an indicator of the success of the reform effort.

Inflation in Russia

The rate of retail price inflation at the end of 1992 was 2,600 percent and industrial wholesale price inflation was 3,400 percent.[2] In the first quarter of 1993, retail price inflation was running at about 26 percent a month (1,500 percent per annum) while wholesale price inflation averaged 30 percent a month (2,230 percent per annum).[3] Inflation stabilized in the fall of 1993 at around 12–15 percent a month, largely due to the responsible budget policies of the finance minister, Boris Fedorov. Based on these figures, comparatively favorable estimates of 700–800 percent inflation were made for 1993 (see Table 9.1). However, both Fedorov and Prime Minister Yegor Gaidar gave in to political pressures before the December 12, 1993 elections and extended close to 1.5 trillion rubles in credits to industry and agriculture.

In January 1994, Fedorov and Gaidar resigned from the government, giving as their reason the near certainty of hyperinflation in Russia if their reforms were not continued. In part reflecting their dismal forecasts, inflation in January rose to about 20 percent.[4] Prime Minister Chernomyrdin rejected Fedorov's demands to dismiss Central Bank President Viktor Gerashchenko, and once again Russia seems headed for even higher inflation. In early

TABLE 9.1 Deficit and Inflation Data for Russia and other Transitional Economies, 1991–1994

Countries	Budget Deficit/GDP(%)				Inflation Rate			
	1991	1992	1993	1994	1991	1992	1993	1994
Russia	21.3	15.0	12–15	15–20	152	2,600 (1,099)	700–800	792
Ukraine	13.5	33.3	35+	n.a.	137	2,500	10–12,875	n.a.
Czech Rep.	2.0	3.3	0	n.a.	52	12.7	15–17	9.7
Belarus	2.2	4.0	n.a.	n.a.	111	1,600	n.a.	n.a.
Kyrgyzstan	-4.6	13.4	3–5	4.5 (8)	180	1,259	1,209	425.7
Estonia	-4.9	-1.5	n.a.	n.a.	211	1,050	n.a.	n.a.
Hungary	3.2	8.1	6.0	n.a.	35	23	20	17
Poland	6.5	6.1	5.1	n.a.	70	43	39	30.2

Source: Stephen Lewarne, *Assessment of the Macroeconomic, Financial and Fiscal Sector Environment in the Kyrgyz Republic*, completed for the U.S. State Department, USAID, December 20, 1993.

Notes: **Russia.** The 1991 actual deficit figures are from European Bank for Reconstruction and Development (1993). All inflation data from the European Bank for Reconstruction and Development are their year-end results for CPI. The 1992 estimates are from Burdekin (1994:25). Burdekin cites Gaspar, "The Fiscal Consequences of Economic Transition in Eastern European Economies," Working Paper, Institute for World Economies, Budapest, Hungary, 1993. The 1993 estimates are from *The Moscow Times*, December 8, 1993 and the author's estimates. Official data from the Central Bank of Russia up to September 1993 have an average monthly inflation rate of 23 percent for a yearly rate of 1,099 percent, but the actual figure may be lower given lower monthly rates in October and November. Estimates for 1994 are based on an average monthly rate of 20 percent. Press reports in Moscow predicted 30 percent monthly inflation if agricultural subsidies were made. As of April 1994 they had not been released, and so inflation was around 12 percent a month. It is anticipated, however, that the subsidies will be released over the summer and fall, and push the average monthly inflation rate to 20 percent. The 1994 budget deficit/GDP is the author's estimate—the assumption is that agricultural subsidies and industrial subsidy reform will slow down considerably over the summer and fall, so that the situation will not get any better (and will probably worsen) compared to last year.

(continues)

TABLE 9.1 (continued)

Ukraine. The 1991–1992 deficit figures are from European Bank for Reconstruction and Development (1993). Inflation figures are annual averages. The 1993 estimates are by the author and the Ukrainian Embassy, Moscow, Russia. The lower bound is based on Ukrainian estimates from the Ministry of Finance, the upper bound from estimates of Cagen-hyperinflation averaging 50 percent a month.
Belarus. European Bank for Reconstruction and Development (1993).
Kyrgyzstan. 1991 estimates are from the IMF, *The Kyrgyz Report-Recent Economic Developments*, September 3, 1993. The 1992 inflation estimate is the IMF's official retail price index in IMF, *Kyrgyz Republic*, IMF Economic Reviews No. 12, 1993. The 1993 estimate is from the Ministry of Economy and Finance, Kyrgyzstan, World Bank data and IMF preliminary estimates. IMF estimates in January for inflation revised this figure upward to 1208.5 percent (unofficial). The 1994 estimates are unofficial from the IMF. The 4.5 percent deficit/GDP ratio is from calculations of the forecast budget deficit to the IMF forecast of GDP. The Kyrgyz estimate is 8 percent.
Czech Republic. The 1991–1993 deficit figures are from the European Bank for Reconstruction and Development (1993). Inflation data for 1991–1992 are from Burdekin (1994).
Estonia, Hungary, and Poland. The 1991–1993 deficit figures are from the European Bank for Reconstruction and Development (1993). 1994 inflation figures for Poland and Hungary are from *The Economist*, April 23, 1994, p. 112.

February 1994, the government was prepared to live up to its promise to slowly reverse reforms and extend up to 34.7 trillion rubles in aid to the agriculture sector. These credit extensions, if approved, will certainly push inflation higher. Estimates by A. Illarionov, Director of the Russian Government Sector for Economic Reform, predict inflation could rise to around 30 percent a month, yielding an inflation rate of 2,230 percent for 1994.[5] Illarionov's estimates may have been too pessimistic however. By May 1994, Prime Minister Chernomyrdin had not issued the agricultural credits nor had Gerashchenko released them. This kept inflation in March and April down to around 10 percent a month. Still, both Chernomyrdin and Gerashchenko have proven records of giving in to special interest groups, and indeed this is one of Chernomyrdin's claims to fame under the guise of "more therapy less shock." He will probably be forced to release these credits in the last quarter of 1994, triggering an increase in the average monthly inflation rate in Russia to around 20 percent a month for the year, for an annualized rate of 790 percent. This credit expansion will be reflected in an increased budget deficit, since much of this credit will be issued via the budget rather than directly from the Central Bank of Russia, continuing the pattern of the old Soviet regime. (Credits were issued by GOSBANK rather than the central bank).

Table 9.1 shows the current rate of inflation and budget deficit ratios for Russia and some of the economies against which it is traditionally compared. This offers us a frame of reference for the discussion below, especially since budget deficits and the level of independence of the central bank are central to this chapter's theme.

The primary sources of inflation in Russia seem to be both seigniorage and credit extension to commercial banks by the Russian central bank. This is due not only to a lack of other revenue sources, given the government's current inability to bond-finance government debt, but also to the Central Bank of Russia's credit policies. Both the ministry of finance and the central bank have an established policy of funneling credits via the new banking system to various enterprises that they want to keep afloat. Table 9.2 shows the predominance of cash issue in the money supply and the low proportion of government securities in the total money supply.

In such a situation the rate of credit growth and currency issue proceeds almost without check. Daily reports in the press quote the prime minister of Russia or the minister of finance about how credit and money growth must be controlled, but they then proceed to allocate credit as they always have. Indeed, this has been one of the fundamental complaints of the IMF and the World Bank about the Russian Federation, that despite its claims to the contrary, the government is continuing the soft-budget constraint of the old regime.[6]

One of the more effective ways to force the government to end its reliance on seigniorage revenues (the inflation tax) is to promote a truly independent central bank, one able to refuse to money-finance government deficits.

Independence of the Monetary Authority Under Normal Conditions

Once the government decides to engage in macroeconomic policy rather than command-administrative microeconomic policy, the credibility of the monetary authority (the central bank) becomes paramount. This is because the government has an incentive to pressure the monetary authority (if possible) to engage in seigniorage, allowing it to collect an inflation tax through monetary expansions. Underdeveloped economies that have a very difficult time imposing or collecting value-added, income or excise taxes are most likely to use the inflation tax. The problem with this is that private agents begin to anticipate the monetary expansion, thus raising price expectations, and causing a decline in actual output below its natural rate. The monetary authority responds by accommodation of these expectations with the effect of higher than desired inflation. As Grilli, Masciandaro and Tabellini (1991:450) have put it, "the lack of credibility results in an excessive reliance on seigniorage revenues."

Therefore, having a separate monetary authority which is inflation adverse should induce the government to seek revenue from traditional taxation sources such as value-added and income taxes. Having an inflation-adverse central bank (which can enforce its preferences because it is independent) will further induce the government to balance its budget. The more independent the central bank, the theory goes, the lower inflation will be, and fiscal policy will be more disciplined. However, independence may not always work this way.

Abuse of Central Bank Independence. There are at least three ways central bank independence can be abused. First, the central banker, despite his legal independence, may be implicitly working with the government and accommodating its deficit financing. This can occur in any regime, be it a developed market economy or a transitional economy. A public choice perspective explains this behavior: the central banker may be maximizing his personal long-term gains. If he was a political appointee and has some loyalty to the individual or party that chose him, then he has an incentive to accommodate his party's policies so as to obtain an appointment elsewhere in the government after his term as central banker is finished. The probability of this occurring may be higher in regimes that have only recently established a separation between the fiscal and monetary authorities (as in Russia and all the other former Soviet republics). Then too, the choice of appointee may be shaped by political considerations: the president may prefer, not a conservative banker, but a supporter from the ranks of his own party. If the appointment has to be confirmed by the legislature, as under the current Russian system, and the legislature is hostile, then the president has an incentive to choose a banker closer to their wishes in order to minimize conflict, especially if he wants to win on other issues he considers more important. Either way the central banker has some loyalty to the fiscal authority.

The second possibility is that the central banker has a political agenda much different from that of the government and may attempt to undermine its policies. The central banker could then use his legal independence to advance his own cause once he was placed in power. If he was appointed by a president trying to placate a legislature hostile to the president's policies, the banker, who represents the legislature's preferences, has an incentive to undermine the power of the executive. There are two main possibilities:

1. The central banker could put more emphasis on hitting an inflation target than the government, frustrating its employment goals, conversely;
2. The central banker could put more emphasis on hitting either an employment or output target than the government, thus frustrating the government's inflation target.

In the former case he would tend to stabilize prices, but in the face of large supply shocks he would raise the variance of output and employment.[7] In the latter case, the banker has what appears to be a short-term objective since his policy only temporarily supports the real sector and damages the financial sector. It is generally agreed that a central banker should focus on the former target, inflation, rather than the latter, employment and output, since in the long run output reaches a natural rate and targeting output (or employment) will only lead to higher prices rather than any change in output.

Third, the central banker may simply try to support the financial sector regardless of the political consequences for the existing government. When credit markets are dominated by banks that are on the whole unhealthy, the central banker may try to maintain the liquidity of the banking system so as to avoid bank failures which may lead to the disruption or collapse of the financial sector. In a way, this is similar to the case where the banker is trying to hit an employment target that is higher than the government's. If we are talking about regimes with something close to hyperinflation (say 20–40 percent a month), then these policies can be in direct conflict with the goals of a government that is very sensitive to hyperinflation because of its often detrimental political consequences.[8]

As a result we can say that central bank independence may be a necessary condition to promote lower inflation, but it is not a sufficient condition. The appointment of a conservative central bank chairman is also crucial if an independent central bank is to promote fiscal responsibility and lower both current and expected inflation rather than aggravating the problem.

Independence of the Monetary Authority Under Transitional Conditions

When we discuss central banking and central bank independence in Russia (and the former Soviet republics) today we have to be aware of some important characteristics of these economies. A few features stand out.

First, the Russians have considerable problems with output and are experiencing high negative growth rates. Industrial production declined by about 20 percent in 1992 and between 12 and 20 percent in 1993.[9] As a consequence, the lower-tier banking sector has many outstanding assets which are potentially in default. If the lower-tier banks are not given incentives to reschedule debt for their loan customers, then there is the possibility that as loans are called in, firms will go bankrupt and unemployment will rise.

Second, given the general ill-health of Russian industry and agriculture, both the government and the central bank have an incentive to either directly subsidize enterprises, or (more importantly from the point of central banking) offer very low interest discount loans to commercial banks that have assets (loans) extended to troubled enterprises. There is substantial evidence of this occurring in the Russian Federation in both banking statistics and in statements made by central bank officials.

As of February 1993, central bank credits to commercial banks alone were 2.8 trillion rubles, which was 33 percent of the broad money supply measure (M3). If we include the central bank entry "credits to the economy," amounting to 6.2 trillion rubles on February 1, 1993, then credits to either banks or failing enterprises amount to 8.8 trillion rubles, which is more than the total estimated Russian M3.[10] The 35 trillion rubles in credits to agriculture under discussion in Moscow for 1994 is about 30 percent larger than total M3 for 1993 (around 25 trillion rubles—see Table 9.2). Further, these are credits to only one sector of the economy. How much will be extended to industry for 1994 is not yet known, but it could be substantial. Such numbers suggest that the Russian central bank chairman may, in fact, be intent on hitting a high-employment target and trying to provide liquidity for lower-tier banks. While these credits are officially offered by the government through the prime minister's office, it would be nearly impossible for the prime minister to issue these credits if the Russian central bank's chairman were not willing to accommodate these policies. Given that the Russian government is unable to raise substantial revenues to finance its deficit from tax collection and non-bank financing sources, it must depend on seigniorage as its primary source of revenue.

Central bank officials have expressed their desire to conduct "social policy" and keep enterprises afloat until the government has put a well-developed social safety net in place. (This was stressed at several points in a 1993 interview with Vladimir Smenkovski, Deputy Head of the International Department at the Central Bank of Russia.) Such a policy provides for a

TABLE 9.2 Russian Monetary Aggregates (trillions of rubles)

Monetary Aggregate 1992	Jan	Feb	Mar	Apr	May	June	July	Aug	Sept	Oct	Nov	Dec
Monetary Base (M0) Cash in Circulation	0.17	0.19	0.22	0.23	0.32	0.37	0.46	0.64	0.83	1.01	1.20	1.45
Reserves	n.a.	n.a.	n.a.	n.a.	n.a.	n.a.	n.a.	n.a.	n.a.	n.a.	n.a.	n.a.
M1 (M0 plus)	0.76	0.88	1.00	1.18	1.32	1.46	1.91	2.44	3.27	4.36	5.57	5.88
Current and Special Accts of Firms/Citizens	0.34	0.44	0.50	0.61	0.66	0.74	1.05	1.33	1.94	2.80	3.74	3.70
Deposits of Firms/Population	0.05	0.06	0.06	0.07	0.09	0.10	0.13	0.17	0.18	0.24	0.29	0.35
State Savings Bank Demand Deposits	0.20	0.21	0.22	0.23	0.25	0.26	0.28	0.29	0.37	0.32	0.34	0.37
State Insurance Deposits	.002	.003	.002	.002	.002	.003	.003	.003	.004	.004	.004	.004
M2 (M1 plus)	0.94	1.05	1.18	1.35	1.48	1.62	2.07	2.60	3.42	4.51	5.72	6.04
Term Deposits of the Population in the State Savings Bank	0.17	0.17	0.18	0.17	0.16	0.16	0.15	0.15	0.15	0.15	0.16	0.16
M3 (M2 plus)	0.95	1.07	1.19	1.36	1.50	1.63	2.08	2.61	3.44	4.53	5.74	6.05
Certificates	.004	.004	.003	.003	.003	.003	.003	.003	.002	.002	.002	.002
Government Bonds	.012	.012	.012	.011	.011	.011	.011	.011	.011	.013	.013	.015

(continues)

TABLE 9.2 (continued)

Monetary Aggregate 1993	Jan	Feb	Mar	Apr	May	June	July	Aug	Sept
Monetary Base (M0) Cash in Circulation	n.a.	1.95	2.32	2.60	3.34	4.04	5.13	6.27	7.45
Vault Cash	n.a.	0.01	0.11	0.23	0.22	0.28	0.21	0.54	0.17
Reserve Account at Central Bank	n.a.	0.57	0.64	0.73	0.89	1.07	1.23	1.39	1.61
Corresponding Account at Central Bank	n.a.	1.95	2.08	2.78	2.76	2.86	2.83	4.18	4.62
M1 (M0 plus) Current, Special and Other Accounts	n.a.	8.30	9.12	10.6	13.0	15.4	15.6	21.5	24.5
	n.a.	5.38	5.66	6.72	8.11	9.55	8.46	12.9	14.2
Deposits at Commercial Banks	n.a.	0.46	0.56	0.69	0.93	1.19	1.23	1.47	1.74
State Savings Bank Demand Deposits	n.a.	0.51	0.59	0.57	0.62	0.64	0.81	0.92	1.03
M2 (M1 plus)	n.a.	8.49	9.34	10.9	13.4	16.0	16.2	22.2	25.3
Term Deposits of the Population in the State Savings Bank	n.a.	0.19	0.21	0.35	0.43	0.56	0.58	0.69	0.80
M3 (M2 plus)	n.a.	8.50	9.36	10.9	13.4	16.0	16.2	22.2	25.3
Government Bonds	n.a.	0.01	0.01	0.01	0.01	0.01	0.01	0.01	0.02

(continues)

TABLE 9.2 (continued)

Notes: The method of accounting and types of accounts have changed since 1992 and hence the "Current and Special Accounts of Firms and Citizens," includes the following items (each item's share of total M1 as of September 1993 is given after its Russian transliteration): basic accounts (*raschetnye scheta*) 23 percent, special accounts (*spetsial'nye scheta*) 0.06 percent, capital investment accounts (*scheta kapvolozhenii*) 18.4 percent, accredited and checking accounts (*akkreditivy i chekovyescheta*) 1.7 percent, accounts of local budgets (*scheta mestnykh biudzhetov*) 6.9 percent, budget accounts of professional trade unions etc. (*profsoiuznye itd.*) 8.3 percent, accounts of the State Insurance Fund (*sredstva Gosstrakkha*) 0.05 percent, long-term deposits (*fond dolgosrochnogo kredbitovaniia*) 0.0 percent.

Sources: 1992 data are from *Ekonomika i zhizn'*, February 1993, No. 8, p. 6 and interviews at the Central Bank of Russia by the author in 1993. The 1993 data are from Tsentral'nyi Bank Rossiiskoi Federatsii, *Tekushchie tendentsii v denezhno-kreditnoi sfere*, vol. 8–9, statistiko-analiticheskie operativnye materialy, December 1993, p. 37.

convenient re-routing of soft credits to faltering enterprises. Rather than making specific budget allocations as under central planning, credits are extended via central bank discount loans to lower-tier banks which in turn are not forced to call in bad loans from enterprises. The familiar soft-budget constraint has not disappeared in the transitional phase—rather it has simply changed form.

Finally, the distinctions of political power have not yet been made clear in the Russian Federation. Thus when one uses a statement such as the "independence of the central bank from the government," as so many of the papers on central banking do, one must be careful to define exactly what or who the government consists of and from which body the central bank should define its independence. In most cases the concern is with independence from the fiscal decision maker so that monetization of the deficit can be avoided.

Thus, to determine the usefulness of the Russian central bank in suppressing inflation, we need to examine the motivation of the central banker and the environment in which he must work. We must investigate both the necessary conditions for controlling inflation—institutional independence of the central bank—and the sufficiency conditions for controlling inflation—a conservative or inflation-adverse central banker as head of an institutionally independent central bank.

Independence of the Central Bank of Russia

The methodology employed here to evaluate the independence of the Central Bank of Russia is a modification of that used in an ambitious study by Grilli, Masciandaro and Tabellini (1991). They divide measures of central bank independence for eighteen countries in the OECD into two categories: political independence and economic independence. The former measures the extent to which the central bank's governing board is politically independent of the government while the latter measures the constraints on the government's ability to borrow from the central bank or influence policy instruments.

To Grilli et al.'s two measures of independence we add other factors to allow for a fuller discussion of central bank behavior. Several other studies have suggested more qualitative measures such as the role the central bank sees for itself in forming social policy (Cukierman, Webb and Neyapti 1992) or, more specifically, seeking a full-employment goal (Bade and Parkin 1980; Burdekin and Willett 1991) and whether or not the central bank has an exchange rate objective (Burdekin and Willett 1991). We would add to this list the relationship of the central bank's governor to the government—e.g., is the position a cabinet post or not?

I divide the analysis of independence into *political* and *economic* as Grilli et al. have done and add the issues of social policy, exchange rate objectives and the nature of the governor's office. The categories of central bank independence are summarized in Table 9.3. Each of the categories will be discussed qualitatively. In this way this paper differs from the work of Cukierman, Webb and Neyapti (1992), Burdekin and Willett (1991), Grilli, Masciandaro and Tabellini (1991), and Bade and Parkin (1980), as well as most others, which attempts to find some quantitative relationship between their independence measures and inflation. The biggest source of disagreement among studies on central bank independence is over how to weight different factors. I avoid this problem by not weighing them, but by simply adding factors to flesh out the various categories. Given the short time the Russian central bank has been in existence and the fluidity of the underlying legislation, this qualitative approach seems preferable.

Political Independence of the Central Bank

Relationship of the Central Bank and the Government

There are three factors determining independence in the areas of monetary policy and board management. A central bank is more politically independent if there is no government approval of monetary policy, if there exists a statutory requirement that the central bank pursue monetary stability and if there are legal provisions that strengthen the central bank in conflicts with the government.

Government Approval of Monetary Policy. Neither the Law of the Central Bank of Russia nor its proposed amendments allow the central bank to make monetary policy without government approval. The Russian Republic law states that the "basic directions of monetary policy will be annually approved by the Supreme Soviet" (article 13, Law of the Central Bank of Russia). The proposed amendments are more direct: "The basic directions of monetary policy developed by the Central Bank of Russia in cooperation with the government of the Russian Federation and presented to the Supreme Soviet will be established by the following methods" (article 14, proposed amendments, *Delovoi mir,* July 2, 1993, p. 5).

The proposed amendments go even further in subordinating the Russian central bank to the government by requiring that monetary policy be developed "by the Central Bank of Russia in cooperation with the government." This clause was probably added by President Yeltsin and Finance Minister Fedorov in an attempt to gain more control over the central bank's actions.

Participation of the Government on the Board, and the Governor/ Government Relationship. There is nothing in the current legislation nor its proposed amendments which prohibits the participation of members of the

TABLE 9.3 Categories to Evaluate the Independence of the Central Bank of Russia

I. *Political Independence*
   1. Central Bank/Government Relationship
      a) Government approval of monetary policy.
      b) Participation of the government in the board.
      c) Relationship of governor to the government.
      d) Nature of special agreements between the government and the central bank.
   2. Central Bank Governing Board Appointments
      a) Appointment of the governor.
      b) Length of governor's term.
      c) Terms of board appointments.
      d) Length of board appointment.
   3. Constitutional Requirements
      a) Requirement that the central bank pursue monetary stability.
      b) Legal provisions that strengthen the bank in conflicts with the government.
   4. Other Objectives of the Central Bank: Is price stability the primary goal of the central bank?

II. *Economic Independence*
   5. Financing the Budget Deficit
      a) Does the government receive automatic credit?
      b) Does the government borrow at market rates?
      c) Is there a time limit on government borrowing?
      d) Is the amount the government borrows limited?
      e) Does the central bank participate in the primary market for public debt?
   6. Use of Monetary Instruments
      a) Setting of the discount rate.
      b) Supervision of the commercial banks.
      c) Exchange rate policy.

Notes and Sources: Most of these categories are derived from V. Grilli, D. Masciandaro and G. Tabellini (1991). Additional categories are from R. Burdekin and T. Willett (1991, category 6c), A. Cukierman, S. Webb and B. Neyapti (1992, category 4), and the author (category 2c and 2d). Cukierman, Webb and Neyapti (1992) have shown that in underdeveloped economies *the frequency of the change in the governor of the central bank* is one of the better proxies for central bank independence. However, to date there has been only one change-over in the two years that the Central Bank of Russia has existed and we cannot include this category in any meaningful way.

government on the board of directors of the central bank. In fact, the position of chairman of the central bank was given cabinet status in March 1993. This move seems to have been entirely political on Yeltsin's part, however. It seems as though Yeltsin thought that by making Gerashchenko a member of the cabinet he could then dismiss him. However, even if he were dismissed from the cabinet, this would not remove Gerashchenko from the governorship of the central bank since only the Duma has this authority.

It is not known if Gerashchenko even attended cabinet meetings. It is not likely, since it was necessary for the minister of finance, Boris Fedorov, and Gerashchenko to hold meetings over the 1993 IMF aid package (see below). Had Gerashchenko attended cabinet meetings, presumably he would have discussed the matter there. Nonetheless, a member of the government can, in theory, sit on the board of the central bank—notably as governor of the bank.

Nature of Special Agreements Between the Government and the Central Bank. Although not usually listed in the standard measures of central bank independence, special agreements between governments and central banks often give us insight into the informal connections between the two bodies.

At present there are two agreements in place between the central bank and the government of Russia. The first was a March 1993 agreement in which various deficit targets were set. The second, negotiated in May 1993, was an agreement negotiated with the IMF in order to obtain access to a new special transitional economies aid package of $3 billion.

Each agreement set money supply growth targets, deficit financing restrictions and inflation targets. The first of these measures is the most important since it defines the use of a policy instrument, whereas the remaining two measures are more or less policy targets.

The current agreement provides for the money supply to grow at a rate between 16–18 percent a month over 1993, the budget deficit to be set at a target level (not specified) and inflation to be in the single digits per month by the year's end. What is of special interest is why the Central Bank of Russia decided to take the IMF memorandum of May 1993 more seriously than the agreement negotiated before the referendum on April 25, 1993.

Prior to the IMF memorandum the Russian central bank was using its ability to issue credits to commercial banks and print money to fuel very rapid inflation. This inflation was in turn damaging the credibility of the Yeltsin reform efforts. Why did the central bank take the IMF memorandum more seriously than the March agreement? To answer this we need to look at political developments in this period.

When the Central Bank of Russia was first established, Yeltsin appointed Grigorii Matiukhin to be its head. Matiukhin was a supporter of Yeltsin's reform strategy, one important aspect of which was the gradual reduction of subsidies to state enterprises and a general slowing down of increases in the money supply. While Matiukhin was not terribly good at slowing down inflation, he was much more conservative than his successor Gerashchenko. For example, from January 1, 1992 to May 1992, Matiukhin's last five months in office, the money supply grew 85 percent. From June to October 1992, Gerashchenko's first five months in office, the money supply grew 171 percent (i.e., its growth rate doubled; see Table 9.2).

One of the reasons why Matiukhin was replaced was that he had allied himself with Yeltsin rather than the "industrialists" in the legislature (of whom the chairman of the Supreme Soviet, Ruslan Khasbulatov, was one). When Matiukhin seemed to be pursuing policies that would force state firms into bankruptcy, Khasbulatov exercised his legal right to dismiss the governor of the bank. In Matiukhin's place he put Gerashchenko whom he knew he could rely on to support his slower-paced policies.

Beginning in August of 1992 (two months after Gerashchenko took office) inflation began to rise after having fallen between June and July by 15 points. Assuming that there is a lag between increases in money and credit and inflation, Matiukhin brought the inflation rate down while Gerashchenko started it rising again. Inflation rose, as did the money supply, until February (from 12 percent between July and August 1992 to 32 percent between December 1992 and January 1993).[11]

In the first half of 1993 the political stature of the legislature began to decline and with it, some of Gerashchenko's power. The decline in the legislature's power can be seen in the referendum of April 25 in which the office of the president had much more at stake than the legislature. The first two questions of the referendum concerned the legitimacy of the presidency whereas the third questioned the legitimacy of only Yeltsin, not the office. (The questions were: Do you believe in the presidency? Do you approve of the government's (i.e., Yeltsin's) economic policies? Should there be new presidential elections?) Had Yeltsin not received a majority on the first and second questions, the whole structure of the government and its current reforms would have had to have been reconsidered.

The legislators had little at stake (the fourth question being: Should there be new legislative elections?). Had they not received a majority, members would have had to run for reelection, disastrous for some but not for the institution as a whole. When Yeltsin gained approval on the first three questions, the presidency greatly increased its stature vis-à-vis the legislature.

Perhaps realizing the waning of his power base and faced with inflationary pressures, Gerashchenko decided to take seriously the IMF memorandum which more or less reinforced the March agreement. The central bank promised to limit money supply (M2) growth to 16–18 percent a month over

1993—about 3 trillion rubles total—and agreed to distribute the credits equally between the government and the commercial banks.[12]

What is of interest to us here is that the Russian case seems to be distinct from other cases of central bank/government relations discussed by such studies on central bank independence as Grilli, Masciandaro and Tabellini (1991), Burdekin and Willett (1991) and Cukierman, Webb and Neyapti (1992). In an attempt to restore the credibility of its faltering reform effort, which was being seriously discredited by inflation, the Yeltsin government (not the central bank) imposed a strict monetary policy. Only after the Russian central bank lost political ground in the referendum (since Gerashchenko, its governor, had tied his fortunes to the legislature) was a fiscally conservative agreement taken seriously by the bank. *In other words, the government forced the hand of the central bank to undertake price stability, not vice-versa.*

Central Bank Governing Board Appointments

Appointment of the Governor and Length of the Governor's Term. An important indicator of political independence is the procedure for appointing the bank's governor. It is preferable that the governor (or chairman of the board) of the central bank not be appointed by the government, but rather by a board of representatives of the central bank, and that he or she be appointed for more than five years. The reason for the last is that most political terms are for four or five years. Some argue that it is not so much the length of the term that matters, but that the appointment of a governor should not fall in an election year.[13] However, five years seems to be a good benchmark.

The legislation and the reality in the Russian Federation are somewhat at odds with regard to the governor's appointment. The legislation governing the central bank and its proposed amendments declare that "the Governor of the Central Bank of Russia is appointed for a term of five years and can be dismissed from office by the Supreme Soviet" (article 36, Law of the Central Bank of Russia). The ambiguity results from the fact that there is no indication of what must occur for the Supreme Soviet to remove the governor from office. This presents a conflict between a five-year appointment and the possibility of dismissal. The proposed amendments to the law are equally vague with virtually no change in the wording.[14]

According to interviews with central bank officials the process for removal is not at all clear. For example, when asked why Grigorii Matiukhin, the former governor of the Central Bank of Russia, left office, Vladimir Smenkovski of the central bank stated, "there is not a well-established procedure for removal of a chairman. Probably he [Grigorii Matiukhin] decided himself to resign."

In fact, according to Grigorii Matiukhin, he was summoned back from

Tver, where he was working with a regional division of the central bank, by Ruslan Khasbulatov, the chairman of the Supreme Soviet.[15] Upon his return to Moscow, Matiukhin was told to submit his resignation because the central bank was not working well (*bank rabotaet plokho*) and that he should claim poor health in his resignation letter. Perhaps not to Smenkovski, but to Grigorii Matiukhin the procedure for removing the central bank's governor is clear: "Khasbulatov simply tells you to resign."[16]

The current confusion on the matter may actually have something to do with the timing of the original central bank legislation and the spirit in which the bank was established. The original legislation was as much a political document as an economic arrangement in that the establishment of a monetary authority separate from GOSBANK was an assertion of greater independence from the Union. All of this was part of Yeltsin's power struggle with Gorbachev and the Union government.[17] At the time Gorbachev was the closest thing the Soviet Union had to an executive branch of government and the Supreme Soviet of the Russian Soviet Federated Socialist Republic was the closest thing the Soviet Union had to a legislature (there were actually fifteen of these Soviets—one for each republic of which Russia's was the most important).

At the time the legislation establishing the Russian central bank was being written, Yeltsin was not president of Russia since that position did not yet exist. He launched his campaign for power from the position of chairman of the Supreme Soviet of the Russian Republic. In writing the central bank legislation, he made sure that he, in his position as head of the Supreme Soviet, would control the appointment of the governor of the Central Bank of Russia. In order to guarantee the autonomy of the position, the document made clear that other than for the appointments of the board of governors and the governor of the central bank, the Central Bank of Russia and the Supreme Soviet would not be responsible to one another.[18] This was necessary in order to distinguish it from the GOSBANK, and to a certain extent Yeltsin's economic policy advisors (Yavlinsky for one) were aware of the benefits of an independent central bank.

Now Yeltsin holds the presidency, Russia's chief executive position. The new legislature, the Duma, however, may not be any more cooperative on matters of monetary policy than was the Supreme Soviet when Ruslan Khasbulatov was its head. The new Duma has a substantial populist membership and is unlikely to make approval of Yeltsin's candidates for the bank's governor easy. The Duma council, like the Supreme Soviet before it, has considerable influence over who is appointed governor of the central bank, and they know that once he is in power the governor will enjoy some degree of independence from the executive branch of government.

Indeed, this was Yeltsin's plan in the first place, as is confirmed by his original appointment of Grigorii Matiukhin as governor of the central bank, whose policies through December 1991 were in stark contrast to the then governor of the GOSBANK, Gerashchenko. Matiukhin tried to slow down subsidies to state enterprises and move more rapidly toward positive real interest rates whereas Gerashchenko continues to this day to increase subsidies to industry and seems to have no intention of moving toward positive real interest rates. Yeltsin probably was not aware at the time that the governorship of the central bank could be used against him.

The new constitution was adopted in December 1993 by referendum, and it has not really cleared matters up. In the first place, the Central Bank of Russia's charter remains in effect. Dismissal of the governor of the central bank must be approved by the Duma; the president has the right to propose dismissal but only the Duma can confirm it. However, refusal to accept the president's proposal three times means that he, in this case Yeltsin, can dissolve the Duma. In these circumstances the struggle becomes highly politicized. The choice then is not over whether the central bank governor will run a conservative or liberal monetary policy, but rather whether Yeltsin and/or the members of the Duma want another election. Rather than making the status of the economy central to their choice of the central banker, all parties involved would place political considerations first.

Terms and Length of Board Appointments. The board of directors of the central bank is appointed by the Duma for the same term as the governor.[19] There are several ways in which this requirement weakens the bank; the most important is that the board is selected by the government rather than by the banking industry. The participation of the government means that board members who support or are indebted to a political faction are more likely to be appointed. Second, because the board's term is the same as that of the bank's governor, there may not be continuity in the administration of the central bank. Thus, both of these rules serve to undermine the independence of the central bank from government control. The constitution itself says nothing about the selection or powers of the board of governors.

Constitutional Requirements

Constitutional requirements refer to the constraints placed on the institution of the central bank and the powers granted it by its charter or establishing legislation. These requirements are distinct from those regulating governor or board appointments since they describe the type of institution the appointed board and chairman will operate.

Requirement That the Central Bank Pursue Monetary Stability. The bank's responsibilities for monetary stability are stated in article 5 of the Law of the Central Bank of Russia and article 8 of the proposed amendments. Among the central bank's basic tasks as stated in article 5 of the existing law, there is only one reference to any kind of monetary stability goal, namely to "insure the stability of the ruble."

The proposed amendments increase the importance of monetary stability. Article 8 states that the basic task of the central bank is "to insure the stability of the monetary system of the Russian Federation." Further in the same article it provides a mechanism to accomplish that goal, namely "to be the creditor of last resort for banks and other credit institutions." The "last resort" term is perhaps a bit premature since at present the central bank provides over half of all credits to the banking system. Nonetheless, the drafters of the proposed amendments were wise to move this requirement from article 14 of the Law of the Central Bank of Russia to be listed with the other fundamental tasks of the central bank in article 8. In this way they increased the perceived importance of this goal.

Legal Provisions That Strengthen the Central Bank in Conflicts with the Government. It is on the final point of provisions regarding legislative changes that the proposed amendments would make some important changes. The Law of the Central Bank of Russia explicitly states that the central bank has the right to appeal legislation damaging to its independence:

> The Bank of Russia is independent of the administrative and bureaucratic organs of government. The Bank of Russia will have the right to appeal to the State judiciary demanding that any laws passed by the State administrative agencies be repealed (made inactive) and the State judiciary will determine if these laws illegally interfere with the activities of the Bank of Russia. (Article 1, paragraph 3, Law of the Central Bank of Russia)

However, this right is not included in the proposed amendments, and this should be a cause for concern. In fact, article 1 of the proposed central bank legislation has been rewritten in a way which suggests that a new relationship between the bank and the government is desired by the authors of the new legislation. Although Yeltsin wrote both the original legislation and the proposed amendments, he wrote the former as the chairman of the Supreme Soviet and the latter as president of the Russian Federation, and his objectives in each case were not the same.

Other Objectives of the Central Bank

Generally, a central bank will have a number of subsidiary goals. The bank may have a mandate to solve financial crises, regulate banks, control inflation or regulate output. The role of the central bank is perceived differently in each country having one and is thus worth investigating.

Is Price Stability the Primary Goal of the Central Bank? The Central Bank of Russia does not have price stability as its only major goal nor does it have an inflation target to hit, as does, for example, the New Zealand central bank.[20] In fact, Russia is not that much different from the United States which, according to Cukierman, Webb and Neyapti (1992), has price stability as one goal but other, potentially conflicting goals such as employment targets.[21]

When Russian central bank officials were asked to rank the priorities of their policy objectives, their answers were often contradictory. However, generally speaking, the Russian central bank places the highest weight on hitting an employment target (currently maintaining the levels of overemployment). This conclusion was reached from statements made in interviews with Vladimir Smenkovski at the central bank, who repeatedly referred to the inadequate social safety net being constructed by the government and the central bank's responsibility to provide credits until the net was in place. "The Central Bank of Russia is pursuing not only monetary stability but also economic growth..." he stated. " Our society does not know all the facets of the unemployment problem.... We now maintain these [loss-making] firms as a social safety net. Economic growth is the main priority."

This presence of conflicting policy objectives makes clear the distinction between the necessary and sufficient conditions for real central bank independence. Even should the Russian central bank be made politically independent, if the bank and its governor see its role as something other than pursuing price stability, then the bank may contribute to both actual and expected inflation.

Economic Independence of the Central Bank of Russia

Financing the Budget Deficit

The economic independence of the central bank focuses mainly on the rules governing the central bank's credit extensions to the fiscal authority (government) and the type of reserve control it exercises. We will first look at the credit facilities of the bank. In order for economic independence to be established in this area, credit should not be automatically extended by the central bank to the government, it should be extended at market interest rates, and it should be temporary and limited in amount.

In these areas the central bank legally possesses some economic independence, although in practice this is questionable. Its establishing legislation states that the central bank has the right to extend credit to the ministry of finance but under the conditions that the term be no longer than six months and the amount cover only the difference between current income and expenditures. The phrase "the bank has the right to" implies that the extension of credit is not automatic upon the treasury's request (see article 17 of the Law of the Central Bank of Russia). There is nothing mentioned about these loans being made at market interest rates, but the article does limit the amount to current year differences in income and expenditures.

The proposed amendments instead state that the rules governing the central bank's financing of the government deficit will be governed by the law "On the State Internal Debt of the Russian Federation."

Does the Central Bank Participate in the Market for Primary Debt?
Next, a central bank is deemed more economically independent if it does not participate in primary markets for public debt. In the U.S. this is an important distinction. The Federal Reserve is a major participant in the market for *outstanding* treasury obligations but it does not participate in the primary issue of these obligations.

According to the agreement passed on May 6, 1993, between the finance ministry and the central bank on the sale and circulation of short-term government debt, the central bank will directly administer the primary market for government debt. The bank has named twenty-one primary dealers and has established a coupon yield equivalence formula for the new treasury bills.[22]

Again, it is difficult to hold the Russians to a western standard on this criteria. Usually it is seen as better that the central bank does not participate in the market for public debt.[23] However, it would be unreasonable to expect the Russians not to start the process via the central bank.

In a way they are using to their advantage some of the centrally planned economy's infrastructure, which had a well-connected payments system (to facilitate wage payments to the real sector) and distribution network through the old GOSBANK network which the Central Bank of Russia inherited. In fact, central bank officials referred to this when I asked them if they were worried about the bank's participation in the primary market for public debt. I think it a positive move that they are at least initiating the sale of government debt, albeit via the central bank.

The Use of Monetary Instruments

The next two elements of economic independence are the setting of the discount rate and supervision of commercial banks. If the discount rate is set by the central bank this implies more independence, and if the central bank is not solely responsible for commercial bank supervision it is deemed to be more economically independent also. This latter point relates to the need to separate the monetary authority from the commercial banks. Separation permits both agents to pursue independent goals and allows the central bank to formulate policy separate from its supervisory role.[24]

Setting the Discount Rate. Article 14 of the Law of the Central Bank of

Russia makes the central bank responsible for setting the discount rate. With this power the central bank defines the conditions for short-term loans. This responsibility is defined more clearly in the proposed amendments to article 14.

Supervision of the Commercial Banks. Supervision of the commercial banking system rests solely in the hands of the central bank. In chapter 6, "Regulation by the Central Bank of Russia of the Activities of the Banks," the regulations governing the relationship between the central bank and the commercial banks are established. The central bank's duties are further specified in chapter 7, "Supervision of Banking Activities," and no mention of an outside review body is made.

Exchange Rate Policy. Burdekin and Willett (1991) and Hochreiter and Tornquist (1990, cited in Burdekin and Willett 1991) both suggest that an exchange rate objective may not have much influence on central bank independence, but it can be an "important mechanism" enhancing the goal of price stability.[25] Burdekin and Willett note that the pegging of the Austrian schilling to the Deutsche mark since 1981 has produced a "hard-currency" policy that has "not only guided the course of monetary policy but also the actions of the unions and government."[26] An exchange rate peg, if it is too narrowly defined, tends to become the central bank's dominant policy objective and constrains its behavior so that it cannot meddle in or fine-tune other areas of the economy. In a sense, the maintenance of an exchange rate peg is a type of price-objective policy since the exchange rate is simply a relative price. To this extent, then, an exchange rate peg may enhance the price stability goal of the central bank and may bring it to the fore in the event of other competing objectives such as employment goals.

The existing central bank legislation does not specify the exchange rate rule to be followed as does, say, the Estonian central bank's charter which makes the Central Bank of Estonia an effective currency board, pegging the Estonian kroon at eight to the Deutsche mark. Both the existing central bank legislation in Russia and the proposed amendments talk about providing stability for the ruble. However, how this is to be achieved seems to be at the discretion of the central bank. When I asked central bank officials whether it was their intention to remain on a floating exchange rate regime, their response was: "The Central Bank of Russia will be involved to the extent of intervention since it will try to control some fluctuations in the exchange rate. But we will not strive for a single exchange rate."[27]

Consequently, the exchange rate targets set by the bank from month to month are not anchors of any kind and do nothing in terms of providing a mechanism for price stability. Moreover, exchange rate anchors seem to work more successfully for small, open economies, and it remains to be seen how the Russian economy will act when it becomes more integrated with the world economy (that is, will it accept world interest rates or influence world interest rates). For now such distinctions may be premature.

Conclusions

The type of monetary policy the Central Bank of Russia conducts at present seems dependent upon the political make-up of the Russian Duma. The Russian central bank is institutionally a separate entity, and this separation is guaranteed in its fundamental legislation (in much the same way and to a similar degree as it is for any other G-7 country). However, the governorship, a crucial element of actual central bank independence, is controlled by the Russian Duma—indeed, the fundamental legislation allows for the governor's dismissal (under no defined terms!) by the Duma. As long as the Duma has some fiscal policy decision-making responsibility, then the governor of the central bank can be dismissed at the Duma's will. This is exactly what happened to Matiukhin in June 1993 under the old legislature, and the new constitution similarly allows for the new governor's dismissal.

While the conditions for the appointment and dismissal of the governor specified in the current law do the most to seriously hamper the ability of the central bank to conduct monetary policy, the personality of the governor has much to do with the current problems. Until quite recently Gerashchenko had politicized the position of the governorship of the central bank, preferring to pursue social policy (i.e., near full-employment policy) in addition to price policy. As a result he has taken the central bank into areas in which it has little expertise and few good reasons to intervene.

Milton Friedman, back in 1968, said of the role of monetary policy: "[T]he monetary authority should guide itself by magnitudes that it can control, not by ones it cannot control."[28] What he meant by this was that the monetary authority will often try to accomplish an ultimate goal when all it can really do is influence an intermediate target. A central bank can only influence nominal quantities and only very few of them at that. The emphasis on price stability comes from the fact that much of the price instability in any economy results from an irresponsible stewardship over the money supply.

The source of this irresponsibility is more often than not an ill-conceived idea that the monetary authority can affect the level of output over the long term. It cannot. The governor of the Russian central bank must realize this and attempt to control only the variables over which he has direct control: cash and credit emission. He should realize that his best monetary policy is "to prevent money itself from being a source of economic disturbance."[29]

Notes

1. The author wishes to thank Bridgette Granville, Perry Patterson, Joel Hellman, Richard Burdekin, Tom Willett, Christopher Waller, David Ascheur, Michael Murray, Ben Slay, Peter Kennen and an anonymous referee, Vladimir Smenkovski of the Central Bank of Russia and Grigorii Matiukhin (former Chairman of the Central Bank of Russia). All views are those of the author and do not necessarily reflect those of the Kyrgyz Government, KPMG or USAID.
2. European Bank for Reconstruction and Development (1993:110).
3. Central Bank of Russia (1993:2).
4. *Moscow Times*, Feb. 4, 1994, p. 11.
5. *Moscow Times*, Feb. 4, 1994, p. 11.
6. See Kornai (1980) for a theoretical explanation of the soft-budget constraint.
7. See Rogoff (1985).
8. This may be the case in Russia today where political reform is generally associated with the erosion of savings and increasing poverty that is brought on by hyperinflation. The sooner the reform government can reduce hyperinflation, the sooner will people associate reform with increased wealth, not decreasing wealth.
9. Latsis (1994:4).
10. Central Bank of Russia (1993).
11. See Central Bank of Russia (1993).
12. Gerashchenko (1993:5).
13. See Waller (1992).
14. See article 37 of the proposed amendments in *Delovoi mir* July 2, 1993, p. 5.
15. This information is from an interview I had with Matiukhin on July 15, 1993.
16. See also G. G. Matiukhin, *Ia byl glavnym bankirom Rossii*, Moskva: Vyschaia shkola, 1993, p. 3.
17. See Lewarne (1991:2).
18. Article 2, Law of the Central Bank of Russia.
19. The Supreme Council of the old legislature is specified in the original legislation; this is apparently now interpreted to mean the Duma. See article 37, Law of the Central Bank of Russia and article 38 of the proposed amendments for specifics of the appointment process.
20. See *Reserve Bank of New Zealand Act 1989*, pp. 8–9 for the bank's inflation goals. For a brief summary, see Burdekin and Willett (1991:634).
21. Cukierman, Webb and Neyapti (1992:358, Table 1; 393, Table A-1).
22. See *O Vypuske Gosudarstvennykh Kratkosrochnykh Beskuponnykh Obligatsii*. Proposals to the Russian Supreme Soviet, February 8, 1993.
23. See Grilli et al. (1991).
24. While it is not included in the present analysis, the Estonian law on central banking (Zakon ESSR o bankakh) fails to separate the central bank from the commercial banks when it comes to the application of such monetary policy instruments as the setting of the discount rate. This is evident in article 7, section 4 which states that: "the Bank of Estonia will consult on the acceptance of decisions as stated in articles 18, 19, 28, 35 and 49 (each of which deal with discounting, reserve requirements and

general monetary policy) with the commercial banks and their union associations."
Fortunately none of the laws analyzed here have the problem so explicitly stated.
25. See Burdekin and Willett (1991:633).
26. Burdekin and Willett (1991:633–34).
27. Conversation with Vladimir Smenkovski at the Central Bank of Russia.
28. Friedman (1968:17).
29. Friedman (1968:17).

References

Bade, R., and M. Parkin. 1980. "Central Bank Laws and Monetary Policy." Mimeo. University of Western Ontario, Department of Economics, London, Ontario.

Burdekin, Richard. 1994. "Budget Deficits and Inflation: The Importance of Budget Controls for Monetary Stability," in Richard Sweeney, Clas Wihlborg and Thomas Willett, eds. *Establishing Monetary Stability in Emerging Market Economies*. Boulder, Colo.: Westview Press, forthcoming.

Burdekin, Richard C. K., and Thomas D. Willett. 1991. "Central Bank Reform: The Federal Reserve in International Perspective." *Public Budgeting and Financial Management* 3(3): 619–51.

Central Bank of Russia. 1993. *Tekushchie Tendentsii v Denezhno-kreditnoi Sfere*. Vypusk 2, April.

Cukierman A., S. Webb, B. Neyapti. 1992. "Measuring the Independence of Central Banks and Its Effect on Policy Outcomes." *The World Bank Economic Review* 6(3): 353–98.

European Bank for Reconstruction and Development. 1993. *Quarterly Economic Review*, April.

Friedman, M. 1968. "The Role of Monetary Policy." *The American Economic Review* 58(1): 1–17.

Gerashchenko, V. 1993. "Current Trends in Monetary Policy and the Development of the Banking System in Russia." Address (in Russian) to the Association of Russian Bankers in *Bizness, Banki i Birzi* 19(86): 5.

Grilli, V., D. Masciandaro, and G. Tabellini. 1991. "Political and Monetary Institutions and Public Financial Policies in the Industrial Countries." *Economic Policy*, October: 341–92.

Kornai, J. 1980. *Economics of Shortage*. Vol. 1. Amsterdam: North Holland.

Latsis, Otto. 1994. "Economy Was Stabilizing Before Government Reshuffle." *Delovoi Mir*, Feb. 14: 4.

Lewarne, S. 1993. "Legal Aspects of Monetary Policy in the Former Soviet Union." *Europe-Asia Studies* 45(2) March: 1–24.

―――. 1991. *Finansovyi vestnik*. Moscow, June: 2.

Matiukhin, G. G. 1993. *Ia Byl Glavnym Bankirom Rossii*. Moskva: Vyschaia Shkola.

Moscow Times. 1994. Various issues.

Rogoff, K. 1985. "Can International Monetary Policy Coordination Be Counterproductive?" *Journal of International Economics* 1: 199–217.

Waller C. 1992. "The Choice of a Conservative Central Banker in a Multisector Economy." *American Economic Review* 82(4) September: 1006–12.

10

Impediments to the Macroeconomic Stabilization of Russia

Manuel Hinds[1]

Introduction

The Parliamentary elections of December 1993 marked a watershed in the process of economic reforms in Russia. Although they reelected Boris Yeltsin as president, the voters seemed to reject the reform program his government had pursued since the formation of an independent Russian state in late 1991. In January 1994, as the new government was being formed, the threat of hyperinflation arose. However, contrary to all expectations, the new government reached an agreement with the International Monetary Fund, reduced the rate of monetary creation, increased interest rates and continued with the privatization program. As a result, the rate of inflation continued to fall and the real interest rate, as measured against the inflation rate of the previous twelve months, went from highly negative to highly positive for the first time since July 1992.

In the summer of 1994, inflation was at its lowest (200 percent) since July 1992 (228 percent). In 1992 it was expected that inflation would rapidly converge to international levels. However, as can be seen in Figure 10.1 below, the relatively low rates of inflation that summer were followed by an outburst of inflation that took two years to tame.

This surge of inflation was the direct consequence of the government's response to the "arrears crisis." As the rate of monetary creation subsided and real interest rates increased in the first half of 1992, there was a squeeze in the financial markets. State enterprises felt the pinch, and they responded by purchasing inputs on credit extended by other firms. The practice was

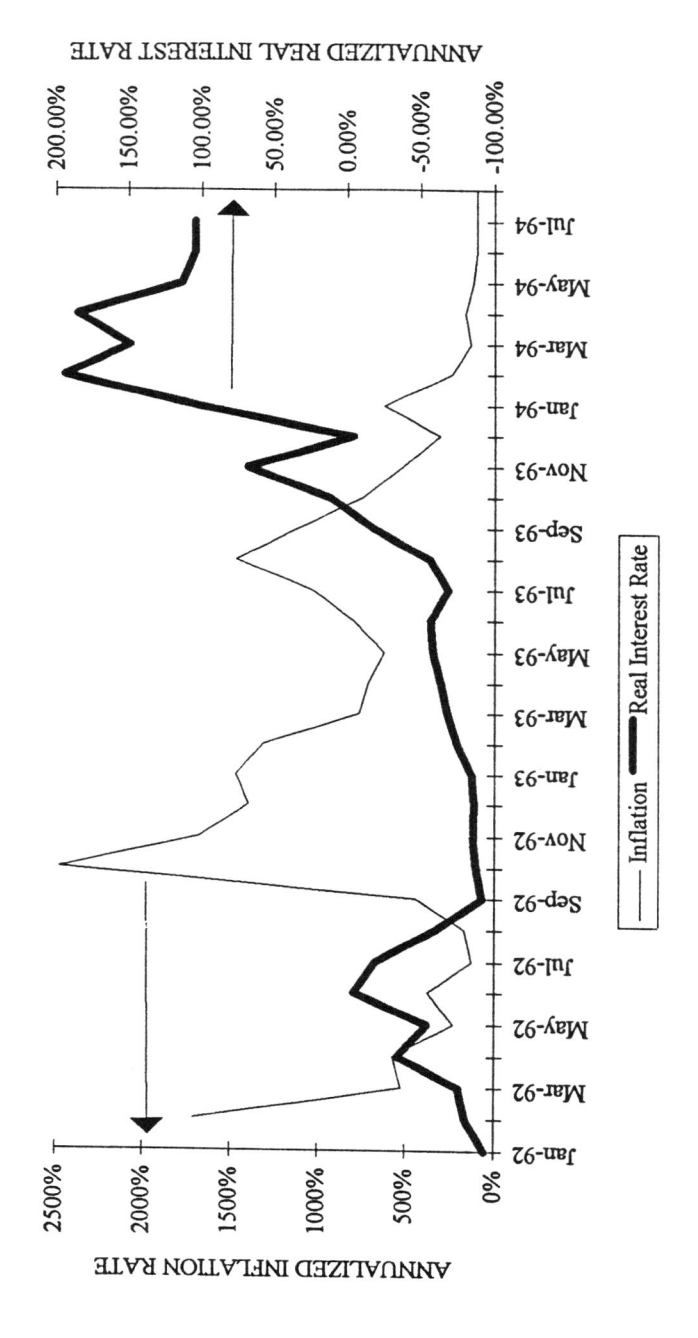

FIGURE 10.1 Inflation and Interest Rates in Russia, 1992-1994

widespread: in the first semester, inter-enterprise gross borrowing went up by approximately the same amount as the country's total industrial GDP. Unfortunately, the enterprises then started to fall into arrears among themselves: having bought inputs on credit, they produced goods at a loss, and were unable to repay their loans.

This process was terribly perverse because the enterprises were able to lend to each other only by depleting their inventories of raw materials, which could otherwise have been put to useful purposes. Instead, raw materials were turned into useless or overpriced final or intermediate goods. Thus, a steel mill transformed iron ore into very expensive and low-quality steel, which was then sold on credit to a factory to make tractors nobody wanted. Since the tractor company was not selling its output, or was selling it at a huge discount in the black market, it fell into arrears with the steel mill, which fell into arrears with the mining enterprises and all its other providers. In this process even the more efficient enterprises, or those that started the game with large inventories of raw materials, were threatened with insolvency because of their credit links to the most inefficient enterprises.

This game could not go on forever, because the stocks of raw materials and intermediate goods were not inexhaustible and enterprises needed cash to pay their own workers' salaries and the cash expenditures of the providers of essential inputs. Yet the managers did not worry much about this, because they knew they would have a strong bargaining position when they asked the central bank for more credit. Because of the financial contamination produced by the network of mutual arrears, when the crunch came most of the enterprises in the country—the inefficient and the less inefficient, the ones that had stocks of raw materials and those which did not—would be in danger of having to shut down if credit was not given.[2] The managers bet the central bank would oblige.

Eventually, their bet paid off. In early August, 1992, *The Washington Post* reported:

> MOSCOW, Aug. 4. The head of Russia's Central Bank said today that, in an attempt to bolster former Soviet industries that employ millions of workers, the bank will cancel debts of about 3 trillion rubles [US$20 billion] that the state-run enterprises owe each other.
>
> "Canceling debts has its disadvantages in that [it] encourages the weak as well as those which boosted their prices to artificially increase the money owed to them," acting bank chairman Viktor Gerashchenko said in an interview in the newspaper Izvestia. "But, what other alternative do we have?"[3]

As shown in Figure 10.1 above, the annualized monthly rate of inflation accelerated immediately after the bailout, from 228 percent in July to almost 2,600 percent in October. The exchange rate jumped from Rb. 161 to the dollar to Rb. 398 in the same period.

Ominously, just as the inflation rate is subsiding again, reports of a second arrears crisis are appearing in the Russian and Western press. This time the inter-enterprise debt problem is compounded by arrears to banks, to the government (taxes) and to workers (salaries). In addition, the government has fallen behind on payments for goods and services delivered to it by the enterprises. On August 23, 1994, the *Financial Times* carried a piece saying, among other things:

> Russia's growing inter-enterprise debt, estimated by officials to exceed Rbs.90,000 bn ($42 bn at the market rate), is at the top of the government's agenda and could determine the fate of Russia's fragile economic reforms... [A high officer of the government] said that the Russian government would assume responsibility for that portion of the debt owed by state ministries and would help pay workers salaries, which in some factories are more than four months late... The Russian rouble hit a new low of 2,190 roubles to the dollar in trading yesterday amid market fears that the government will continue to bail out insolvent enterprises.[4]

At the time this chapter was written in the summer of 1994, it was still not known how the government would respond. If it expands the rate of monetary creation to bail out all the debtors, Russia will experience another outburst of inflation, which could take years to tame. If it does not, and maintains monetary discipline, the economic adjustment would lead to many enterprise failures and a rapid increase in the rate of unemployment. This is an unfortunate consequence of the extremely rigid economic structure that Russia inherited from its socialistic past.

There are two aspects to Russia's production problems: flows and stocks. The root of the flows problem is that the set of incentives that led to the misallocation of resources under central planning is still largely in place. In consequence, economic resources are being misallocated as badly as they were in the past. The stock problem is that past misallocated flows congealed into an inadequate capital structure. When the old regime collapsed, Russia was left with substantial stocks of machinery and equipment that are obsolete, or badly designed, or simply in the wrong place, leaving its industries in an internationally uncompetitive position.

Impediments on the Real Side of the Economy

At the beginning of the reform process there were two main impediments to the functioning of market incentives on the real side of the economy:

1. price controls prevented the transmission of market signals, and
2. the principal-agent problems inherent in the communist system of ownership made market signals irrelevant. The weak state control over the enterprises during the last decades of central planning gave

way to open workers' and managers' control. The latter used the enterprises' assets for their own advantage, to the detriment of the interests of the enterprises themselves, by raising their own wages, doing business on the side with the enterprises' output, and by "spontaneously privatizing" the enterprises' assets.

The government moved to solve these problems by liberalizing prices early on and by staging the largest privatization program in history.

The problems, however, returned through the back door, as it were. Price liberalization has been countered by price controls set, openly or covertly, by local and provincial authorities, and even by the federal government. In addition, export quotas on essential inputs result in domestic prices of these goods being much lower than those prevailing in international markets. The privatization program has also failed to resolve the principal-agent problems. Ownership of the enterprises is spread so thinly, among millions of persons, that there are no owners who have enough of a stake in the companies to attempt to discipline the managers. The latter have continued to behave largely as they did when their enterprises were nominally owned by the state. The lack of market discipline has been worsened by the provision of large subsidies to insolvent enterprises. These subsidies are usually conveyed through loans to failing enterprises with the assumption either that these loans will not be repaid, or will be partially or fully repaid under negative real interest rates.

Impediments on the Financial System

Banking Under Central Planning

The financial system was not a major factor in the allocation of resources under the old regime. Under central planning, banks had four main functions:

1. to convey cash resources to enterprises and other economic units in accordance with the central plan;
2. to manage the payments system;
3. to mobilize resources from the population and convey them to the government; and
4. as central planning gave way to market incentives, the banks were supposed to impose financial discipline on the enterprises. Banks, however, could not do so, since in practice there was little difference between loans and direct transfers. Enterprises ignored repayments with impunity.

A handful of institutions were to implement these goals: the central bank, which issued the currency; one bank for each major sector in the economy; the foreign trade bank, which financed international trade and held a substantial portion of the country's foreign exchange assets and liabilities; and the savings bank. These were huge institutions in terms of number of branches and staff, but small in financial terms as a result of the demonetization of the economy.

The savings bank was (and in 1994 is still) the only institution authorized to accept deposits from the general population. It transferred all of these resources to the government, which transferred them to the other banks or to different government agencies. The other banks received deposits only from enterprises and government dependencies, mostly for payments purposes.

The Birth of the Russian Financial System

In the late 1980s, the traditional control problems of central planning had reached enormous proportions: the enterprises lied more than ever to the central planners regarding their production capacity and costs structure, did not comply with the plans based on those lies, and sold increasing portions of their output on the black market for their managers' private gain, as a means to acquire consumption goods for their employees, or both. The Gorbachev government attributed these problems to the centralization of the economy. Its solution was decentralization, but leaving in place all the incentives of the socialist economy.

As part of the general program to decentralize the economy, the government allowed the creation of what were called "private banks"— financial institutions owned by state-owned enterprises, alternatively called "zero" banks because they started from zero. The government's idea was to use these banks to impose financial discipline on the enterprises, which they would do by lending only to firms presenting a credible plan for profitable activities. These banks, however, carried within them a contradiction that would prevent their ever playing the role they were expected to play: the banks were controlled by the same enterprises they were expected to control.

Enterprises created these banks with great enthusiasm. By the end of 1990, there were already several hundred of them; in 1992, there were more than two thousand. The enterprises' enthusiasm was based on two very attractive features of the banks. First, by controlling a bank the enterprises had a guaranteed source of financing. Second, they could use the banks to evade government regulations intended to discipline them. Legally, enterprises could not pay bonuses or even salaries if they did not sell their output. This regulation was aimed at ending the common practice of producing unsalable goods and storing them for posterity. The banks, however, could be created in combination with "trading companies," enterprises that bought and sold products among the enterprises. These companies were invented by the government to solve the pervasive supply problems of the parent enterprises. Factories would have to stop production because they lacked raw materials that other enterprises had in excess, sometimes without any plan to use them. According to the reasoning that led to their creation, the trading companies would end this problem because their profits would come from promoting trade among the enterprises.

The enterprises thought otherwise. They created trading companies to buy their own output, financed by their own banks. In this way enterprises could claim they had sold their output, even if it was sitting in their warehouses. They could then proceed to pay salaries and bonuses, and to build houses and provide other facilities for the workers.

The fledgling "private banks" did not accumulate deposits directly from the public. The funds came from the large banks (which were initially directly owned by the central government of the Soviet Union and later by the Russian federal government), provincial governments, local authorities, and state-owned enterprises in a rather obscure form of joint ownership. These large banks obtained money from the central bank and the savings bank and lent the money to the private banks, which financed the trading companies, which purchased the output of the parent enterprises.

Private banks were created not only by industrial enterprises but also by research institutes, universities, scientific communities and other groups having trouble paying or increasing their salaries. Typically these banks were "owned" by groups including all these kinds of institutions.

The Current Situation

Over time the new banks diversified into different kinds of institutions. Some of them have continued to act as financial agents for their owner-customers, others have evolved into financial agencies for the spontaneous privatization activities of the managers of the institutions owning them, and some evolved into independent financial institutions whose aim is to maximize their own profits. All of these get their funds from the "interbank" market, which gets its liquidity from the savings bank, the central bank, the traditional banks and from enterprise deposits thrown back into the market by the receiving banks.

The large, old, traditional banks have also undergone a substantial transformation. During the institutional collapse of the last few years of Gorbachev's regime, local enterprises and government agencies took over the local branches of these banks, effectively dismantling them. The banks' central headquarters, however, continued to operate as before.

This arrangement was convenient for all parties involved because the federal government kept on using the traditional banks to convey resources to local enterprises, particularly after the bailout following the first arrears crisis. The amounts of credit conveyed through these banks have been huge, and have been focused on keeping afloat enterprises that are not generating enough cash to survive. This goal was not attained in many cases for the following reasons.

1. The payments system is extremely inefficient. In 1992, payments inside Moscow could take as long as two weeks, while payments between two other cities could take three months. At the high inflation rates prevailing in Russia, the real value of the transfers had diminished substantially by the time they reached their destination. Today, payment transfers between two cities take three to four weeks, and transfers within Moscow can be very fast. Still, for the enterprises outside the capital the delays are important.
2. The subsidized resources are frequently diverted into the interbank market where they are lent at much higher interest rates. The lenders of these resources can be branches of the traditional banks (before they deliver them), the receiving enterprises themselves, or the private banks where they deposit the resources. The profits may accrue to the managers of any of these institutions, or they may be shared among all of them. Many of the private banks thrive on this arbitrage.
3. In many cases the borrowers of the subsidized funds are the managers of the receiving enterprises who use the funds for their own "spontaneous privatization" activities, such as buying assets from their own or other enterprises, or deposit the resources abroad.

Subsidized credits are not the only mechanism by which resources are transferred to ailing enterprises. One of the most important among the others is state orders. These purchases by the government are frequently made not to supply the state, but to support enterprises. This practice was facilitated by the lack of a state budget (1994 was the first year since the breakup of the former Soviet Union that Russia has had a budget). Ministries were able to place orders with enterprises without telling the Ministry of Finance.

The subsidized funds, even though often diverted and intermediated in complex ways, plus the subsidies transferred to the enterprises through other means, allowed the enterprises to pay their bills during the second half of 1992 and for most of 1993. It was in early 1994, as the rate of credit creation diminished, that the second arrears crisis started to build up. The explosion of state orders strained the Ministry of Finance's ability to pay all its bills, and the government, too, fell into arrears. The government's finances have been further strained because many enterprises fail to pay their taxes (they are not necessarily unable to pay, but simply refusing to pay). Arrears to banks have already increased substantially. As reported by the *Financial Times* in the piece quoted above, some enterprises have even stopped paying wages. The enterprises are demanding a new bailout.

Thus, as long as the government remains willing to support inefficient enterprises, the deficit that is relevant in an analysis of Russia's monetary problems is much larger than the difference between the government's revenues and its expenditures. It also includes the losses that the enterprises are generating because, ultimately, these are financed by printing money. This combined deficit is huge, several orders of magnitude larger than the deficit as traditionally defined.

The Core Problem

In summary, the main problems in the financial sector, as evidenced by the recent increase in arrears by all kinds of borrowers in Russia, stem from rigidities in the domestic transformation process. Arrears are simply one way by which enterprises transfer to the rest of the economy the losses which they incur by not adjusting to the new economic environment. Other mechanisms serving the same purpose include direct subsidies; price controls imposed on goods and services used by the domestic enterprises; export quotas imposed on basic inputs, which reduce the domestic prices of these inputs to levels well below those prevailing in international markets; substantial delays in tax collection, which are leading to what is called "tax arrears" but amounts to effective subsidization; high rates of credit creation, which keeps enterprises liquid even when they are operating at a loss; and subsidies conveyed through negative real rates of interest. Whenever the volume of resources transferred to the enterprises through these mechanisms is reduced, enterprises begin to default on their debts.

Thus, the increase in arrears should not be seen as the problem in itself, but as a manifestation of a larger problem affecting the Russian economy throughout the transition period. As long as the enterprises remain unable or unwilling to increase their efficiency and adjust to the continuous shifts in relative prices associated with the operation of a market economy, they will continue to run losses. The burden of such losses will then be transferred to the rest of the economy through either higher rates of inflation and negative real interest rates, or higher arrears.

The problem of adjustment arises because Russia inherited a supply structure that was not, and still is not, consistent with the economic needs of the population. The lack of consistency is evident in two main dimensions. First, the enterprises produce many things that no one wants. Second, they produce many others at costs much higher than those prevailing in international markets. These excessive costs reduce the welfare of the population because Russia could get higher prices by exporting its raw materials than it gets by using them to manufacture unwanted or inefficiently produced goods. Industries that cannot survive paying international prices for their inputs actually *destroy* wealth—they subtract value from the raw materials and components they use. Unfortunately, many enterprises in Russia subtract value, and therefore cannot survive without transfers from the rest of the economy.

Thus the government urgently needs to accelerate the process of economic transformation: first, to eliminate the losses generated by production that destroys value; second, to allow the emergence and growth of competitive enterprises that can operate within a system of market-determined relative prices. The best way to accelerate this process is to increase the flexibility of the economy.

The main obstacle to accelerated change is the continued effort to keep inefficient enterprises operating, which crowds out the operation of efficient ones by preempting the use of resources by the latter. The more resources enterprises can get through means other than selling their output, the lower the amounts that are available in the market for the development of competitive enterprises and the weaker the incentives to change the structure of supply. Every rouble sunk into the losses of inefficient enterprises is subtracted from the savings available to invest in competitive firms.

The continued bailout of enterprises is, to a very large extent, a manifestation of the political power of the enterprise managers. As is widely recognized in Russia, many of the enterprises are not paying their debts, not because they do not have the resources, but because they want the government to pay their bills. Many Russian enterprises, or their managers, have sizable sums deposited abroad or in the interbank market. However, the government does not know which enterprises are faking their financial problems.

In fact, knowing which enterprises are faking and which are truly in financial trouble is immaterial to the solution of the basic problem: the refusal of producers to adjust to the new market conditions and its manifestation in the form of arrears. The transformation of the Russian economy will succeed only when enterprises are forced to generate funds to finance their operations and repay their loans from the market itself. Thus, the solution to the problem is for the government to refuse to fix it. The government should declare that debts between agents other than the government are private affairs, so that enterprises and banks should take good care to lend only to enterprises that can repay their loans and to collect these loans when due. The government, however, worries about the economic and political implications of a collapse of payments.

The Government's Concerns

The transition to a market economy is complicated because the stocks and flows aspects interact dynamically in a very complex way in the economic, social and political dimensions. Through these interactions the distribution of stocks tends to hinder the efficient allocation of the new flows, and the introduction of a capitalist system cannot immediately improve the situation. In many respects, the market seems to have worsened the situation, because it emphasizes all the inefficiencies in the original allocation of stocks and tends to eliminate them in the rash way markets work: by the elimination of the inefficient. This is anticipated by the government and other economic actors, and their responses are delaying the solution of the flow problem.

The factors complicating the process can be seen by assuming that the government is able to introduce market forces fully, solve the principal-agent problem in the enterprises, and impose financial discipline so that the Russian economy starts to work like a market economy. The new owners and their managers would start improving production methods, streamlining procedures, and reducing staffs. They would close down loss-making production and invest in profit-generating assets. Since the unproductive assets would likely be taken out of production before the new investments were in place, the physical production of the country as a whole would decline, both because of the streamlining of enterprises and because many enterprises would go bankrupt. This would have three main consequences: very high rates of unemployment, a deindustrialization of the country, and a financial crisis.

Production Declines

The decline in production is already occurring, mainly through the collapse of the centralized marketing system. Its arrangements ensured a market for many enterprises producing goods not in demand in the new economy, such as weapons, obsolete machinery and equipment, and poorly designed, low-quality consumption goods. Production has fallen by more than 25 percent in the country as a whole and has fallen even more in some industries.

Unemployment

One of the manifestations of the Russian economy's rigidity is the failure of unemployment to increase substantially in the face of a large decline in production. In a system where the enterprises still hope that the government will eventually bail them out to prevent political problems, having large staffs is valuable because they provide the threat with which to blackmail the government. This is true of both privatized and state-owned enterprises. Many of the state-owned enterprises are in addition effectively controlled by their workers.

But even if we assume that the principal-agent problems are solved and financial discipline imposed, declining production and improved efficiency in the surviving enterprises would cause an increase in unemployment, leading to a reduction of domestic demand. Since most Russian goods are not yet competitive in international markets, a reduction in domestic demand is likely to result in a reduction of *total* aggregate demand, which, in turn, would lead to a second reduction in production, this time affecting enterprises that would be viable if demand had not contracted. This would lead to another wave of unemployment.

This process would have a limit. However, given the extent of the inefficiencies of the existing enterprises, the number of people that would be left without employment given a full introduction of market forces could be staggering. The most current estimate of the extent of overstaffing in Russian enterprises is 30 percent, which means that this percentage of the industrial and agricultural labor force would be left unemployed if production were managed efficiently. This figure, however, assumes that all the enterprises would survive—it is the number of people who could be fired without reducing the volume of production. But many enterprises would go under because their products are not wanted, or because their costs are too high regardless of the size of their labor force, or because of the recession that would follow the drop in demand. Thus, unemployment figures over 30 percent would not be surprising, and they could reach much higher levels, conceivably over 50 percent.

It is important to emphasize that this problem could be alleviated, but not solved, by devaluation of the currency. This would raise the relative prices of manufactured tradable products, but also those of the raw materials used in their production. Thus, domestic producers would be squeezed and forced to operate as efficiently as foreign producers—while their capital equipment and the design of their products are not adapted to the international relative costs of the inputs. In general, Russian production is more intensive in its use of expensive raw materials than production in capitalist economies, particularly in energy. Given the efficiency of international markets, the margin left to compensate for this disadvantage would be very small.

Some automatic adjustment would come from the low price that the existing capital equipment would command in the Russian market as a result of its inefficiency. But in a market economy, the price of an asset just reflects its ability to generate profits, so that physical capital would be correctly priced, giving no advantage to its owners. Furthermore, the rental costs of capital—interest rates and the rate of expected profits—would be the same or higher than in the Western economies, because risks are higher in Russia. Thus, most of the adjustment would have to come from a reduction of labor costs. Many enterprises might be able to compensate for poor equipment by reducing their payrolls, but many could not.

One of the arguments in support of a policy of devaluations is that the country would not be able to import more than it could export. The high price of imports, the argument goes, will provide a natural barrier against foreign competition. However, if domestic consumers cannot afford imported goods as a result of a heavily depreciated currency, much less will they be able to afford domestic goods, because the cost of tradable raw materials—and in many cases the excessive amount of them used in production—would price them out of reach. The threat to Russian industry will come from the tradable inputs markets: raw materials, if priced at international prices, will become too expensive for the domestic producers.

The government knows this very well. This is the reason for the export quotas now imposed on essential inputs (such as oil and gas), which divert a substantial portion of these materials into the domestic market at prices much lower than those prevailing in international markets.

The Shift in the Composition of Production

As a result of these price increases, the composition of aggregate output must change dramatically. Since manufacturing is the sector hardest hit by the changes in relative prices and facing the least demand for its output, its share in GDP would decrease while that of primary production would go up. Massive investments would flow first toward the production of primary materials because these have an assured demand, not only internally but also in the world market. Thus, in the initial years of reform Russia would tend to become less industrialized than it is now and more dependent on the production of oil, gas, gold, diamonds and food. This pattern is already evident in foreign investment. But even if production in the primary sector increases, it cannot absorb enough labor in the initial years to offset the decline in the manufacturing workforce. In fact, the labor force may fall there too, even as production is increasing, because the primary sector is also overstaffed.

The incidence of unemployment would not be uniform. There are entire cities that depend on one enterprise for their living. If such an enterprise proved to be inviable, tens or even hundreds of thousands of people would find themselves unemployed, unable to move because there is no housing market in Russia, and because, even if there were, they would have no money to buy or rent a dwelling elsewhere.

Financial Crisis

Another effect of market forces would be to drastically reduce—sometimes to zero—the value of the liabilities incurred in financing the obsolete assets and their operation. This would turn the economic losses that were incurred when the assets were built into financial losses. Experience in other countries shows that it is difficult to decide who will absorb these losses. Foreign creditors can curtail the flow of international credits if they are not repaid, and having domestic depositors bear the losses can be politically very costly. In all recent cases, the claims of foreign creditors and domestic depositors on the valueless assets have been met by the government, that is to say, through taxes imposed on the people and enterprises that are leading the economic recovery. This is one of the most perverse ways in which the flow and stock effects interact with each other.

The Effects on the Flows

The protection of the domestic depositors is likely to prove a light burden on the government because high negative real rates of interest have effectively wiped out the real value of the savings bank deposits. But even if this problem is eliminated, the government must still satisfy foreign creditors and care for displaced workers. The government will have to tax the efficient to subsidize the inefficient—it cannot allow the unemployed to starve to death. In the most transparent form of intervention, the government would tax the productive part of the population to subsidize the consumption of the unemployed. The amount of taxation the government would have to impose to subsidize the unemployed could be very high and would reduce the resources available for the productive part of the population to invest in generating growth. This is true in all countries with a social security system, but the magnitudes make a difference.

Conclusion

Thus, the following are the main problems preventing the financial system from becoming an efficient allocator of resources.

1. The enterprises suffer from acute principal-agent problems which lead them to misallocate resources in a wholesale manner.
2. A substantial portion of the banks are not independent in their credit decisions because they are controlled by their borrowers. This would continue to be a problem even if the principal-agent problem in the enterprises was solved.
3. The government's motivation to improve the allocation of the flow of resources and its political ability to make the necessary changes are weakened by the serious social problems that would follow.
4. As long as a credible solution to these social problems is not at hand the government will hesitate to carry out the most fundamental reforms and will be tempted to use the financial system as a substitute for a proper social security system—which is what a good portion of it is now... and a very expensive one.

Notes

1. An earlier version of this paper was presented at the International Symposium of Economic Modeling at the University of Göteborg in 1992.

2. See Hinds, *Issues in the Introduction of Market Forces in Eastern European Socialist Economies,* March 1990, EMENA Technical Papers, The World Bank, for an analysis of the havoc that the lack of owners causes to stabilization programs through the inter-enterprise credits and other mechanisms.

3. Eleanor Randolph, the *Washington Post*, August 5, 1992, p. A28.

4. Chrystia Freeland and Agencies in Moscow in the *Financial Times*, August 23, 1994.

11

The Collapse of the Ruble Zone, 1991-93

King Banaian and Eugenue Zhukov[1]

The Commonwealth of Independent States that succeeded the former Soviet Union inherited from it a monetary system that had a single source of cash emissions, the Central Bank of Russia, and a single common currency, the Soviet ruble, and a multitude of other banks extending credit to state enterprises of all sorts. Almost immediately this system came under pressure. Besides wanting separate currencies as symbols of national independence, many of the new republics found practical problems in relying on the Russian central bank as their source of base money. The Russian government and the Russian central bank in turn found it difficult to control Russia's own cash emissions when credits could be issued by any of the other republics' banks.

The result of this situation was very high inflation in the former Soviet states. Except for Estonia, which left the ruble zone before 1992, these countries saw an average tenfold rise in prices. Obviously such rapid inflation placed strains on the operation of the ruble currency zone. When payments between member countries were delayed, as they often were, the value of receipts fell. Periodic cutoffs of gas deliveries by Russia and the Central Asian nations to the other republics for non-payment (or delayed payment) were common. In 1992 and 1993, the stresses inherent in the institutional structure of the ruble zone led to its destruction.

This chapter discusses the events that led up to and immediately followed the dissolution of the ruble zone. Since its breakup, the formation of smaller currency blocs has been contemplated by several of the commonwealth states. Russia and Belarus may form a zone of their own; a customs union in Central Asia may yet lead to a unified currency there.

TABLE 11.1 Inflation Rates in the Commonwealth of Independent States, 1992

Armenia	829%
Azerbaijan	1174%
Belarus	1116%
Estonia	19%
Kazakhstan	799%
Kyrgyzstan	1487%
Latvia	2655%
Lithuania	1850%
Moldova	1276%
Russia	1314%
Turkmenistan	1799%
Ukraine	1213%
Uzbekistan	698%

Source: OECD. Data on Tajikstan not available.

With the adoption of new currencies, each republic faced the necessity of forming a central bank. Some banks were formed hurriedly in response to the disintegration of the ruble zone; others appear to have been carefully planned well in advance. All have developed new relationships with commercial banks and the successor republics' governments.[2]

The issues involved in issuing new currencies in the former Soviet Union are discussed here in three sections. We first describe the factors motivating a decision to remain in or exit from a currency zone.[3] Using an optimal currency areas approach, we conclude that the collapse of the ruble zone was predictable. While many of the former Soviet republics were satisfied with the arrangements of the ruble zone, Russia was not. Russia was also willing to sacrifice the short-term political benefits from cooperation in order to gain the arrangements it preferred.

Much of the trouble that followed the creation of the Commonwealth of Independent States (CIS) stemmed from the monobank financial system inherited from the old Soviet banking system, described in the second section. Russia had little choice but to accept the lack of control it had over the issue of ruble credits by the other republics' state banks. We next describe the events of 1993, when the ruble zone finally collapsed. We conclude with an appraisal of the inherent difficulties faced by the republics in adopting fully independent currencies.

Currency Zones in Theory and Practice

A currency zone can only function properly with a single monetary authority. If two or more central banks co-exist, each can capture the full benefits of issuing currency (for example, by monetizing social expenditures) that make the government popular, while imposing some of the costs (i.e., inflation) on other members of the currency zone. That in a sense was the problem with the old ruble zone. Although only the Central Bank of Russia could issue household money, any of the republics' state banks could issue non-cash credits to state enterprises,[4] and each republic had an incentive to inflate the money supply. Each enterprise in turn had incentives to convert non-cash rubles into currency to buy inputs. The result was excessive inflation.[5]

Interest in currency zones has increased recently with the discussion of a single European currency, and application of this literature to the former Soviet Union has been widespread.[6] One sharp difference between these two cases is their starting points: the former Soviet states began by sharing a single currency and had to decide how the republics' new central banks would use it; the European Community already had independent currencies in place and had to negotiate a treaty to subsume them. Since there are significant transaction costs in each setting, it is reasonable to expect the status quo to hold. The appearance of new currencies in the former Soviet states would suggest, therefore, that the cost of introducing new currencies was less than that of negotiating a treaty to continue common use of the ruble.

The traditional approach to optimal currency areas focuses on elements of a macroeconomy that are likely to influence or be affected by movements in exchange rates. If the exchange rate can be an effective instrument in stabilizing output, countries will be better off introducing independent currencies. Nominal wage rigidities serve as an argument against a common currency, since changes in the exchange rate can help equilibrate the real wage. A common pattern of shocks among potential zone members, however, makes exchange rate changes less effective in stabilizing output and reduces the desirability of flexible exchange rates.

Such criteria lead Gros (1991) to conclude that the ruble currency zone was optimal. Labor, based on the Soviet experience, was quite mobile across the commonwealth states, and these countries have historically had extremely large trade flows with each other. Goldberg, Ickes and Ryterman (1994) cite anecdotal evidence of large wage variations within Russia; since this is accomplished without a North Caucasus ruble and a Kamchatka ruble, there is no need to have independent currencies on these grounds. However, most of the industrial base of the former Soviet Union lies west of the Urals while the agricultural and energy sectors lie to the south and east; a demand shock is likely to affect the Baltics and Central Asia differently. Last, Vavilov and

Vjugin (1993) show that while trade between the republics has historically accounted for more than 80 percent of total trade, the breakup of the Soviet Union is likely to reduce trade flows to 20–30 percent of total trade in the newly independent republics.

Based on the traditional criteria, the former Soviet Union appears not to have been an optimal currency area. Goldberg, Ickes and Ryterman (1994), however, argue that in the former Soviet Union the traditional criteria for an optimal currency zone "are irrelevant since *the exchange rate will not be able to effectively perform the task of short-run stabilization to which it is assigned*" (p. 295, emphasis in original). The other republics still initially benefited from membership in the ruble zone in order to obtain transfers from Russia. Russia made it clear as early as 1991 that countries leaving the ruble zone would be charged world prices for energy and other goods. Tarr (1994) shows that the effect of these subsidies was to provide large transfers to the western commonwealth states, particularly Ukraine and Belarus. Only the Central Asian republics appear to have been harmed by these subsidies.[7]

Yet the timing of the introduction of new currencies, as we shall see, goes against the argument that prospective subsidies held the ruble zone together: new currencies were issued first in the Baltics and Ukraine. As we discuss below, the three largest energy producers of the former Soviet Union—Turkmenistan, Kazakhstan, and Azerbaijan—were among the last to leave the ruble zone. Goldberg et al. (1994:320) ask themselves, "Why...is our analysis of the costs and benefits of independent currencies yielding opposite predictions from events for some countries?" They reply that introduction of a new currency is in part a political signal that other reforms are to be undertaken, and that "countries most likely to leave the ruble zone are those that seek a reform path that is more progressive than that of Russia" (p. 321). They point to Estonia and Ukraine as examples. However, Ukraine's recent slide towards hyperinflation, and the indecision of its Parliament, hardly appear to reflect a search for a more progressive reform path. Likewise, Kyrgyzstan cannot be viewed as undergoing a more reform-oriented transition, and it left the ruble zone before Russia moved to dissolve it.

While we argue that the traditional criteria give an incomplete answer to the question of a currency zone, we also think that Goldberg et al.'s analysis of the ruble zone focuses too much upon the other members of the commonwealth and too little upon Russia.[8] The set of implicit transfers through selective credits and subsidized pricing of energy was not negotiated in a treaty that was costly to break. Repeatedly, Russia would use the threat of charging world energy prices to induce concessions from the other commonwealth states. Russia, like the rest of the former Soviet Union, faces large budget deficits and has an inefficient system of taxation. In its search for additional revenue it could be expected to attempt to reduce subsidies to the other republics. This lowered the benefit of remaining in the ruble zone for the others, and a few countries exited. But in our final analysis, the events leading to the collapse of the ruble zone were engineered by Russia itself.

The decision to leave the ruble zone was apparently influenced by the size of the transfers to a republic from the Central Bank of Russia. Table 11.2 lists the dates on which the zone's member countries adopted either an independent currency, such as the Azerbaijan manat, or coupons, such as the Ukrainian karbovonets, and the size of transfers from the Central Bank of Russia to the republics in 1993. Those countries that indicated from the outset that they did not wish to join the Commonwealth of Independent States (e.g., the Baltic states) received only small amounts of financial aid from Russia. Many of these transfers to the commonwealth's members came in the form of currency transferred from the Russian central bank to the republics' central banks. The last column shows financial transfers with these currency transfers removed. It makes little difference however; as shown by the significant correlations at the bottom of Table 11.2, those countries most dependent on transfers from Russia were the slowest to exit the ruble zone.

TABLE 11.2 Financial Flows from Russia and the Timing of the Introduction of National Currencies in the Former Soviet Union

Country	Date of Introduction[a]	Russian financing as share of GDP	Financing net of currency transfers
1. Belarus	5/25/92	10.7%	7.2%
2. Estonia	6/20/92	4.0%	4.0%
3. Latvia	7/20/92	1.0%	1.0%
4. Lithuania	10/01/92	3.2%	3.2%
5. Ukraine	11/12/92	21.7%	21.7%
6. Kyrgyzstan	5/10/93	22.9%	14.5%
7. Moldova	7/27/93	11.3%	7.5%
8. Georgia	8/02/93	51.5%	36.1%
9. Azerbaijan	8/20/93	25.8%	17.4%
10. Turkmenistan	11/01/93	53.3%	34.4%
11. Kazakhstan	11/15/93	25.5%	16.7%
12. Uzbekistan	11/15/93	69.9%	44.2%
13. Armenia	11/22/93	49.0%	28.6%
14. Tajikstan	still in zone	90.7%	58.7%

Rank correlation coefficients:
   Including currency transfers   0.84
   Excluding currency transfers   0.80

[a] Date is for either introduction of coupons or final currency.
Source: World Bank and author calculations.

The Remnants of the Soviet Monobank System

The old Soviet system created two types of money: currency, which was used largely to pay wages and by consumers to buy goods (if available), and credit, which consisted of accounts of transactions between enterprises. Since nearly all enterprises were state owned, these paper claims were often offsetting—the state largely owed the money to itself. Excessive currency issue was not expressed as inflation since prices were controlled; it was more often expressed as a shortage of goods and the accumulation of savings by consumers who found nothing to buy.[9]

When the Soviet Union gave way to the Commonwealth of Independent States, most of the new republics allowed the establishment of private enterprises but did not immediately privatize their state enterprises. Most of these firms experienced large increases in their costs as the prices of raw materials imported from other republics were driven up by bids from other enterprises and Western firms. The best employees often left to work for themselves, reducing productivity at the state enterprises. The state enterprises were able to stay afloat largely by borrowing from the former state banks (Promstroibank, Agroprombank, Sberbank). In 1992 these banks loaned Rb 4.6 trillion (or 31 percent of GDP) to state enterprises. The balance of lending to enterprises was largely from the government deficit and the state pension fund. While it was popular to blame the "near abroad" within Russia, Figure 11.1 shows only 20 percent of the monetary expansion by the Central Bank of

FIGURE 11.1 The Composition of Credits Issued by the Central Bank of Russia, May 1992

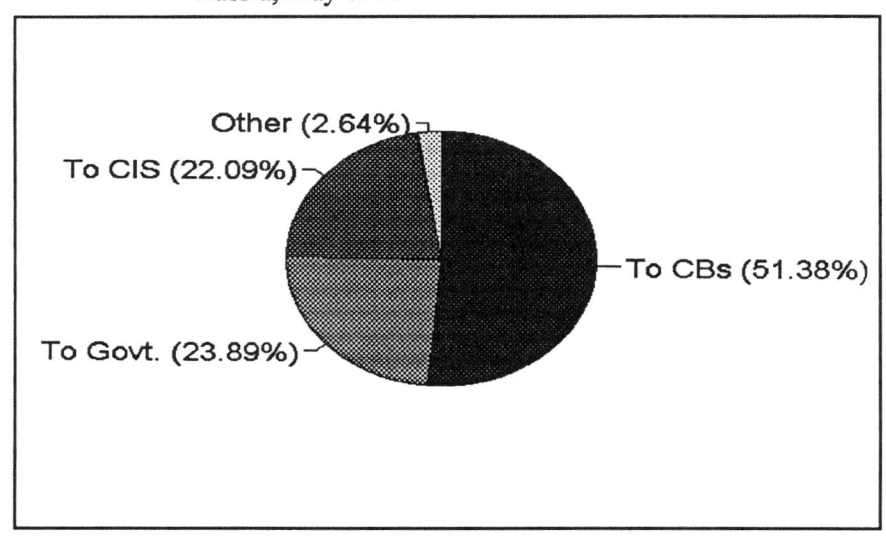

- Other (2.64%)
- To CIS (22.09%)
- To Govt. (23.89%)
- To CBs (51.38%)

Russia went to other commonwealth countries. Most of the growth in lending to the other commonwealth states occurred in mid-1993 as the Russian central bank created and converted lending to a system of correspondent accounts.

How were these loans or subsidies to be financed? In a country with an independent currency they could be financed by issuing currency. However, the other republics in the ruble zone had ceded that right to Russia. Consequently, the Central Bank of Russia created correspondent accounts for the other republics on July 1, 1992. This was done in part to alleviate interenterprise arrears between state-owned firms in different republics in the commonwealth. This had the additional effect, however, of functionally separating the republics' non-cash rubles from non-cash Russian rubles. Conversion of rubles for these accounts would occur at a 1:1 rate up to some set limit, but above this limit non-Russian non-cash rubles would be discounted. The Central Bank of Russia would post rates of conversion between Russian non-cash rubles and other commonwealth countries' non-cash rubles. So in some sense the republics had their own currencies as early as July 1992. However, the countries within the ruble zone continued to rely on Soviet (pre-1992) and Russian rubles for cash transactions. In order to issue currency, the other republics' central banks had to acquire the funds from the Russian central bank. These credits could then be converted into rubles in any other republic. Since the level of inter-republic trade was so high, the expansion of credit by any republic in the ruble zone would be felt in the other ruble-using republics.

Russian policy towards the ruble zone was guided by an attempt to establish the Central Bank of Russia as the sole issuer of both types of money: cash and credit. This would secure for Russia most of the benefits that arise from issuing currency. There were two issues of contention:

1. How would the benefits of issuing currency be divided among the member states of the ruble zone?
2. How would states leave the ruble zone?

The first issue is contentious but in theory easy to resolve. There would be a mechanism to periodically issue currency to each member of the ruble zone in a manner that would maintain the loyalty of the rest of the commonwealth. Surprisingly, in discussions of the ruble zone there has been little debate about this question.[10]

The second question was much harder. The treaty of September 1992 specified that states had to pre-announce a decision to leave the ruble zone and specified how multilateral trade balances were to be settled. It did not settle, however, how the currency switch would be conducted. It did not require that old rubles be returned to the Central Bank of Russia when a new currency was introduced. The agreement was more concerned with the narrow issue of settling trade balances rather than dealing with control of the money stock. Subsequent events in 1993 demonstrated the error of not settling these broader issues.

The Collapse of the Ruble Zone

Foreign opinion of the ruble zone was mixed. The United States and the International Monetary Fund initially supported it, whereas the European Bank for Reconstruction and Development advised against attempting to maintain the ruble zone, owing to the lack of coordinated currency and budget policies. The European Bank felt the republics would be better served by independent currencies.

In March 1993 reports from Bishkek stated that Kyrgyzstan was awaiting delivery from London of new bank notes for introducing its own currency. Kyrgyz officials gave assurances that these were to be introduced only upon collapse of the ruble zone. Still, according to Radio Free Europe, "[Kyrgyz president] Akaev has been a supporter of the ruble zone in the CIS states, not least because the international financial organizations that are trying to help Kyrgyzstan overcome the collapse of its economy have generally discouraged the introduction of a national currency."[11]

Other international organizations eventually came to the European Bank's view. On May 3, 1993, Kyrgyzstan opted to leave the ruble zone, encouraged by an IMF stabilization package that eventually totaled $62 million and by a $60 million development loan from the World Bank. It gave no warning to Russia or its other trading partners before doing so. This step created certain problems within the ruble zone. Countries within the zone settled and financed their trade balances in rubles and had a unified exchange rate against the hard currencies. Other commonwealth countries settled and financed trade in hard currencies, and the exchange rates between them were determined by cross-reference to hard currencies. When a country left the ruble zone, it typically set an exchange rate below the current ruble rate in hard currencies. The difference in rates thus caused a loss to its trading partners in the ruble zone, if it was allowed to settle at the new, lower exchange rate. The notification period was to allow the countries to agree on some amount in a hard currency that would settle the outstanding balance. The Kyrgyz, by making a rapid departure, increased their leverage in negotiations over this settlement, and the other countries, particularly Uzbekistan, felt betrayed. In reaction, Uzbekistan cut gas supplies to Kyrgyzstan until a special agreement was signed to settle bilateral trade accounts.

Another consequence of withdrawal from the ruble zone is that rubles in the exiting country will be transferred to neighboring countries still in the ruble zone. Ideally, any rubles swapped by the Kyrgyzstan National Bank for the new som should have been returned to the Central Bank of Russia, but again no such arrangement was made. Between May 6 and May 20 the ruble lost over 15 percent of its value against the dollar as rubles flowed back into Russia. The effect on other countries was even more severe. Both in Tashkent, Uzbekistan, and Alma-Ata, Kazakhstan, the ruble traded at about 20 percent less than it did in Moscow. It became obvious to others in the ruble zone that the game played by Kyrgyzstan could be played again and again. Azerbaijan announced on June 15 that it would introduce the manat by the end of the month. Only the overthrow of the Elchibey government by Geydar Aliev prevented this from happening.

Others in the commonwealth, however, still wished to remain in a currency zone. On May 14, at a commonwealth summit to discuss the exit of Kyrgyzstan from the ruble zone, President Nazerbaev of Kazakhstan revealed that his country had been in confidential talks with Belarus and Russia to form a new union.[12] But plans for this prospective union soon fell apart. The issue once again was the settlement of debts between these two countries. According to the Kazakh prime minister, Sergei Tereshchenko, Russia insisted that the trade deficit be transformed into sovereign debt and denominated in a hard currency. This demand apparently caught the Kazakhs by surprise. Tereshchenko claimed that Russia's tough stance in the negotiations was intended to push Kazakhstan out of the ruble zone and that Russian negotiators even explicitly suggested that it introduce its own currency. The Russian representative, Deputy Prime Minister Alexander Shokhin, said in reply that Kazakhstan had threatened to halt deliveries of grain, coal and iron ore if an acceptable settlement could not be reached.[13]

Reaction in Alma-Ata was swift. The vice president of Kazakhstan called for macroeconomic shock therapy along the lines of Poland, but noted in the same speech that his country was being forced from the ruble zone. Uzbekistan sympathized with Kazakhstan. The Uzbek government finally had its new currency, the sum, printed. Both countries joined the other Central Asian republics and Azerbaijan in signing a treaty with Turkey which called for an economic union (the Economic Cooperation Organization). This last act was sharply criticized by Shokhin, who stated that these countries must decide whether to orient themselves towards Moscow or Istanbul. "If our friends in the CIS, in their search for a better life, are looking towards the south, then they will have to choose between integration with Russia or with their southern neighbors."[14]

Other signs of Russian discontent emerged. A telegram sent from Moscow to the Belarussian National Bank on June 15 set down harsh conditions for Belarus to continue to receive rubles. The conditions included establishing the ruble as the only legal currency in Belarus,[15] giving the Russian central bank the power to regulate credit and cash, changing Belarus's banking and hard currency laws to match Russia's, and granting Russia control over the implementation of agreements. This naturally raised the question of sovereignty among Belarus's government. Western leaders advised Belarus to introduce the thaler, a permanent national currency, without further delay. Belarussian prime minister Vyacheslau Kebich went to Moscow to work out terms for continued participation in the ruble zone. Discussion at this time also revolved around debts owed by Belarus to Russia for natural gas.

In short, as 1993 progressed the Russians began to set much harsher conditions for continued membership in the ruble zone. They were demanding either agreement on pursuing a common monetary policy or for member countries to leave the ruble zone. Russia's main lever to push the republics towards the latter choice was interenterprise debts: Russia could provoke action by insisting that debts be converted into sovereign debt denominated in hard currency. With both Kazakhstan and Belarus, it was using that lever.

In the midst of these negotiations, the Central Bank of Russia on July 6 ordered all banks to begin conducting transactions in new, 1993-issue Russian rubles. At that time about Rb 4.7 trillion was in circulation, of which the government estimated that Rb 3.25 trillion were new Russian rubles. By the time of the cancellation order three weeks later, only Rb 250 billion (about 4 percent of circulation by then) in old rubles remained. But the other countries in the commonwealth were not informed of the decision to cancel the old rubles. Both Uzbekistan and Kazakhstan reported on July 10 that they had experienced a shortage of the new rubles. According to one report in *Commersant*, the republics quickly realized what was in the air and sent requests for Rb 2 trillion in cash, with the hope that the Central Bank of Russia would have to ship some of this money in new rubles.[16] When rumors spread that the Russian central bank's employees had been asked to work on Saturday, July 17, even individuals in Moscow knew enough to trade old rubles for hard currency.

The ruble swap effected one week later struck the republics the hardest. Since they could only settle accounts with Russian firms in the new rubles, the other republics had to decide to either introduce their own currencies or enter into agreements with Russia to form a new ruble zone under Russia's terms: convert technical debts to sovereign debt and relinquish the right to issue their own currencies.

Four countries chose to leave the zone at once. Georgia and Azerbaijan quickly announced their intentions to introduce the lari and the manat, respectively. By September 1 the Russian ruble was foreign currency in both countries. Armenian finance minister Levon Barkhudarian condemned the action, saying "The decision...virtually means the introduction of a new Russian currency...It is a direct violation of all previous agreements on currencies" (*Reuter*, July 25, 1993). The move in essence forced all republics out of the ruble zone; they would have to seek re-admission.

Moldova's National Bank declared all ruble accounts in local banks national property starting July 1, 1993. Payments with other commonwealth countries were made through special correspondent accounts opened in Moldova's national bank. By doing that, in preparation for a full-fledged national currency, Moldova wanted to avoid mistakes made by Kyrgyzstan, which introduced its som currency without proper preparations, disrupting settlements with neighboring Kazakhstan, Uzbekistan and Russia. In consultation with their trade partners, including Russia, the authorities decided to formally introduce the leu on November 29, 1993. Reflecting the trade deficit and high inflation, the Moldovan ruble depreciated steadily against the U.S. dollar and stood at Mrub 2,500 per US$ on average in October compared to about Mrub 1,700 per US$ in August. Against the Russian ruble it fell from 1 to 1 in July to almost 1 to 3 in November.

The remaining governments decided to keep the old ruble with the hope that Russia would honor its commitments by providing 1993 rubles. This encouraged the inflow of old rubles from republics that were leaving the ruble zone. According to one report, Georgian citizens, whose own country had abandoned the ruble, were offering rubles at any price for hard currency.[17] The old ruble began to sell at a 25–30 percent discount versus the new ruble, as Soviet rubles began to flow in from Russia and elsewhere.

Kazakhstan and Uzbekistan demanded a commonwealth summit, deriding the other republics for "pursuing selfish, isolated policies."[18] Russian central bank chairman Viktor Gerashchenko meanwhile said that the currency swap had compelled commonwealth countries to opt in or out of the ruble zone. Said his deputy Alexander Khadruyev, "It will go down into history some day that on (July) 26 we introduced a national currency.... This shows we have thought everything out very clearly."[19] Echoed the business weekly *Commersant*, "[central bank chairman] Viktor Gerashchenko in two days solved a problem that the best minds of the Ministry of Finance had tackled for years."[20]

Without Russian rubles and with few levers to use against Russia, however, those countries that did not immediately leave the ruble zone acceded to Russia's demands. After the Central Bank of Russia carried out a threat to slow the rate at which the republics could transfer rubles to the bank—which meant further losses as the value of the Soviet ruble dipped lower—the presidents of Russia, Kazakhstan and Uzbekistan signed an agreement on August 7 to preserve the Russian ruble as the sole currency in these republics. The agreement included recognition of trade debts as sovereign debts to be treated like international loans and recognition of the Russian central bank as the sole issuing bank for rubles. A new treaty was signed on September 7. It specified that the signatories would have to adjust their customs, tax, bank and credit policies to Russian standards before they would be allowed to swap for Russian rubles. Goods, labor and capital were to move freely among the members.

There were two major problems with this framework for the Russians. First, all remaining interstate debts were to be settled through the correspondent accounts set up the previous year, and rubles were to be swapped at a 1:1 exchange rate. By this time most of these accounts had been exhausted. The remaining trade debts, the Russians insisted, had to be converted to state debt. By granting all national non-cash rubles equal status with non-cash Russian rubles, the republics were getting bargains on their debts and were given an incentive to speed repayment.

Second, the Russians foresaw that it would be difficult to bring cash ruble rates into alignment. Most foreign exchange markets in the rest of the commonwealth were quite rudimentary. This would place most of the cost of adjustment onto the Moscow exchanges, which would disrupt the orderly exchange rates the Central Bank of Russia had worked so hard to create over the summer. This problem would be most severe if Russia distributed the new rubles among the other members of the ruble zone. Said Federov, "The biggest problem is the policy on the ruble zone, which has not been fully thought out. The biggest danger would be to deliver cash to the CIS countries before they have coordinated their economic policies."[21]

Almost immediately after the September 7 agreement Russia began to seek strict interpretations of the gray areas still under discussion. Statements from Moscow emphasized that the treaty was to create a wide economic union rather than a currency zone. Commonwealth embassies in Moscow received draft agreements on co-production of defense goods and cooperation in taxation. But even if these were agreeable to the other republics, Russia was rapidly backing away from rebuilding the ruble zone. *Tass* reported on October 21 that Russian finance minister Boris Federov found the speed of integration "dangerous and unacceptable." Federov warned that the republics were using the agreement to get access to cash rubles. He was supported on the 25th by Vladimir Mashits, in charge of Russian policy for economic cooperation with the Commonwealth of Independent States. Mashits stated that even if the member states were willing to harmonize policies with Russia, Russia might insist on independent currencies that were not legal tender in Russia. This was in clear contradiction to the agreement signed one month earlier.[22]

Meanwhile, Deputy Prime Minister Shokhin flew for talks with Kazakhstan and Uzbekistan. On the 27th, he echoed Mashits's comments. "The presence of interim or national currencies is the most convenient way to create a unified monetary system." Kazakh president Nazarbayev stated that he felt compelled to start printing a new currency, as the currency shortage in his country had become severe. The breaking point was reached in discussions when Shokhin demanded that Kazakhstan place hard-currency and gold reserves on deposit as collateral for new rubles. This demand was also mentioned by Uzbekistan.[23] Shortly thereafter, on November 3, both countries announced they would issue their own currencies within a week. The tenge and the som were issued to the public on November 15.

The reaction in Russia was predictable. As the final preparations were made for issuing the tenge and the som, Shokhin stated that the exit of the two Central Asian states was a success for Russian economic diplomacy.[24]

> I do not think the single ruble zone is finished ... Kazakhstan and Uzbekistan have announced that they are rejecting the ruble and introducing their national currencies. However, the ruble will continue to play the key role in financial transactions inside the CIS. In addition, along with the consolidation of the economic alliance of the former USSR republics, for which all of them are now working with the exception of the Baltic states, the exchange rate of national currencies with regard to the ruble will become more clear. So, it will be possible to cooperate in a more reliable and effective way. (*Tass*, Nov. 11, 1993)

The reluctance of the last member countries to leave the zone was overcome by the flood of Soviet rubles into their economies. Armenia at first insisted it would remain in the ruble zone. But as happened in Central Asia after the introduction of the Kyrgyz som, old rubles began to flow out of Kazakhstan and Uzbekistan and into Armenia and Tajikistan. One way to compare the data is to take the cross rate between the Soviet and Russian rubles in Yerevan, Armenia. This rate rose from 1.3 Soviet rubles per Russian ruble at the beginning of the Russian currency swap to 1.5 in late September and 1.6 on November 8. After the announcement on November 12 that the Kazakh and Uzbek swaps would begin three days later, the cross rate soared to 3.4, and a week later to 8.5. One week later, Armenia issued the drah'm.

A Phoenix Rising from the Ashes: The Belarussian-Russian Monetary Union

Tables 11.3 and 11.4 describe the current status of the national currencies in the former Soviet Union. Only the Baltic states of Estonia and Lithuania have elected to fix their currencies to some external standard. As seen in the last column of Table 11.4, the currencies of these countries and Latvia have appreciated against the Russian ruble. The Transcaucasian and Central Asian economies, most of whom left the ruble zone unwillingly and hurriedly, have seen their currencies depreciate dramatically against the ruble. In some cases these countries' leaders decided to overvalue their currencies in the belief that the rates they experienced after large ruble inflows from neighboring republics were temporary. This was clearly true in Central Asia and in Armenia.

TABLE 11.3 Currency Arrangements in the Former Soviet Union

Country	Currency	When introduced	Exchange Rate Regime
Armenia	Drah'm	11/22/93	Floating rate regime.
Azerbaijan	Manat	08/20/93	
Belarus	Belarussian rubel	11/24/93	Signed an agreement on monetary union with Russia to swap rubel for Russian ruble.
Estonia	Kroon	06/20/92	Currency board, with peg of 8EK = 1DM; current account convertibility.
Georgia	Lari	01/01/94	Floating rate regime.
Kazakhstan	Tenge	11/16/93	Floating rate regime.
Kyrgyzstan	Som	05/10/93	Floating rate regime. Full convertibility.
Latvia	Lat	06/28/93	Floating rate regime and current account convertibility.
Lithuania	Lit	07/15/93	Fixed to $US at L 4 = $1.
Moldova	Leu	11/29/93	Floating rate regime.
Russia	Russian ruble	07/26/93	Floating rate regime. Current account convertibility.
Tajikistan	Russian ruble		Never left ruble zone. Signed an agreement on monetary union with Russia.
Turkmenistan	Manat	11/01/93	Floating regime.
Ukraine	Karbovanets (temporary currency), hryvna (final currency)	11/12/92 hryvna to be introduced in early 1995	Floating regime.
Uzbekistan	Sum	11/16/93	Floating regime.

Note: Exchange rate regime classifications by IMF.

TABLE 11.4 Exchange Rate Depreciation of the New Currencies

Country	Currency	Intro. Date	Intro. Ruble	Ruble Rate on 4/27/94	Depreciation
Armenia	drah'm	11/22/93	90	6.1	-99.71
Azerbaijan	manat	08/20/93	10	10.08	~0
Belarus	rubel	11/24/93	10	10.0	0[b]
Estonia	kroon	06/20/92	10	133.9	+274.06
Georgia	coupon	08/02/93	1	.0028	-99.95
Kazakhstan	tenge	11/16/93	500	64.79	-98.61
Kyrgyzstan	som	05/10/93	200	146.3	-24.9
Latvia	lat	06/28/93	1662[a]	3174.6	+97.29
Lithuania	lit	07/15/93	100	450.0	+523.70
Moldova	leu	11/29/93	0.33	.0022	-99.99
Turkmenistan	manat	11/01/93	500	180.0	-85.86
Ukraine	karbovanets	11/12/92	1	0.05	-99.11
Uzbekistan	sum coupon	11/16/93	1	0.3	-91.95

[a] In terms of Latvian rubles, issued parallel to Russian rubles at par. At time of issue, Latvian rubles traded at LvR 8.31 = 1 RRb
[b] In expectation of monetary union with Russia.
Notes: Exchange rates set in terms of new Russian rubles per unit of currency. Depreciation at annualized rates. On April 27, 1994, the rate of exchange of the Russian ruble was Rrb1800:U.S.$1
Sources: Radio Free Europe; International Monetary Fund; *Commersant*.

For example, in Figure 11.2 we show the depreciation of the Armenian drah'm versus the dollar and the Russian ruble.[25] The early decline in the drah'm came from its overvaluation; the drah'm was initially valued at the old Soviet ruble's official exchange rate with the Russian ruble. This was 2.4 at a time when the street rate of exchange for the two rubles was over 8. There was similar overvaluation versus the dollar. The exchange rate depreciated substantially more as the blockade of the country by Azerbaijan, Iran and Turkey,[26] particularly crucial for energy imports, caused heavy demand for foreign exchange for imports. As summer weather reduced energy demand, the country became better able to ship exports and re-acquire foreign exchange.

The most significant development in 1994 was the signing of a monetary union treaty between Russia and Belarus. The signing was long expected. Discussions were underway during the November exodus of the other commonwealth countries, in conjunction with the treaty signed in September. An initial accord was reached in early February, but it would have given the Belarussian central bank authority to issue Russian rubles. At the insistence of the Central Bank of Russia and Russian economics minister Shokhin, this plan was replaced by one in which the sole right to issue rubles would remain with the Russian central bank. In return for this, the agreement allowed

FIGURE 11.2 The Armenian Drah'm, Nov. 1993–Sept. 1994

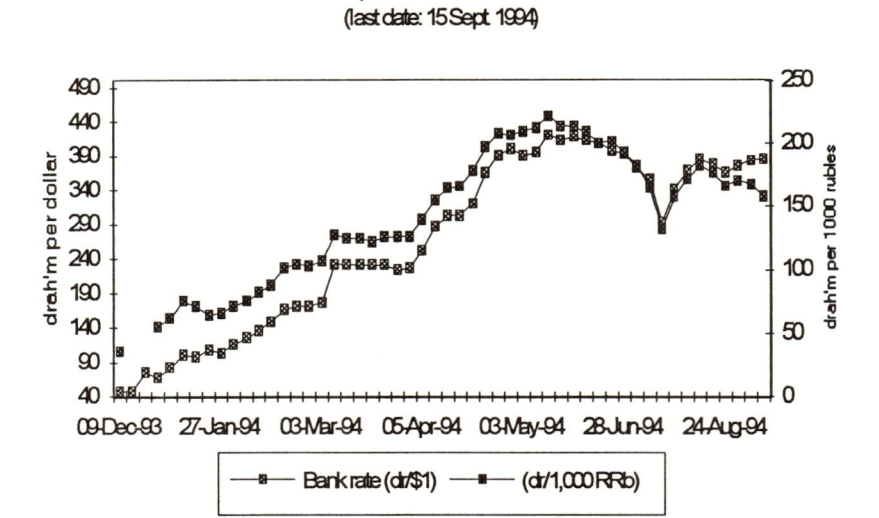

Depreciation of the Drah'm
(last date: 15 Sept 1994)

Belarus the right to exchange up to 200,000 coupons (zaichiks) at a 1:1 rate. The zaichik was trading at 10 per ruble. An agreement to this effect was signed April 12, 1994.

The main opposition to this reform has come from the banks in Belarus, in particular its central bank. This bank will end its autonomous existence when the union is enacted. Its chairman, Stanislav Bogdankevich, contends that the government is substituting the agreement for enacting reforms of the Belarussian economy. Belarus had approximately 40 percent inflation per month over the first six months of 1994, in comparison to 10 percent for Russia. Currency in circulation in Belarus increased 2800 percent between January 1993 and April 1994, the time of the agreement. The overvaluation of the zaichiks compensates Belarussian savers for Russia's acquisition of exclusive rights to seigniorage revenues. An additional reason for the agreement may be to guarantee the value of Russia's credits for gas shipments to Belarus, which at the time of the signing equaled $265 million.

One apparent factor in bringing the republics to negotiate currency union with Russia is Russia's control of gas shipments. At several times over the winter of 1993–94, Russia reduced or stopped gas shipments to other commonwealth countries, demanding some payment of debt in either rubles or dollars. Those countries able to generate hard currency exports, in particular the Baltic states, were able to induce Russia to restart shipments and renew credits. Belarus had much less ability to do so, and thus was led to join a union in part to assure continued energy shipments. Russia's dominant position could also prevail in its negotiations with Ukraine, Moldova and, to a lesser extent, Georgia and Armenia.

Conclusion: Prospects for Reformation

While a large commonwealth-wide ruble zone has collapsed, subsets of the commonwealth have started to form smaller alliances. Kazakhstan, Uzbekistan and Kyrgyzstan formed a trade area effective from February 1994. No customs or tariffs exist between these three economies. The effect of this is mixed. Kyrgyzstan exports largely manufactured goods (including substantial amounts of textiles) that require inputs from Russia and other commonwealth countries. After introducing the som, Kyrgyzstan has had difficulty making payments within the commonwealth and has suffered output losses as a result. Uzbekistan and Kazakhstan conduct about 5 percent of their total trade with each other (approximately $500 million in 1993). Both governments have expressed hope that they could substitute another $400 million in trade with each other for trade outside the ruble zone. With roughly similar economic structures, including substantial energy reserves, Kazakhstan and Uzbekistan have some potential for forming a currency union.[27]

The clear lesson from 1993 is that the ruble zone was an artifact of the Soviet era. Spanning nine time zones and a myriad of levels of economic development, it was likely to fail. Without direct Russian action, the incentives for the other republics were to remain in the ruble zone and attempt to export some of their inflation to the other members. While the breakup of the ruble zone did not solve the problems for the other republics, it has made several come to grips with the difficult choices each faces in the transition to a market economy.

Appendix
Key Dates in the Evolution of National Currencies in the Former Soviet Union[28]

January 1992. The Central Bank of Russia establishes the system of correspondent accounts with the central banks of the former Soviet republics. These accounts replaced the inter-branch payments mechanism, and allowed the Central Bank of Russia to observe payments imbalances.

June 20, 1992. Estonia introduces the kroon, backed by a currency board pledged to maintain an exchange rate of 8 kroon to 1 Deutsche mark.

July 1, 1992. The Central Bank of Russia centralizes all cross-border payments of Russian enterprises in order to control the amount of credit extended to other republics. Imbalances were to be financed through the system of "technical credits." As a result of newly imposed restrictions non-uniform exchange rates between the various republics' non-cash rubles emerged.

January 22, 1993. Ten former Soviet states agree to found an Interstate Bank (ISB) designed to process interstate payments.

May 2, 1993. Kyrgyzstan announces it will leave the ruble zone on May 10 and introduces the som. Exit of rubles to neighboring Central Asian states depresses temporarily the exchange rate of rubles for dollars in Alma-Ata to one-fifth the rate in Moscow.

End of June, 1993. The Central Bank of Russia and the Russian government ask the former constituent republics to take a stand on the matter of their national currencies. Russia's government sends telegram to Belarus, suggesting that they either pursue a common monetary policy with Russia or introduce a national currency beginning July 1st.

July 6, 1993. The Central Bank of Russia orders commercial banks to stop giving old bills to their clients.

July 26, 1993. The Central Bank of Russia announces the withdrawal of all pre-1993 banknotes from circulation. Russian citizens would have until August 7 to exchange up to 35,000 ($35) worth of rubles. The other former Soviet republics were not informed in advance. This step by the Central Bank of Russia completed the separation of the currencies begun in 1992 by separating non-cash circulation.

August 18, 1993. Stolichny Bank (Moscow) affiliates began offering transactions with the currencies of the other commonwealth countries.

September 7, 1993. Armenia, Belarus, Kazakhstan, Russia, Tajikistan and Uzbekistan signed a treaty "On Practical Measures to Create a New-Type Ruble Zone." The treaty provides for uniform monetary, credit, budgetary and currency policies with the leading role to be assumed by the Russian Central Bank.

September 24, 1993. By that date signatory countries closed standard bilateral agreements with Russia "On a Merger with the Russian Monetary System." The first clause says that "the ruble zone of a new type is understood by the parties as a system in which the only legal tender is the ruble issued by the Central Bank of Russia."

October 27, 1993. At a press conference Deputy Prime Minister Aleksandr Shokhin states that establishment of a new ruble zone will take time and asks the other signatories to formulate plans about their relations with Russia.

November 3, 1993. Kazakhstan announces it will leave the ruble zone. Cites Russia for imposing "unacceptable conditions"—i.e., requiring the deposit of large gold and hard currency reserves in Russia—for using the new ruble. Uzbekistan announces the same day that it is considering joining Kazakhstan.

November 24, 1993. Belarus announces that the Belarussian rubel will be its sole legal tender. By converting the Russian ruble to a foreign currency, officials hope to better establish the relative value of the two currencies.

April 12, 1994. Russia and Belarus sign monetary union treaty. Russian ruble will be sole legal tender in both countries. Belarussian citizens will be allowed to exchange 200,000 Belarussian rubels into Russian rubles at a 1:1 rate, though they trade in the open market at 10:1. Tajikstan announces the next day that it will join the Belarussian-Russian union.

July 8, 1994. Kazakhstan, Kyrgyzstan and Uzbekistan sign a treaty to form economic and defense unions. Each country will chair the committees for one year. Other states are invited to join. Financial policies of the three countries are to be coordinated.

Notes

1. Pitzer College and St. Cloud State University, and Rice University. We thank without implication Levan Efremidze for research assistance and Nurhan Davutyan, Pamela Martin and Thomas D. Willett for comments on an earlier draft of this paper.

2. Steven Lewarne presents a detailed account of the development of the Central Bank of Russia in chapter 9 of this volume.

3. For more detail, see our paper in a forthcoming volume in this series (Banaian and Zhukov 1995).

4. These issues are discussed by Krugman (1991:chp 11), Casella (1992), and Miller (1993).

5. As explained by Zwass (1979:9-21), the Soviet system exercised much stricter control over household currency, which was issued in cash notes, than over "enterprise money" which was chiefly a set of accounting entries. Each enterprise would be allocated non-cash rubles as a share of its working capital, along with some retained earnings from the previous year. If production fell short of target, more would be given. When the Soviet Union broke up, state banks still maintained this relationship to the firms they financed.

6. Recent examples are the papers in Williamson (1991), those by Goldberg, Ickes and Ryterman (1994), Willett and Al-Marhubi (1994) and our forthcoming paper in the next volume (Banaian and Zhukov 1995).

7. Since the Central Bank of Russia obtains all the seigniorage as sole issuer of cash rubles, it would be necessary to give back to Central Asia more than their losses from selling energy at below world prices. See Casella (1992) for more on this issue.

would impact poorly on Russia's designs to maintain some influence in the region" (p. 316). We doubt Russia had any qualms about declaring economic war; its military position makes it a force to be reckoned with, regardless of the currency it keeps.

9. This led many writers to fear a "monetary overhang" that would cause inflation as goods appeared on the shelves after economic liberalization. However, the price increases in the former Soviet states were so large they all but wiped out the value of this overhang.

10. This is different from the question of how member countries were to receive cash rubles from the Russian central bank. As we shall see, that question was hotly debated.

11. Radio Free Europe/Radio Liberty transcripts (hereafter RFE/RL), March 19, 1993.

12. *Commersant*, "Enigmatic C.I.S. Economics Union," May 19, 1993, p. 26.

13. *Commersant*, "Enigmatic C.I.S. Economics Union." See also RFE/RL, June 23, 1993.

14. *Financial Times*, July 14, 1993.

15. Belarus had previously declared it would introduce the rubel in 1994 and introduced a dual coupon, the zaichik, earlier in 1993.

16. It is unknown how many of these requests were met in new rubles. The government, contrary to its own orders, did pay government workers with Soviet rubles the week before the swap.

17. *Respublika Armenii*, July 30, 1993.

18. *Reuters'* wire report, July 28, 1993.

19. *Commersant*, "Central Asian Republics Join Russian Ruble Zone," (English edition) August 4, 1993, p. 6.

20. *Commersant*, "Central Asian Republics Join Russian Ruble Zone."

21. *Reuters*, October 14, 1993.

22. *Tass*, October 21, 1993; *Reuters*, October 26, 1993; *Tribune Business News*, October 26, 1993.

23. Guy Chazan, "Minister Says Ruble Zone States Should Introduce Their Own Currencies," UPI ClariNet computer network, October 27, 1993 and Janet Guttsman, "Rouble Out of Favor as Russia Gets Tough," *Reuters*, October 29, 1993.

24. UPI, November 10, 1993.

25. The rate reported is an average of buy and sell rates for six to ten banks in Yerevan, gathered by the authors from the Aragil News Service.

26. The blockade was imposed on account of the Karabagh conflict. Additionally, civil war frequently cut transportation of exports and imports through Georgia.

27. One might also expect that the other Central Asian states—Tajikistan and Turkmenstan—would join this union. However, the Tajiks use the Russian ruble and joined the Russian-Belarussian union. It was revealed that in negotiations Russia agreed to provide a loan of 80 billion rubles to Tajikstan, perhaps as an inducement to join. Turkmenstan signed a trade agreement with Russia a few days after the other Central Asian states formed their union and seems increasingly likely to tie its manat to the ruble.

28. Many dates for introduction of national currencies are omitted here. These dates can be found in Tables 11.2 or 11.3.

28. Many dates for introduction of national currencies are omitted here. These dates can be found in Tables 11.2 or 11.3.

References

Banaian, King, and Eugenue G. Zhukov. 1995. "Developments in the Former (and Future?) Ruble Zone: An Appreciation Using an Optimal Currency Areas Approach," in Thomas D. Willett et al., eds., *Trade and Currency Policies for Emerging Market Economies*. Boulder, Colo: Westview Press, forthcoming.

Casella, Alexandra. 1992. "Participation in a Currency Union." *American Economic Review* 72(4): 847-63.

Goldberg, Linda S., Barry Ickes and Randi Ryterman. 1994. "Departures from the Ruble Zone: The Consequences of Adopting Independent Currencies." *World Economy* 8(2): 293-322.

Commersant. 1993. "Central Asian Republics Join Russian Ruble Zone," (English edition), August 4, p. 6.

Gros, Daniel P. 1991. "Economic Costs and Benefits of Regional Disintegration in the Soviet Union." Center for Economic Policy Studies Working Document No. 55.

Krugman, Paul. 1991. *Currencies and Crises*. Cambridge, Mass.: MIT Press.

Miller, Marcus. 1993. "The Break-up of the Ruble Zone and Prospects for a New Ukrainian Currency: A Monetary Analysis," in *The Economics of New Currencies*. Pp. 113-35. London: Centre for Economic Policy Research.

Tarr, David G. 1994. "The Terms-of-Trade Effects of Moving to World Prices on Countries of the Former Soviet Union." *Journal of Comparative Economics* 18 (March): 1-24.

Vavilov, Andrey, and Oleg Vjugin. 1993. "Trade Patterns After Integration into the World Economy," in John Williamson, ed., *Economic Consequences of Soviet Disintegration.* Pp. 99-174. Washington, DC: Institute for International Economics.

Willett, Thomas D., and Fahim Al-Marhubi. 1994. "Currency Policies for Inflation Control in the Formerly Centrally Planned Economies." *World Economy* 8(4): in press.

Williamson, John, ed. 1991. *Currency Convertibility in Eastern Europe*. Washington, D.C.: Institute for International Economics.

Zwass, Adam. 1979. *Money, Banking, and Credit in the Soviet Union and Eastern Europe*. White Plains, New York: M. E. Sharpe.

12

The Latvian Monetary Reform

George J. Viksnins and Ilmars Rimshevitchs[1]

After Latvia regained its political independence in September 1991, the economy contracted rapidly, experiencing both negative growth and exploding inflation. In 1992, as the Comecon or CMEA trading system collapsed,[2] GDP fell by more than 30 percent while consumer prices rose by a factor of ten. (The inflation rate from December 1991 to December 1992 is estimated at 958.1 percent.) In 1993, however, the economy began to turn around. Both growth and inflation improved considerably, with prices rising by only 35 percent and the decline in output slowing. Still, by mid-1994 real output had fallen to about half of its previous level. In the recent past, due to systemic biases toward vertical integration and large-scale enterprise, the ratio of exports to "Gross Republic Product" in all three Baltic countries exceeded 60 percent, and more than 90 percent of export production went to CMEA destinations. With market signals now supplanting Gosplan directives both ratios will decline, but the short-term dislocations are a serious matter, both economically and politically. Official unemployment figures are still low, but they are rising and there is a lot of hidden unemployment. The seriousness of the restructuring problem is starkly reflected by the decline in caloric intake per capita—from 3522 calories in 1990 to 2533 calories in 1992—as rents and utilities take a larger share of family spending in the presence of declining real wages.

Latvia joined the International Monetary Fund, after extensive discussions and a review of its economic situation, on May 19, 1992, with a total quota of 61 SDR million (at that time approximately $85 million). In 1991, Latvia recorded an external current account surplus of more than 12 percent of GDP, as well as a general government surplus of about 7 percent of GDP. This was largely because the prices of finished industrial products in the "ruble zone" were freed first, while the prices of energy and other raw materials continued to be controlled. However, the fiscal situation deteriorated significantly in the first half of 1992, with a central government budget deficit of about 3.5 percent of GDP being recorded. For the year as a whole, the government budget deficit was a relatively modest 1.5 percent, but in 1993 a small surplus was realized. In 1992, Latvia's current account in its balance of payments showed a surplus of about $43 million; a merchandise trade deficit of about $119 million was more than offset by a positive balance of $161 million in services, primarily from the transport sector. In 1993 Latvian exports were significantly larger than imports, and there was an inflow of foreign exchange on both the current and capital accounts.

The law establishing the Bank of Latvia was adopted on May 19, 1992, with a considerable majority of the members of Parliament voting in favor. This legislation was largely based on the central bank law in Germany, with provisions made for current domestic conditions in Latvia.

The "Law of the Bank of Latvia" granted the bank independence from government control. Its president and board of governors are appointed for a term of six years; this is to allow them to design and pursue an independent monetary policy, free from government pressure to monetize budget deficits, with the aim of controlling inflation.

The Board of Governors of the Bank of Latvia convenes once every two months. At these meetings the board discusses monetary policy and assigns quarterly quantitative targets, and issues central bank directives for the commercial banks. The Executive Board, which consists of six members and deals with everyday activities (refinancing banks with short-term credits, foreign exchange dealing, banking supervision, and similar issues), meets more often and carries out the tasks set by the board of governors. Tight monetary policy and the stabilization of the lats, combined with relatively high real interest rates, have led to a noticeable inflow of capital from abroad. The foreign exchange reserves of the Bank of Latvia have more than doubled since the beginning of 1993 and are currently valued at nearly $600 million.

After regaining independence Latvia began to carry out monetary and banking reforms remarkably quickly and effectively. The president of the Bank of Latvia, Einārs Repše, put a temporary currency unit, the Latvian ruble (LVR), in circulation on May 7, 1992. At the time various Soviet financial experts foresaw a disastrous end to that experiment—after all, Repše was a physicist and not a "finansist," the new money had no backing or cover, and so on. A few experts likened the issue of the new Latvian currency to economic suicide. However, by the end of 1992 Latvia had negotiated a successful divorce from the ruble zone. The Latvian ruble appreciated significantly against the Russian ruble, and in time even began to float upwards against so-called "hard currencies," such as the dollar and the Deutsche mark.

The lats returned to the pockets of Latvians on March 5, 1993, when a paper currency of five lats denomination was introduced. The currency was exchanged at the rate of LVR 200 to one lats, or, in practice, two of the 500-unit Latvian ruble notes for a Ls 5 note.[3] Even though the Latvian ruble notes were quite well printed for a temporary currency, some counterfeit LVR 500 notes had started turning up, and because of this the lats was placed in circulation a bit sooner than originally planned. This monetary policy move once again had to be defended against self-selected experts, in Latvia as well as abroad. These people said: How can the lats be worth more than a dollar? As the lats appreciates, will this not destroy Latvia's exports? Does a stable and strong currency benefit anyone other than the "mafia"? In 1993 the lats was, in fact, one of the world's strongest currencies—the exchange value of the lats in terms of U.S. dollars rose even more than did the Japanese yen (the yen rose about 10 percent, but the lats by approximately 30 percent). Today one U.S. dollar is about 55 santimi, a little over half a lats. It is probable that the actual purchasing power of one lats in terms of Latvian commodities is considerably higher than even two dollars, especially outside of Riga. It is important to note that the relative stability of a currency is much more important than the attainment of a precisely correct purchasing power parity. The fact that in 1993 Latvia had a balance of trade surplus and that the central bank's foreign exchange reserves rose by more than Ls 150 million seems to suggest that the appreciation of the national currency has not destroyed the competitiveness or profitability of exports—although it is possible that instead of a 100 percent profit margin, exporters will now have to be satisfied with "only" 40–50 percent returns.

Thus, during the past two years the Bank of Latvia has accomplished a great deal, successfully separating the country from the ruble zone and strengthening the credibility of the national monetary unit. The bank has also developed the instruments of monetary control and assisted in the propagation of new securities and means of payment. The network of financial transactions has been extended and improved, and local banks are beginning to participate in most significant international communications systems (for example, SWIFT). Still, the financial market in Riga is developing rather slowly—many banks hold excess reserves which pay no interest, while other banks are offering their depositors unbelievably high interest rates. Looking at this from the outside, one is tempted to ask why they do not borrow from each other or make more use of the central bank's discount facility.

All in all, the very high interest rates offered by some Riga banks today seem a cause for concern. Even though inflation in 1993 was about 35 percent, some banks are offering deposit rates that are significantly higher than that, and they charge their borrowers still higher rates, even as high as 100 percent per year. The fact that such transactions are even taking place shows that bankers and their customers are still looking at the past to predict the future. It is certainly true that in 1992 some borrowers were still making a healthy profit by exploiting the arbitrage possibilities in the disintegrating USSR. Many are undoubtedly thinking that they will make a nice profit in the east in 1994 and 1995 as well. People in Ukraine and Belarus are fleeing the local currency, and those who act quickly can still earn large profits. However, it is difficult to guess what will happen in Russia itself. Will the ruble try to catch the karbovenets?

Although the Latvian economy will continue to be significantly influenced by events to the east, it would be foolish to base the development of its banking system on permanent speculation in the countries of the former Soviet Union. In a normal economic situation the majority of commercial bank assets are short-term loans to domestic trade, industry, and agriculture, or low-risk government securities. The Bank of Latvia has participated in several auctions of two-month credits for banks, and there have also been quite a few auctions of short-term government securities, with interest rates in the 20–30 percent range. (The central bank discount rate was 27 percent in the fall of 1994.) It seems much more appropriate and logical for commercial banks to hold these assets given Latvia's current economic situation.

It is interesting that even though U.S. inflation in 1993 was 3 percent and Latvia's was 34.9 percent, the value of the lats rose quite steadily. One interpretation is that the lats was initially significantly undervalued and only now is beginning to approach purchasing power parity. Let us recall the forecast made by Mr. Repše, the president of the Bank of Latvia, in 1993: he said that the exchange rate of the dollar in Latvia might be "in a range between 150 and 50 LVR per one dollar" (quoted from *Dienas Bizness*, February 18, 1993). In santimi, that would be between 75 and 25 to the dollar—and the exchange rate today has stabilized near the midpoint of this range.

Until it was pegged in 1994, the exchange rate of the lats was determined by supply and demand in the foreign exchange market. During 1993 and 1994 the Bank of Latvia bought significant quantities of foreign exchange, mainly U.S. dollars, keeping the value of the lats *lower* than it would have been without intervention. As our colleague, Bank of Latvia senior consultant Uldis Klauss, wrote in the U.S. Latvian-language newspaper *Laiks*: "If the buying of foreign exchange were to be stopped or interrupted, the consequences could be truly catastrophic, with the value of the lats suddenly soaring. The equilibrium exchange rate of the lats will have been reached, when the buying and selling of foreign exchange will be of an approximately equal level." This situation has already been reached.

In 1993, however, Latvian exports were significantly larger than imports, and there was an inflow of foreign exchange on both the current account and the capital account in the balance of payments. Although statistical data concerning capital flows is not complete, the deposits of nonresidents in commercial banks rose from Ls 3.1 million to Ls 27.2 million. From the Latvian point of view the latter number is fairly large (about 6 percent of the broadly defined money supply).

Let us end with the carefully chosen words of the Bank of Latvia's president, Einārs Repše. In a May 1994 speech he said: "It is gratifying to note that the foreign exchange value of the lats is becoming even more stable. Even today we can cautiously speak about a possible stabilization of the lats in relation to the basket of currencies called the SDR. Everyone, who follows the foreign exchange rates, will have noticed that we in fact have used such an anchor." A few readers, who follow such matters, may remember that a fellow named Viksnins suggested such an idea in August 1989.

Notes

1. This paper was first given at a workshop on "Financial Sector Issues in the Transitioning Economies" at Georgetown University, April 23, 1993. A revised version was given at a seminar on Baltic financial sector issues in Tallinn, Estonia, in August 1993.

2. CMEA, the Council for Mutual Economic Assistance, was called Comecon in the U.S. Membership in this Moscow-organized trading system varied, but roughly embraced the Soviet Union and its satellites.

3. The lats is further subdivided into santimi, one santims being the equivalent of a cent: 100 santimi = Ls 1.

13

Fiscal and Monetary Policies in the Transition: Searching for the Credit Crunch

Pierre Siklos and István Ábel

Introduction

The fundamental economic transformations currently sweeping central and eastern Europe provide economists with a unique opportunity to study the role and impact of monetary and fiscal policies. The former command economies have chosen to adopt some of the macroeconomic tools routinely applied in the industrialized world. However, both the speed and nature of the reforms attempted differ across the transforming economies, presenting an opportunity to explore whether any one road to a market economy has, so far, been more successful, in terms of delivering better macroeconomic performance, than other paths to market liberalization. There exist many dimensions, of course, along which "success" or "failure" in macroeconomic terms can be assessed. We wish to suggest, however, that the successfulness of a transition, measured in terms of delivering a rising standard of living over time via rising output and low and stable inflation, is dependent on financial sector reforms as well as developments in monetary and fiscal policies. What follows below is an examination of the role played thus far by the financial sector in the transformation of selected Central European economies, and the ability of this sector to finance the needs of a market-oriented economy. As Phelps et al. (1993) have argued:

If history is any guide, periods of extraordinary demands for investible funds have often brought forth large and sophisticated commercial banks providing large amounts of outside finance to firms over which they receive in return certain rights to control. (p. 40)

One of the most pressing macroeconomic issues facing the transitional economies is the financing of reforms to permit or facilitate the transition from central planning toward market-driven outcomes. From the outset of the transition the need for monetary and fiscal reforms has been great. On the fiscal side there is the legacy of large deficits, a consequence of the need to finance inefficient state-owned enterprises as well as the large-scale subsidization of everything from foodstuffs to housing in the social sector. On the revenue side, the absence of an efficient, modern tax collection system severely limits the government's budget position.

In the realm of monetary policy, an immature financial system (in a sense to be defined below) combined with the absence of monetary policy tools or the wherewithal to manage them pose serious economic threats. Moreover, the large-scale price liberalization and the devolution of commercial banking operations from the government to, at least initially, quasi-governmental institutions also influence monetary and fiscal policies.

Although Hungary, Poland, and the former Czechoslovakia, broadly speaking, faced the same initial macroeconomic conditions, their monetary and fiscal policy responses have differed in many ways, as we shall see. One common element in the transitional experience, perhaps, is the role reforms played in generating a shortage of liquidity, often referred to as the "credit crunch," and the persistence of this shortage. In the initial stages of the transition a credit crunch could have been triggered by the fear of, say, high inflation following price liberalization. If market reforms are stalled by liquidity constraints,[1] then the question which has preoccupied much of the literature, namely whether the big bang approach is preferable to a gradualist approach to economic reforms, is misdirected. Instead, the problem is the credit crunch and its potential impact on economic performance. What is of interest, too, is whether the crunch is a legacy of the economic distortions introduced by central planning alone or whether the conduct of monetary and fiscal policies once in the transition phase has played a part. It is this distinction, usually ignored in the literature, which this paper addresses. While a credit crunch is a standard feature of recessions in industrialized countries, we argue that there are institutional characteristics in the transitional economies which can either exacerbate or ease the shortage of liquidity over time relative to what would be expected in a market economy in the recessionary phase of the business cycle.

Thus the purpose of this study is twofold: first, to summarize the institutional changes implemented thus far in the financial sphere in selected

Central European countries; and second, to provisionally determine whether the financial reforms implemented have produced a shortage of credit, usually referred to as a "credit crunch." This is an important question because, as several authors have suggested (see the following sections), the presence of a credit crunch threatens the success of the transition from a command to a market economy.

Our analysis is restricted to Hungary, Poland, and Czechoslovakia (before its division into the Czech and Slovak Republics) for obvious reasons. These three countries have moved the farthest toward market economies and now have sufficiently long historical and economic records to attempt to draw some preliminary conclusions about their progress in the financial sphere.

The chapter is organized as follows. Section 2 provides a very brief overview of the current macroeconomic performance of the three countries. Section 3 provides a brief comparative survey of the principal financial sector reforms in Hungary, Poland, and Czechoslovakia since the late 1980s. Section 4 asks whether a credit crunch has occurred in these countries. Section 5 concludes and summarizes what we have learned so far about the macroeconomic transition to market economies.

The Current Macroeconomic Situation: A Brief Overview

Reforms aimed at lessening the role of central planning began much earlier in Hungary than in the other Central European countries. Beginning in 1968, prices of selected commodities were liberalized and limited forms of private enterprise were permitted. Nevertheless, 1989 was the watershed year in which central planning was repudiated and market-oriented reforms began to be instituted. The transition phase has been marked by negative rates of growth in GDP from 1990 to 1993—though as 1994 began there were forecasts of a turnaround and the resumption of positive economic growth. At the same time, a surge in consumer prices also delineated the old from the new regime.

This study is motivated in part by the monetary and fiscal policies implemented in the attempt to disinflate. As Montias (1994) points out, the central-planning regimes formerly in place did not provide a viable institutional framework within which to conduct the "stabilization" policies required in the transition to fully market-determined economies. As a consequence, the central governments of all three countries experienced worsening budgetary problems, at least until 1993. Finally, the large international debts accumulated under the former regimes and the constraints these impose on financing the transition have posed a serious problem. Table 13.1 summarizes a few key economic indicators for Hungary, Poland, and Czechoslovakia. The figures clearly show an acceleration in negative GDP growth beginning in 1989 or 1990 in all three countries. Of the three,

TABLE 13.1 Macroeconomic Performance

Indicator	Year	Hungary	Poland	Czechoslovakia
GDP Growth	1987	4.1	2.0	2.1
(% Change)	1988	-.1	4.1	2.3
	1989	-.2	.2	.7
	1990	-4.3	-11.6	-.4
	1991	-10.2	-7.2	-15.9
	1992	-5.0	-1.0	-5.0
CPI Inflation	1987	8.6	25.2	.1
(% Change)	1988	14.8	60.2	.2
	1989	18.9	251.1	1.4
	1990	33.4	585.8	10.8
	1991	32.2	70.3	58.7
	1992	22.0	45.6	10.2
General	1987	-3.5	-.8	-.7
Government	1988	NA	NA	-1.5
Balance	1989	-1.3	-7.4	-2.4
(% of GDP)	1990	.4	3.1	.1
	1991	-3.3	-5.6	-2.0
	1992	-10.6	-7.2	-4.4
International Debt	1987	19.6	33.5	6.7
(Billions of	1988	19.6	39.1	7.3
U.S. Dollars)	1989	20.4	40.8	7.9
	1990	21.3	49.0	8.2
	1991	21.0	48.4	9.6
	1992	20.8	48.6	9.9

Sources: Calvo and Kumar (1993, Table 1). Data for 1992 are estimates. GDP for Czechoslovakia until 1989 is real net material product.

Czechoslovakia has been most successful at avoiding a high-inflation trap, but all were able to sharply reduce inflation by 1992. In contrast, and with the exception of the Czech Republic, government deficits have risen sharply as a percentage of GDP, especially in Hungary. Finally, international debt, evaluated in U.S. dollars, has generally remained stagnant.

As will be explained below, the key determinants of these countries' macroeconomic performance so far lie largely with differences in their monetary and fiscal actions during the transition.[2] Hungary and Poland both had difficulty in obtaining IMF support. However, Poland's political system is in considerably greater disarray than those in the other two countries. Both Poland and Czechoslovakia took a "big bang" approach to price and exchange rate liberalization, whereas Hungary's approach has been more gradual in this respect. Also, privatization schemes seem to have preoccupied the Polish governments to a greater extent than in Hungary. In Czechoslovakia, even the process of privatization was subjected to a type of "big bang" strategy.

Finally, Poland has benefited from external financial support to a greater extent than either Hungary or Czechoslovakia.

As noted above, several authors have commented on the dangers of a credit crunch during the transition period. What we have in mind in this study is a credit crunch created by public borrowing requirements that displace private borrowing, or simple crowding-out. In what follows we make no distinction between direct lending by governments, consolidation banks or other financial institutions which remain creatures of the state.

A Review of Financial Sector Reform

It may be helpful to briefly consider when and how financial reforms were implemented in Hungary, Poland, and Czechoslovakia. As financial reforms began earliest in Hungary, we begin with a description of that country's experience. Moreover, since reforms in the three countries covered in this study parallel each other, much of the emphasis in what follows will be about the Hungarian situation. For Poland and Czechoslovakia we shall only discuss the differences vis-à-vis Hungary in their approach to financial reforms. While there now exists a vast literature on the overall reform or transformation process,[3] few authors have provided a comparative review of the financial reforms.[4]

Hungary

Although the reform process is usually said to have begun in 1968,[5] for our purposes the year 1987 marks the beginning of the reform period since this is when Hungary introduced a two-tier banking system. Commercial-banking type operations were transferred from the National Bank of Hungary to newly created commercial banks. Specialist (i.e., merchant or investment banks) and savings banks were also created and these, for the most part, follow the German-Austrian universal banking model. Nevertheless, the state retains a controlling interest in the commercial banking sector and was not expected to divest itself of its commercial banking holdings via privatization until the end of 1993.[6] Significantly, the New Banking Act stipulates that financial institutions comply with the proposals of the Basel Committee on Banking Supervision to achieve a risk-weighted asset-reserve ratio of 8 percent by January 1, 1993.[7] Escape clauses in the legislation permit exemptions to be granted, but ostensibly only until December 31, 1994, and only on an individual basis.[8] Although meeting these standards is not itself an issue[9] (Ábel and Bonin (1992b:15) show that by 1990 these standards were well on their way to being met), the necessary portfolio reallocations no doubt have had significant macroeconomic effects (see section 4 below).

Complementing the banking reforms were reforms aimed at establishing a central bank wielding modern policy tools. Nevertheless, the reformed central bank continues to be hampered by the legacies of the past.[10] For example, the National Bank of Hungary continues to be involved in refinancing the bad debts of enterprises, in part because commercial banks have no incentive under the present "rules of the game" to provide long-term financing. Instead, the current incentive structure is entirely skewed toward the shorter end of the maturity structure.[11] This creates a mismatch between the needs of enterprises and the supply of loanable funds. The present state of affairs is akin to that of segmented markets in the sense that while enterprises prefer long-term financing, commercial banks are largely constrained to supply short-term liquidity. Similarly, domestic and foreign investors have no wish to hold long-term government bonds, preferring instead to hold short-term Treasury bills. And since sources of capital are primarily foreign,[12] the mismatch problem is exacerbated. Moreover, as in the other former command economies, Hungary's state-owned sector is saddled with significant inter-enterprise credit, partly a legacy of the rationing of credit under central planning, but even more the result of the imposition of tight "western style" monetary policies.[13] Thus, for example, by 1989 inter-enterprise credit represented over one-third of available short-term credit (34.6 percent),[14] up from 14 percent in 1982.

While the central banking and commercial banking sectors were reformed in line with existing European models, most notably that of Germany, no substantial reforms of fiscal operations have been implemented except for attempts to privatize state-owned companies.[15] Thus, by 1992, public debt equaled 79.8 percent of GDP and was only 65.3 percent a year earlier.[16] These figures would give Hungary the fourth highest debt/GDP ratio among the twelve OECD countries, behind only Belgium, Italy, and Canada.[17] This raises the question of whether the current rate of growth in the public debt is sustainable.[18] Moreover, the current statutes of the central bank (see *Act on the National Bank of Hungary* 1991, par 19) permit the granting of credits to the state in an amount up to 3 percent of "planned revenues of the central budget in that year."

As is true elsewhere in Central Europe, a nascent money market[19] and an inefficient payments system, combined with the effective absence of competition in the wholesale and retail banking sectors, imply that the functions of the present banking system are narrow by the standards of western industrialized countries.[20] This problem is further exacerbated by other policies which have had major repercussions on commercial banks' balance sheets, skewing their asset holdings toward liquid and low-risk government debt and away from commercial lending.[21]

A second problem with the reformed banking system has been the imposition of high reserve requirements, at least by western standards. Thus, the mandatory reserve ratio was originally set at 16 percent of deposits to be met on a daily basis; the reserve ratio was lowered to 14 percent in January 1993.[22] However, banks will earn interest on such deposits at 50 percent of the National Bank of Hungary's base rate while foreign exchange reserves will earn the market rate. The National Bank of Hungary argues that such high reserve requirements are justified on two grounds.[23] First, the balance sheets of the corporate sector continue to deteriorate, necessitating the write-off of bad loans.[24] Second, the growing pressure on commercial banks to finance government expenditures, via relatively low-risk loans, provides an incentive to skew lending toward the government. As in Italy until very recently, high reserve requirements thus provide seigniorage income to the government.

Finally, the National Bank of Hungary has a specific exchange rate policy.[25] While the domestic currency, the forint, is pegged to a basket of foreign currencies, it is primarily driven by fluctuations in the U.S. dollar and the National Bank of Hungary is actively involved in influencing the forint's course.[26] Thus, the "National Bank of Hungary implements its monetary policy ... by influencing or determining exchange rates" (*Act on the National Bank of Hungary*, par. 8). Moreover, "the National Bank of Hungary quotes and publishes the exchange rates serving to convert foreign currencies into forint and the forint into foreign currencies.... The order of fixing and/or influencing the exchange rate is determined by the Government in agreement with the National Bank of Hungary" (*Act on the National Bank of Hungary*, par. 13). Nevertheless, there are relatively few capital controls for large-scale investors although some controls remain on the transactions of private individuals. Because of the desire and need for large capital inflows to finance necessary reconstruction and modernization of the infrastructure and formerly state-owned enterprises, failure to sterilize foreign exchange transactions produces significant monetary growth.[27]

Poland[28]

A two-tier banking system was introduced in Poland in 1989. The National Bank of Poland became a western-style central bank but, as in the Hungarian example, the National Bank of Poland automatically extends credits to the state up to a maximum of 2 percent of planned expenditures. Operations formerly conducted by the National Bank of Poland devolved onto a newly created commercial banking sector which also assumed many of the existing bad debts of state-owned industries. Unlike Hungary or Czechoslovakia, however, no consolidation fund was created to improve the viability of the commercial banking sector.[29] The Polish financial sector was aided by the Polish government's success in obtaining loan forgiveness from the U.S. and European Community countries. These same countries have been less generous toward Czechoslovakia and Hungary. Second, the IMF and western banks have been more directly involved in Polish financial affairs than in the affairs of either Czechoslovakia or Hungary. As in both the other countries, reserve requirements are steep. However, unlike Hungary, and more akin to the approach followed in western industrialized countries, reserve requirements vary by type of deposit (e.g., 30 percent on savings deposits and 10 percent on fixed-term deposits).[30]

Poland also retains strict capital controls, so the domestic currency, the zloty, is not convertible to the same degree as is the forint.[31] However, Poland was the first of the transitional economies to introduce a form of convertibility—limited convertibility was implemented at the same time as other financial and economic reforms were put in place, while the Hungarian forint's convertibility was established long after other financial and economic reforms were introduced.[32] Moreover, again unlike Hungary or Czechoslovakia, an exchange rate stabilization fund was set up in 1990. Both Hungary and Poland, following initial devaluations, maintain a crawling peg exchange rate.[33] Having switched away from a dollar peg in 1991, the Polish zloty's value is now more heavily influenced by the deutschmark than is the forint. In the fiscal policy sphere, Poland's problems are similar to those experienced by Hungary, despite debt relief from international lenders.

Czechoslovakia[34]

The principal distinguishing characteristic of the Czechoslovak financial reforms was the adoption of a central bank based on the Bundesbank model and the implicit acceptance of a program of price stability following price liberalization on January 1, 1991. Unlike Hungary and Poland, Czechoslovakia also set up a consolidation fund as part of the initial package of reforms leading to the creation of a two-tier banking system. In addition, while banks formed after 1990 must adhere to the Basel capital-adequacy standards, existing banks' balance sheets need to attain this level only gradually (no target date currently exists).[35] In addition, reserve requirements for banks are considerably lower than in Hungary (8 percent for monthly deposits) perhaps because many bad loans are off the books of the newly formed Czechoslovak commercial banks. While Czechoslovakia did not set up a stabilization fund of the kind created in Poland, a large stand-by arrangement with the IMF (of 105 percent of their quota) was negotiated which together with foreign exchange reserves (see below) permits foreign exchange market intervention. The crown (koruny) is convertible on current account transactions and is pegged (with adjustments permitted) to a basket of currencies. Combined with a relatively low foreign debt load and a healthy budgetary situation,[36] Czechoslovakia's financial sector was transformed more quickly and perhaps at lower cost in economic terms than was the case in Hungary, which followed a gradualist approach.[37] Czechoslovakia has also led the way in privatization schemes with the introduction of the voucher system in 1992 which also applied to former state-owned banking enterprises. Although the Czech Republic has continued the fast pace of reform since the break-up of Czechoslovakia, reforms in Slovakia have lagged. Moreover, in the face of rising budget deficits, the Slovak crown has depreciated relative to the Czech crown. The Czech crown is currently pegged to a basket of currencies whose weights are adjusted periodically. In June 1993, the basket was comprised of the German deutschmark (65 percent weight) and the U.S. dollar (35 percent weight).[38]

Despite the apparent ease of the transition there are disquieting signs of impending financial difficulties even in the Czech Republic. For example, Hrnčíř (1993) reports that between December 1991 and June 1993 there has been a large substitution in the ownership of shares of bank credit away from (former) state firms toward the "private" sector.[39] But since the "private" sector now includes former state-owned firms, which own most of these shares, the data give a misleading picture of the health of the Czech financial sector. We thus have a situation where former state-run firms own practically a majority stake in bank credits issued by commercial banks, which advanced these credits to the former state firms in the first place. This makes for an questionable banker-client relationship since banks manage most of the funds underlying the share issue and, consequently, face additional pressure to extend credits which are not backed in any real sense. Despite the creation of a consolidation bank, in 1994 the Czech government had begun to prepare yet another bailout of the commercial banks as this study was being written.

Was There or Is There Now a Credit Crunch?

The potential shortage of liquidity we have alluded to is akin to a credit crunch in that "if firms have limited access to credit or if interest rates are high, the increase in production costs would lead to a credit crunch" (Calvo and Coricelli 1992:71). A credit crunch means that firms are able to borrow funds only with considerable difficulty or not at all.[40] There has been considerable renewed interest in identifying credit crunches, particularly in the United States where the savings and loan scandal, combined with the tight monetary policy pursued by the Federal Reserve, has led some to argue that a new credit crunch emerged in the U.S. during the early 1990s.[41]

In industrialized countries with sophisticated money markets, a tightening of monetary policy by the monetary authorities leads to higher nominal and real interest rates and thus to lower aggregate demand. Alternatively, the tightening of monetary policy can occur via non-price aspects of banking behavior, such as regulatory changes. Hence, a credit crunch can still appear even when nominal interest rates are low. Banks may also contribute to a credit crunch through a contraction of their own as reflected on the asset side of their balance sheets.[42] Thus, for example, when the banks reduce the amount of commercial loans, (large) enterprises in industrialized economies can offset the fall in liquidity by issuing more commercial paper.[43] This option, however, is not yet available to firms in the transitional economies due to the underdevelopment of capital markets. Nor is self-financing much of an option as enterprise arrears grow (see below) and losses are the order of the day since relatively few enterprises are able to consistently generate profits.[44]

Figure 13.1 plots real balances for narrow and broad monetary aggregates. A single vertical bar in each figure marks the date of the beginning of the transition in each country. Admittedly, dating the beginning of the transition has an element of arbitrariness. However, doing so permits some rough comparisons to be made between the "old" and "new" economic regimes. Except for Czechoslovakia, real balances are only moderately lower than before the transition began. However, for Poland it could be argued that real balances simply reflect the elimination of the monetary overhang. The situation is quite different for Hungary where the monetary overhang problem was of little practical relevance. Only recently has the steep decline in real balances been reversed, thereby raising the distinct possibility that Hungary alone has experienced a credit crunch. The data for Czechoslovakia may simply reflect the failure of the Czechoslovak National Bank to hold monetary growth in line with its stated targets.[45] If lower money demand in Hungary and Poland is associated with the output contraction and anticipations of higher future inflation then, as argued by Calvo and Coricelli (1993), this may lead to a "bad" equilibrium, in part because of the resulting impact on the government's budget. The public, expecting higher inflation despite the government's promise to lower inflation through a restrictive monetary policy, will reduce its holdings of money. In order to generate the necessary revenues the government could be pressed to increasingly rely on a combination of policies such as monetization of the deficit (including the deficit of existing and former state enterprises) or a currency devaluation. The end result is more inflation and continuing reductions in money demand and the vicious circle to the "bad" equilibrium.

Taken at face value, real balances in Figure 13.1 reveal no such likelihood of a bad equilibrium for Czechoslovakia, but possibly one for Hungary and Poland. If the deficit-financing scenario outlined above is a credible one, then it will mean more crowding-out and the continuation of a credit crunch in these two countries. This is because it has been common for economies stabilizing in the aftermath of high inflation to ensure credibility via high real interest rates.[46]

Another indicator of credit conditions is the currency-money ratio. Thus, if the banking sector can attract funds away from the holding of currency—the

FIGURE 13.1

Hungary

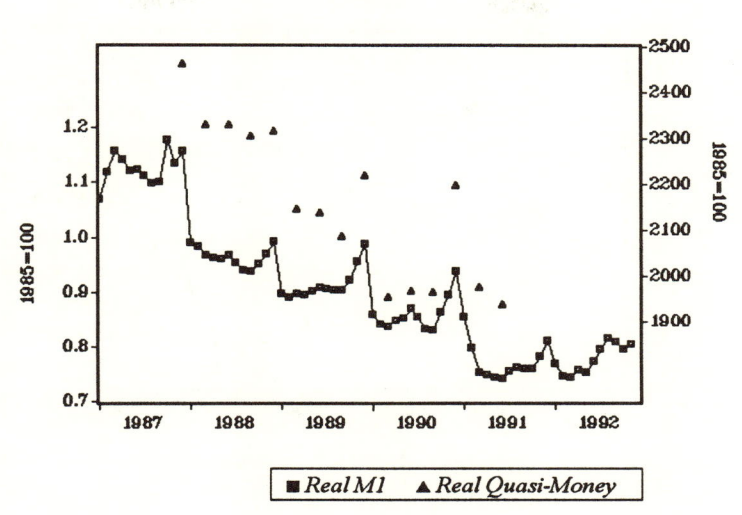

■ *Real M1*   ▲ *Real Quasi-Money*

Poland

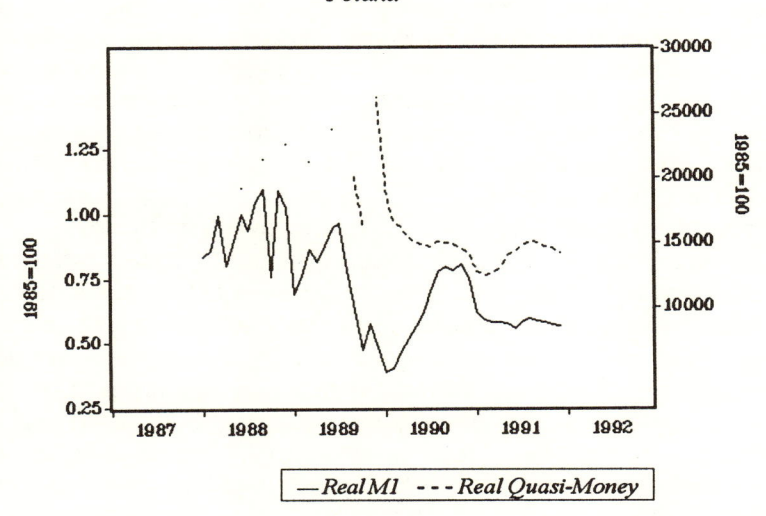

— *Real M1*   - - - *Real Quasi-Money*

(continues)

FIGURE 13.1 (continued)

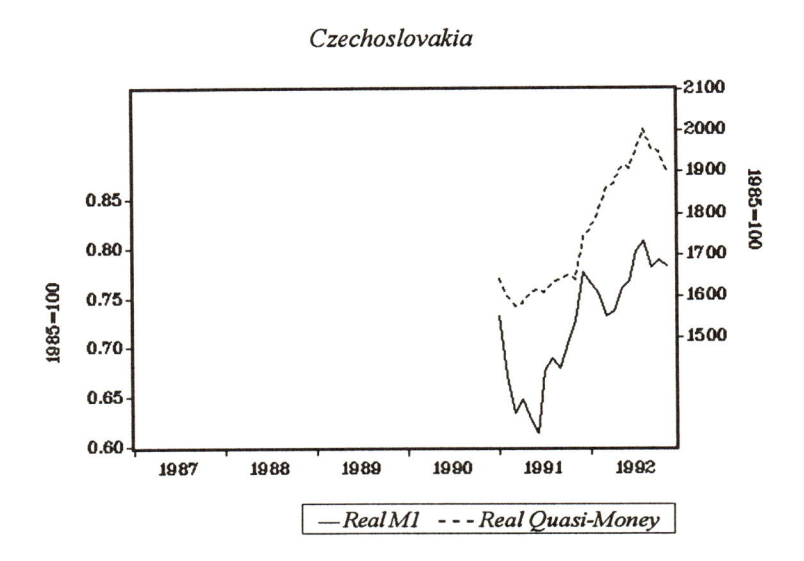

Czechoslovakia

— Real M1   - - - Real Quasi-Money

primary financial asset in a command economy—the currency-money ratio would fall. If, however, the banking system does not provide an attractive environment in which to hold financial assets, this would be reflected in a currency-money ratio which is not falling. Figure 13.2 plots the currency-money ratio for Hungary and Poland, the two countries for which there was sufficient data. There is a downward trend in Poland's currency-money ratio following the "Big Bang," and a small downward trend is also apparent in Hungarian data until the end of 1991.[47] Thereafter Hungary's currency-money ratio jumps to a higher level where it appears to remain stable.[48]

One would expect, other things being equal, portfolio reallocation to result in shifts away from currency toward interest-earning assets such as those included in a broad money measure. The behavior of the currency-money ratio suggests that banks are not acquiring the liquidity necessary to foster financial development, as occurred during the historical development of banking systems in western industrialized countries.[49] Part of the reason may be that real ex post interest rates, as seen in Figure 13.3, have yet to be high enough to entice money holders to reallocate their liquidity toward the banking system.[50] While ex post real interest rates have often hovered around zero, they have also been volatile, a relevant consideration given the fact that much of the available liquidity is short-term in nature.[51,52] This outcome reflects the fact that the central banking authorities are caught in a difficult bind. To attract

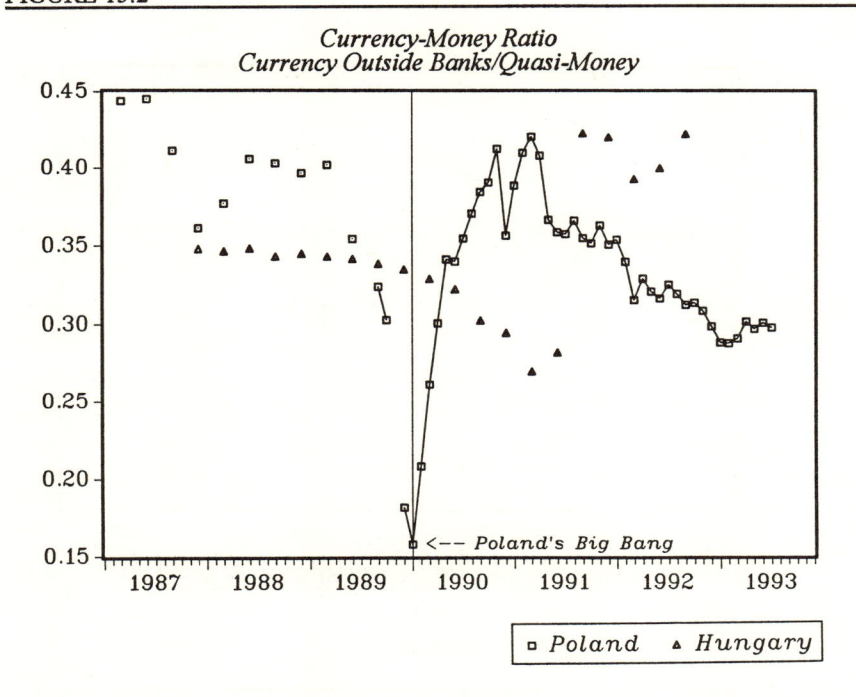

Fiscal and Monetary Policies in the Transition

FIGURE 13.2

Currency-Money Ratio
Currency Outside Banks/Quasi-Money

[Chart showing Poland and Hungary currency-money ratios from 1987 to 1993, with a marker indicating "<-- Poland's Big Bang" at the beginning of 1990. Y-axis ranges from 0.15 to 0.45.]

□ Poland   ▲ Hungary

liquidity into the financial system, sufficiently high real interest rates are necessary. But enterprises would be discouraged from borrowing since real interest rates on loans would also have to be high for the newly independent banking system to be profitable. Thus, it could be argued that a new kind of subsidy has replaced the previous arrangement of granting credits to enterprises via state budgets. Or, using the terminology attributed to Kornai and used to describe financing under central planning, a different soft budget constraint has replaced the old soft budget constraint devised by the former communist states. This approach is most apparent in Czechoslovakia and least evident in Hungary since, as noted above, nominal interest rates remain somewhat regulated whereas prices are more market determined.[53]

The real interest rate is, of course, in part a function of inflation performance. In this respect it is interesting to compare the inflation performance of the three countries.[54] By 1992 inflation in Hungary stood at 20.3 percent while Poland's and Czechoslovakia's inflation rates were 37.7 percent and 11.0 percent. Czechoslovakia benefited from a combination of low foreign debt together with growing foreign exchange reserves, which meant in effect that the real value of the crown was relatively well backed in the "real bills" doctrine sense of the term. By contrast, Hungary's high foreign debt load

FIGURE 13.3

Hungary

□ *Enterprise loan rate less CPI inflation* ▲ *Zero*

Poland

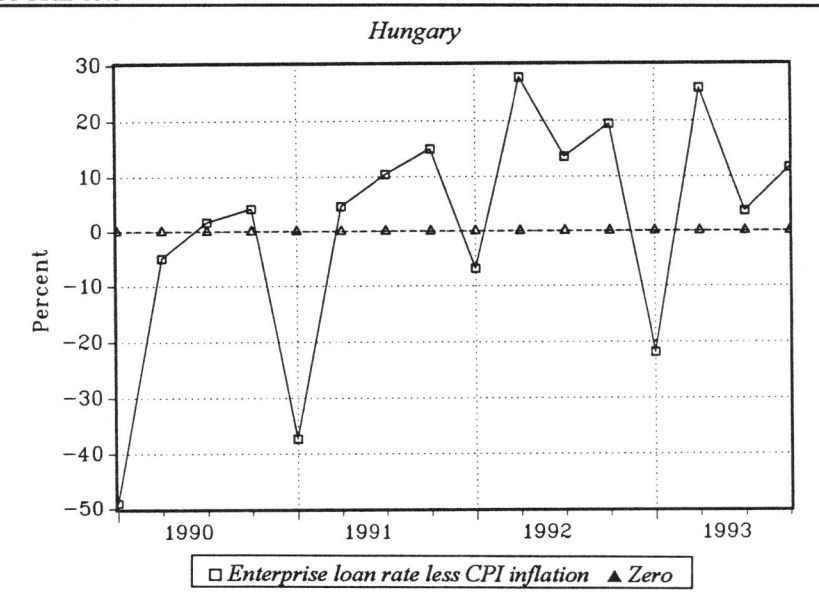

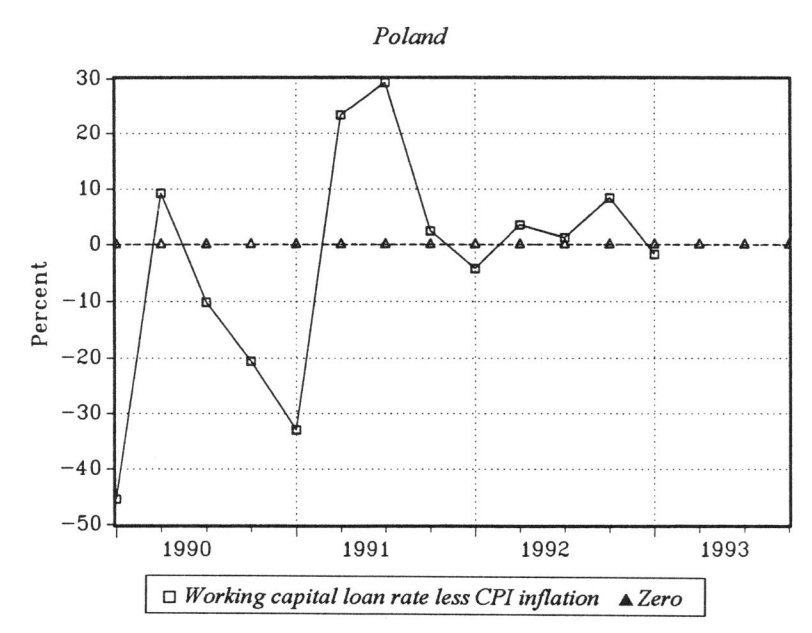

□ *Working capital loan rate less CPI inflation* ▲ *Zero*

(continues)

Fiscal and Monetary Policies in the Transition 251

FIGURE 13.3 (continued)

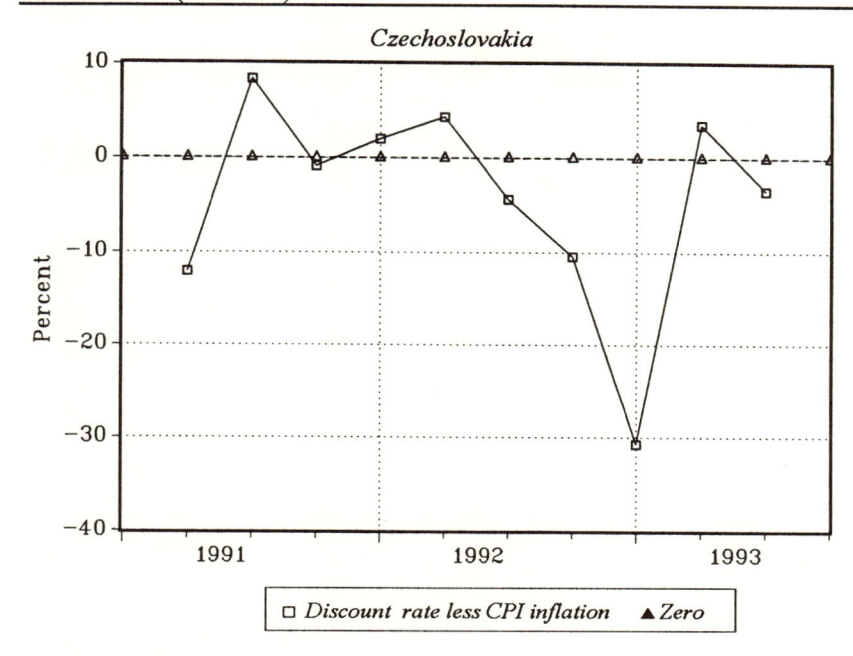

Czechoslovakia

[Chart: Discount rate less CPI inflation, Zero; x-axis 1991–1993; y-axis Percent, −40 to 10]

□ Discount rate less CPI inflation   ▲ Zero

and deeply indebted banking system meant that low inflation credibility had to be gained via the credit-crunch policy. Sharply rising foreign exchange reserves, however, assisted in backing the value of the Hungarian forint. Poland appears to represent an intermediate case. Inflation reached a peak of almost 600 percent in 1990, but since then foreign loan forgiveness and rising foreign exchange reserves have helped to dampen inflationary expectations and the rate has fallen.

Another useful indicator of credit conditions is the velocity of circulation (shown in Figure 13.4). Other things being equal, a lesser reliance on cash to finance transactions would be reflected in a higher velocity of circulation.[55] Velocity does not appear to have risen in any of the three countries, except temporarily, as would be expected in a credit crunch. The release of the monetary overhang may simply have overcompensated for the monetary impact of the credit crunch.[56] Nevertheless, there is some evidence that the joint behavior of velocity and the currency-money ratio is consistent with a model in which velocity is positively related to the currency-money ratio.[57] Thus, as commercial banking spreads, the currency-money ratio should fall to reflect a reduction in the public's reliance on currency and the growing volume of deposits and the increased sophistication of the financial system. This would lessen the impact or likelihood of a credit crunch.

FIGURE 13.4

Velocity in Levels

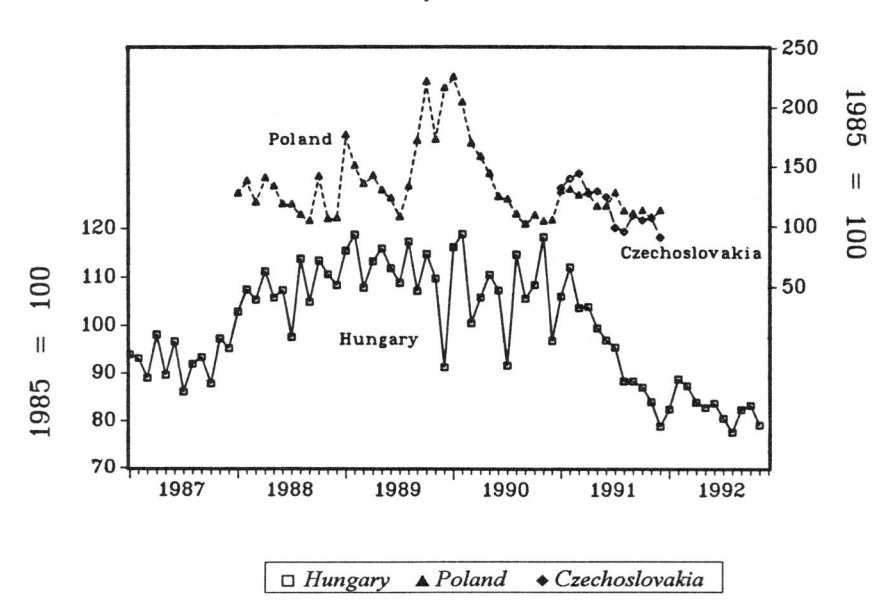

[Figure: Line chart showing velocity in levels from 1987 to 1992 for Hungary (left axis, 1985=100), Poland (right axis, 1985=100), and Czechoslovakia (right axis, 1985=100). Legend: □ Hungary ▲ Poland ◆ Czechoslovakia]

A few other broad indicators of the possibility of a credit crunch were also examined. For example, a credit or monetary crisis should significantly affect the money multiplier and the monetary base. Figure 13.5 plots the M2 money multiplier for Hungary and Poland (there were too few observations available for Czechoslovakia). One would expect the multiplier to fall as banks reduce their assets and as the demand for currency rises.[58] The latter occurs especially if the public is skeptical about the safety of the banking system. Figure 13.5 appears to show that, for Hungary at least, the behavior of the multiplier is consistent with the existence of a credit crunch until the beginning of 1992 when the multiplier starts to rise.[59] By contrast, the data for Poland suggest that the economic crisis may have led to a precipitous fall in the multiplier, which is suddenly reversed a few months after prices and exchange rate systems were liberalized. The rise in the multiplier continues through the months during which some of Poland's foreign debt was forgiven and a privatization scheme was announced. Thus it may be that the credit crunch is a purely Hungarian phenomenon. This might also help explain Hungary's better inflation record relative to Poland's. Of course, differences in deficit and exchange rate behavior between these two countries may also have been important.

FIGURE 13.5

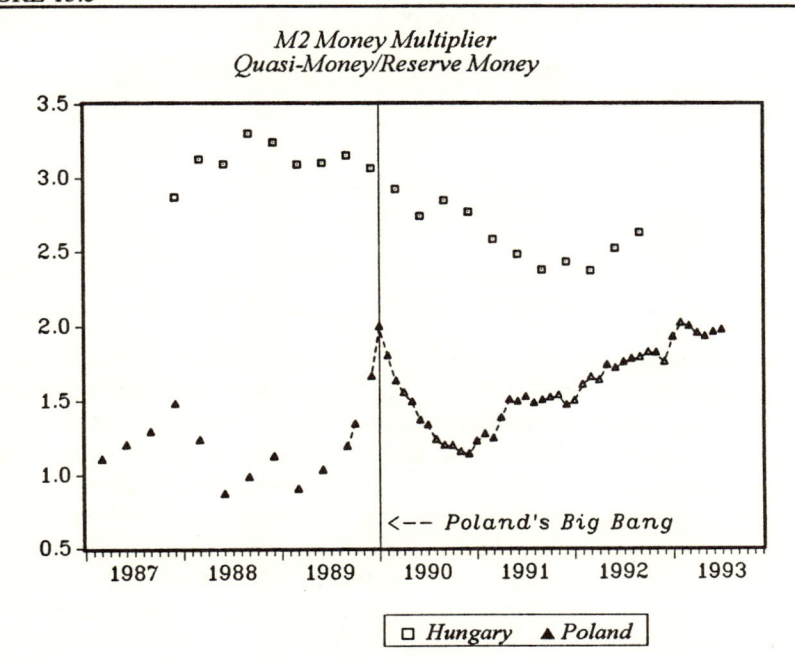

M2 Money Multiplier
Quasi-Money/Reserve Money

□ Hungary   ▲ Poland

So far our analysis has concentrated on the purely financial aspects of the transition. However, as noted in the introduction, the amplitude of the business cycle may be directly affected not only by monetary considerations but also by the behavior of the banking sector.[60] To investigate the role of aggregate credit in influencing economic activity, Figure 13.6 plots industrial production and real domestic credit for the three countries in our sample.[61] Note that the two series move roughly in tandem with each other in the three countries. Indeed, one striking difference between Hungary and Poland or Czechoslovakia is that in the latter two countries real domestic credit rises after the transitional reforms were introduced, whereas in Hungary, where no such big bang occurred, real domestic credit continued to fall until 1991. At the same time, industrial production in Poland and Czechoslovakia reversed its precipitous slide and stabilized. One way of analyzing the connection between industrial production and real domestic credit is to test whether one series causes the other in a statistical sense. One such test, widely used and well known, is the Granger causality test. Table 13.2 presents the results of Granger causality tests between real domestic credit and industrial production. Note the differences in the test results between Hungary and the other two countries, which are suggestive of the phenomenon described above. Real domestic credit

TABLE 13.2 Granger-Causality Tests of Real Domestic Credit (RDC) and Industrial Production (IP)

Country	Null Hypothesis	F-Statistic	Significance Level
Hungary	RDC is not caused by IP	1.18	.32
	IP is not caused by RDC	10.02	.00
Poland	RDC is not caused by IP	2.59	.09
	IP is not caused by RDC	1.79	.19
Czechoslovakia	RDC is not caused by IP	.62	.45
	IP is not caused by RDC	4.40	.06

is found to Granger-cause industrial production in the Hungarian data, but the reverse appears to be true for Poland and Czechoslovakia as one cannot reject the null that industrial production is not Granger-caused by real domestic credit. By contrast, one is able to reject the null that real domestic credit is not Granger-caused by industrial production.[62] Consequently, the test results are suggestive of an output effect stemming from credit constraints or the credit crunch for Hungary but not for Poland or Czechoslovakia.

As noted above, foreign sources of capital are vital in ensuring the liquidity and viability of the commercial banking sector, and exchange rate policy has an important role to play in this regard. All three countries considered here chose to introduce an adjustable peg exchange rate system after an initial devaluation and a period of fixed exchange rates.[63] As Figure 13.7 reveals, foreign exchange reserves in all three countries rose sharply, particularly after 1990. In the case of Poland this can be attributed to the reforms introduced that year,[64] and the same pattern holds for Czechoslovakia after the reforms of 1991. If the markets for these currencies were freely floating and operated as they do for the western industrialized countries—which, of course, they do not—then this would be an indication of undervaluation in the respective currencies. As Figure 13.8 reveals, this appears to be the case since real exchange rates for Poland and Hungary have been steadily rising.[65] For Hungary, the rise in the real exchange rate has been steady since its banking reforms in 1987. For Poland, the rise in the real exchange rate of the zloty resumed a pattern which predated the big bang of 1990. Because these currencies appear to be undervalued, existing asset purchases, direct or indirect via the banking system, can be expected to be worth less in the future because revaluation is expected. But so long as the prospective capital gains are in the future, this implies a tightening of credit flows thereby further exacerbating the severity of a credit crunch.[66]

Finally, evidence about the existence of a credit crunch is apparent from two other sources. As noted above, a credit crunch can be signalled by firms

255

FIGURE 13.6

Hungary

Poland

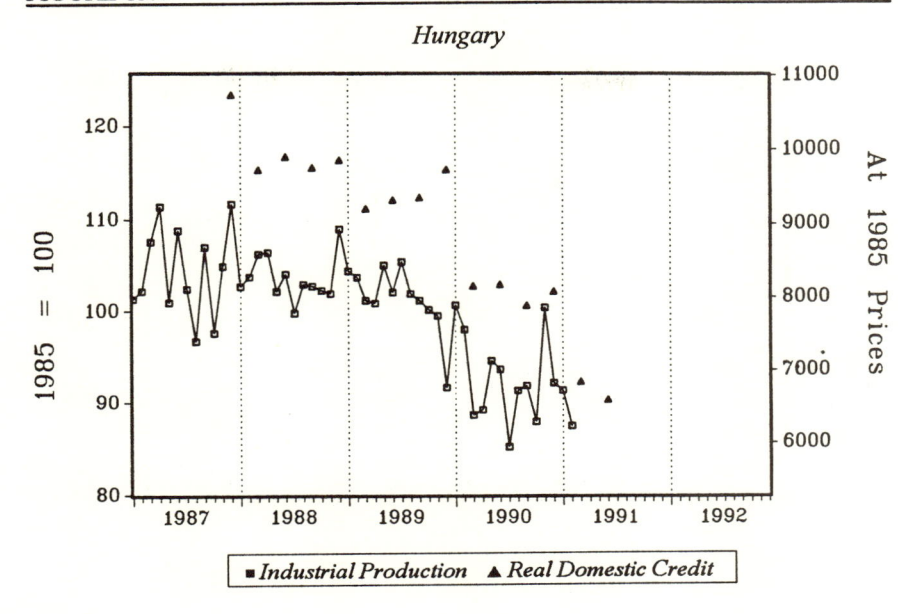

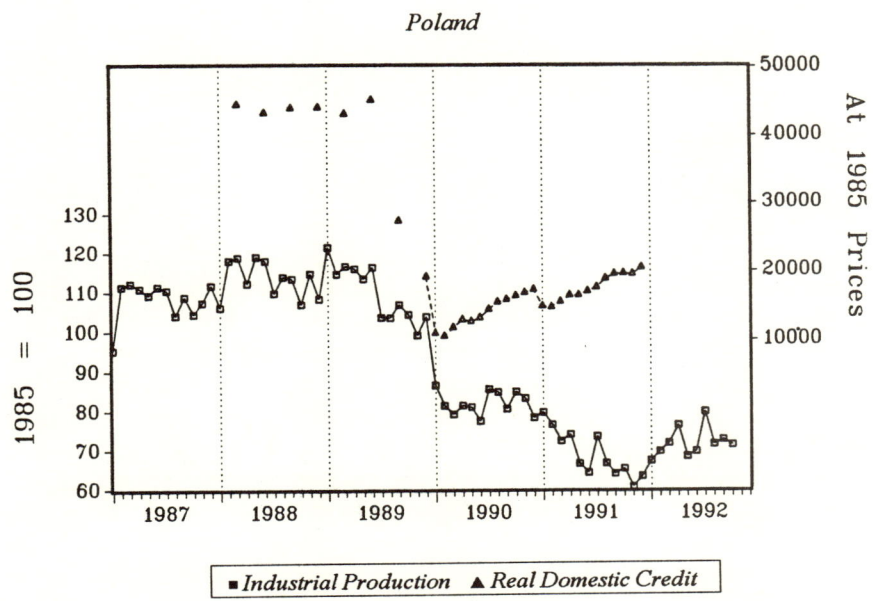

■ *Industrial Production*   ▲ *Real Domestic Credit*

(continues)

FIGURE 13.6 (continued)

Czechoslovakia

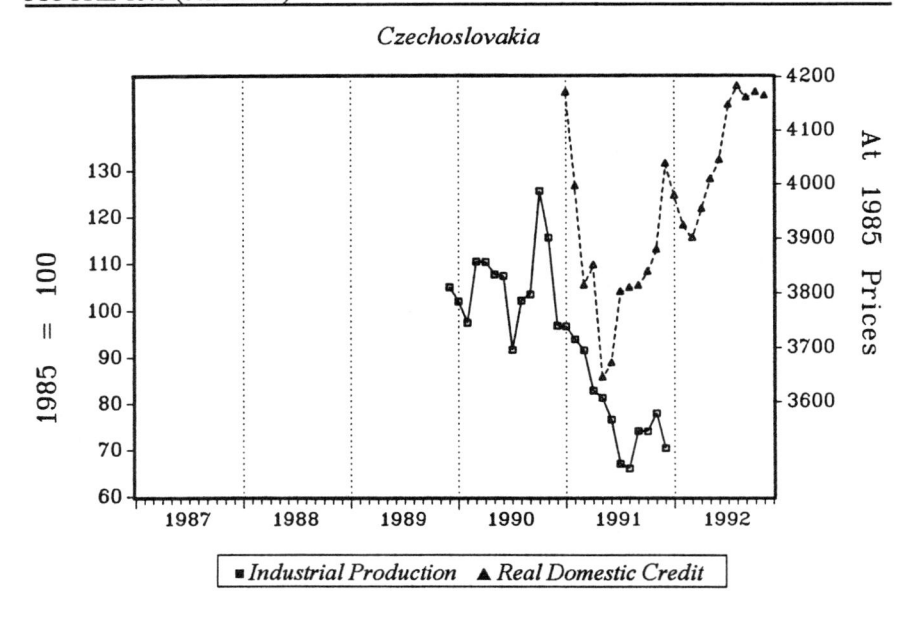

■ *Industrial Production* ▲ *Real Domestic Credit*

FIGURE 13.7

Foreign Exchange Reserves (Millions of Dollars)

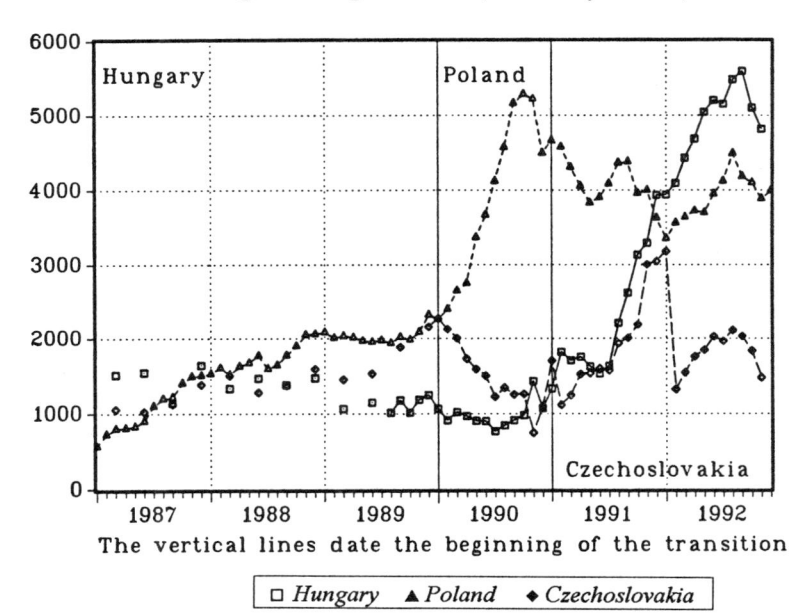

The vertical lines date the beginning of the transition

□ *Hungary* ▲ *Poland* ♦ *Czechoslovakia*

FIGURE 13.8

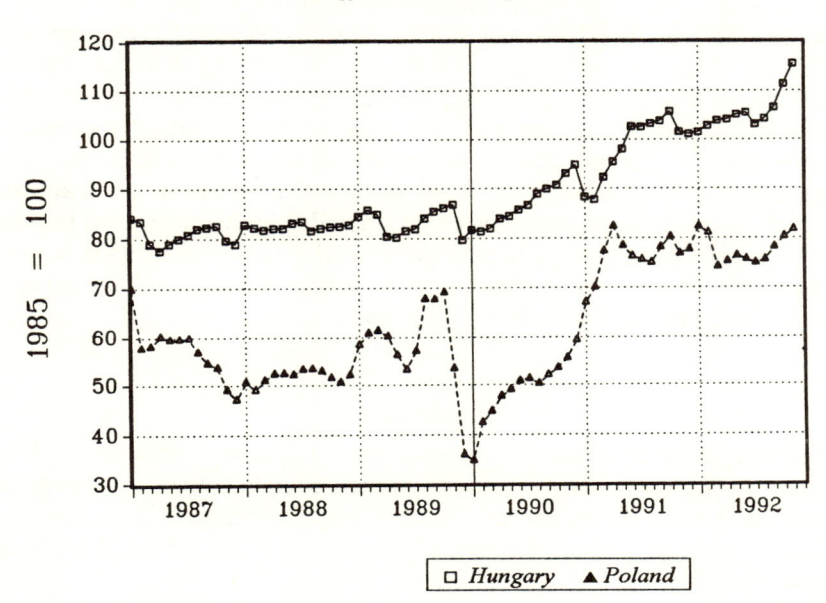

Real Effective Exchange Rate

1985 = 100

□ Hungary ▲ Poland

attempting to obtain funds from alternative sources, for example via inter-enterprise credits. Hungary's experience is illuminating in this respect. Between January 1987 and May 1992 total inter-enterprise debt rose 1300 percent while the number of firms engaged in such transactions also rose by over 1300 percent.[67] There is, however, a sharp reversal in both trends beginning in April 1992. Thus, Hungarian monetary policy seems to have been instrumental in generating a credit crunch. The costs of such a policy would be reflected in the contraction of output whereas the principal benefits would be in the form of lower inflation and additional IMF support as well as a greater inflow of foreign investment. Hrnčíř (1993:Table 13.1) reveals that for Czechoslovakia inter-enterprise debt rose 948 percent between June 1989 and September 1992. The number of firms involved also rose by a similar proportion. There is no evidence of a sharp reversal, and so it appears less likely that a credit crunch was engineered for Czechoslovakia.[68]

An additional source of credit constraints arises from a problem alluded to above, namely the reluctance of the commercial banking sector to act as a source of long-term funds. Thus in 1991 long-term corporate lending stood at less than 20 percent of total assets, which represents a 50 percent fall since 1988.[69] In the meantime, the spread between average deposit and loan rates in all three countries rose sharply. In Hungary, for example, the spread at the short-term end of the maturity structure (i.e., one year or less) stood at less than 1 percent in 1988 and rose to over 8 percent by early 1992,[70] reaching 12 percent by 1993.[71] The experiences of Poland and the current Czech Republic are similar. This may be taken as evidence of the growing risk premium on commercial loans. Broadly speaking, the data so far point to a credit crunch occuring foremost in Hungary and, to a lesser extent, in Poland, and one is least evident for Czechoslovakia. Nevertheless, the data are not especially informative about the sources of the credit crunch which, as pointed out above, reflects a crowding-out phenomenon and confounds purely transitional factors with monetary and fiscal policies implemented since the transition began. Addressing some of these issues awaits further research which we are presently undertaking for the Hungarian case.

Conclusions

Taken together the evidence presented above suggests a credit crunch has occurred in Hungary, while this is less apparent for the other two countries considered. Because the crunch appears most severe in Hungary, this raises the question of what the gradualist approach has accomplished for the Hungarian financial system.

To the extent that our data are faulty, it is possible that our interpretation of the credit crunch is misleading. For example, Sachs (1993) argues that industrial production data are biased since they do not reflect the growing importance of the nascent private sector. Second, since savings rates are high (unfortunately, the data in this respect are equally likely to be unreliable) financing the transition may not be so problematic. While one cannot entirely dismiss these caveats, we believe that the weight of the evidence is on our side. The lessons from Canada's own experience earlier this century serve to illustrate the importance, even with relatively high savings rates, for economic growth or large-scale capital inflows of an efficient banking system and few capital controls.[72] Moreover, so long as governments in the transitional economies, and Hungary and Poland especially come to mind here, continue to constantly draft new legislation the resulting regulatory uncertainty can only delay the maturation of commercial banking, preventing banks from providing the intermediation services necessary to foster economic growth. In this connection, there are also lessons to be learned from neighboring countries such as Austria. As Glück (1994) clearly points out, the Austrian experience is one of a slow and cautious road to full convertibility, credible inflation and financial liberalization over a twenty-year span. Although the transitional economies may not be able to afford quite so leisurely an approach, a more systematic and orderly set of reforms is, at the very least, desirable.

Notes

1. This point has already been made by several authors, among them Calvo and Coricelli (1992), and Ábel and Bonin (1992c).

2. In the working paper version of this chapter, available from Pierre Siklos, we have compiled a chronology of economic and political events for the three countries that may be useful to some interested readers who are not familiar with the details of the transition process.

3. See, among others, Székely (1992,1990), Hardy and Lahiri (1992), Duchatczek and Schubert (1992), Bruno (1992), Balassa (1992), Jindra (1992), Rudka (1992), Ábel and Székely (1992a), Kemme (1992), Commission of the European Communities (1991), *The Banker* (July 1992).

4. See, however, Calvo and Kumar (1993), Borensztein and Masson (1993), and the forthcoming volume edited by Székely and Bonin (1994).

5. See also Székely and Newberry (1993) for additional details about Hungary's transitional problems.

6. There are still considerable doubts about whether privatization will take place on schedule since a first attempt to privatize Budapest Bank has failed.

7. For the details, see Siklos (1994a:chp. 10).

8. *New Banking Act in Hungary II*, p. 33. See also Ábel and Székely (1992a).

9. In part, Ábel and Bonin (1992b) note, because loan consolidation schemes help improve banks' balance sheets. Also, much of the data discussed tends not to adjust for risk categories. When risk-adjusted weights are incorporated, Hungarian banks have not yet, strictly speaking, achieved the Bank of International Settlements standards. (See *Bank Research-Eastern Europe* 1991). The ratios referred to are percent of adjusted capital, which consists of the paid-in portion of registered capital, capital reserves, retained earnings, profit (loss) during a particular year, general provisions and subordinated debt. See *New Banking Act in Hungary I* (1991), Annex, Appendix 2. Siklos (1994:chp. 10) lists the principal risk-weights developed by the Bank of International Settlements.

10. See Ábel, Bonin and Siklos (1994).

11. For example, at the end of 1990 only .4 percent of loans of the Budapest Bank were long term. Moreover, most of these loans were to companies in which the World Bank and the International Finance Corporation are also actively involved. See *Bank Research-Eastern Europe* (1991).

12. Data for the Hungarian banking sector reveal that in 1991 almost 80 percent of funds were obtained from foreign sources. Except for 1989, when the supply of foreign funds fell to 74 percent, the proportion of funds to the domestic banking sector coming from abroad has varied between 77 percent and 80 percent. See Nagy (1992).

13. For further discussion see Ábel and Siklos (1994), Ábel, Bonin, and Siklos (1994), and see below.

14. Ábel, Bonin and Siklos (199:Table 3).

15. The fiscal problems are not so much due to increases in spending but rather to problems with reducing the massive scale of subsidies and social programs built up under the central-planning regime as well as the slow pace of the reforms on the tax

side of the budget equation. Centrally planned economies tended to rely on turnover style taxes, and the move toward ad valorem or value-added style taxes, as well as the introduction of income taxes, has been hampered by an inefficient tax collection structure. Moreover, as taxes are relatively high, there exists an incentive for enterprises to avoid taxes by generating losses instead of profits. As Cukierman, Edwards, and Tabellini (1992) have shown, countries with a poor tax collection infrastructure tend to resort to seigniorage which leads to persistently high rates of inflation.

16. Jaksity (1993:Table V).

17. Based on data from *OECD Main Economic Indicators*, various issues.

18. There is insufficient space here to discuss the separate question of the sustainability of public debt. See, however, Cohen (1991). Concern over this question is heightened by the fact that negative industrial productivity or real GDP growth combined with positive real interest rates have produced the "unpleasant monetarist arithmetic" scenario. This also raises the question of central bank independence in Central Europe discussed in Siklos (1994b).

19. In 1992, the National Bank of Hungary introduced two types of repurchase agreements. "Passive" repurchase agreements are meant to be used as a conventional money market instrument, as in several western industrialized countries such as Canada. "Active" repurchase agreements are meant to assist commercial banks with short-term liquidity problems.

20. See Ábel and Bonin (1992b) and *OECD Financial Market Trends* (1992) for further discussion of the deficiencies of the Hungarian banking system.

21. See Szabó (1991), Nyers and Lutz (1992), National Bank of Hungary (1993, various issues) and the discussion below.

Some of the data for the banking sector in Nagy (1992:Table 2) is instructive in this regard. Thus, between 1987 and 1991, commercial loans fell from 79 percent of total assets to 58 percent, whereas holdings of securities rose from 1 percent to 12 percent of total assets over the same period.

22. Balassa (1992:23). There are a host of other prudential requirements which depend on whether outstanding loans are classified as "bad" or otherwise. See *New Banking Act in Hungary I* (1991), par. 28.

23. See National Bank of Hungary (1992:111).

24. This is reflected in two different statistics. First, the passage into law of the Bankruptcy Act of 1992 has led to proceedings in the case of 2881 incorporated entities by July 31, 1993. Second, corporate tax revenues during the first seven months of 1993 were only one quarter of the projected figure. See National Bank of Hungary (July 1993:21).

25. As argued in Siklos and Ábel (1994), the National Bank of Hungary acts as if it is pursuing a real exchange target. One reason for pursuing such a policy is that, by 1993, the National Bank was borrowing mainly from German and Japanese money markets. See National Bank of Hungary (April 1993:24).

26. See International Monetary Fund (1993) for a description of exchange rate regimes.

27. Kemme (1992), and section 3 below.
28. A detailed account of the first year of the Polish stabilization program is contained in Lane (1992). Wyczański (1993) points out that there have been many changes in the legislation affecting the banking system and the central bank since 1989.
29. This is partly reflected in the fact that, by the end of May 1993, 4950 enterprises were reported by commercial banks not to be credit worthy. This figure represents an increase of over 11 percent relative to the May 1992 figure. See Narodowy Bank Polski (1993:5).
30. See Kemme (1992).
31. Capital controls can be viewed as a device, though not the only one, to ensure that a chosen exchange rate remains credible or stable. See Portes (1993) for a discussion of these questions as they apply to the European Monetary System. See also Kokoszczynski (1993).
32. This may also have been precipitated by the general belief that dollarization is relatively more advanced in Poland than in either Hungary or Czechoslovakia.
33. See Borensztein and Masson (1993:chart I).
34. See Aghlevi, Borensztein, and van der Willigen (1992), Hrnčíř (1991), and Prust (1990) for additional details about the Czechoslovak transition program.
35. One can speculate that despite the consolidation fund, the balance sheet situation of Czechoslovak banks was even less favorable than that of either Polish or Hungarian banks. See Hrnčíř (1993).
36. According to Hrnčíř and Klacek (1991:Table 2), Czechoslovakia's foreign debt stood at 104 percent of exports in 1989. By contrast, Hungary's and Poland's external debt stood at 319 percent and 486 percent of exports, respectively, for the same year. By 1992, Czechoslovakia's external debt as a percent of exports fell to an estimated 56.7 percent (Institute of International Finance Inc.:Table 6).
37. Among others, see Kemme (1992).
38. See Hrnčíř (1993).
39. Ownership has fallen from 66.89 percent of these credits at the end of 1992 to 42.53 percent at the end of June 1993. By contrast, the "private" sector's share has risen from 9.78 percent to 40.10 percent over the same period. See Hrnčíř (1993: Table 1).
40. Sundararajan and Baliño (1991:2).
41. See, for example, Bernanke and Lown (1992), Owens and Schreft (1992) and Peek and Rosengren (1993) for empirical evidence.
42. This is called the credit channel effect of monetary policy by Bernanke and Blinder (1988). Analyses which ignore the role of banks in the monetary transmission process are said to focus instead on the monetary channel of monetary policy. For our purposes, the terms credit or money crunches are used interchangeably.
43. Even in Hungary, where capital markets are relatively advanced compared with elsewhere in Central Europe, only 0.4 percent of corporate funding occurs via the bond market and an even smaller percentage of capital is raised via stock issues. All data are from the National Bank of Hungary (October 1993:123).

44. Unless the effect is an output-induced one, in which case nonbank credit would also fall. See Kashyap, Stein and Wilcox (1993) on this point. As Bruno (1992) points out, a credit crunch is not surprising in the aftermath of hyperinflation. Bolivia, Mexico, and Israel all experienced the same effect after their stabilizations.

45. This is certainly consistent with the evidence presented in Hrnčíř (1991).

46. See Siklos (1990) for a survey.

47. We discuss the behavior of the currency-money ratio further below when we describe the behavior of velocity. While it is plausible that the absence of deposit insurance, except in Hungary where it was introduced in 1993, may have influenced the currency-money ratio, there is no evidence of such an independent effect stemming from the creation of deposit insurance in several of the industrialized economies unless it is viewed as being part and parcel of what is meant by financial development, broadly speaking. See Siklos (1993).

48. I have not been able to determine whether the jump is due to a change in the definition of either the currency or the quasi-money series. However, the jump does not appear to be due to some regulatory event.

49. Siklos (1993:chp. 3).

50. Also, the data reveal the impact of interest rate ceilings on various bank deposits. See Kemme (1994) for a chronology of these ceilings for the three countries examined in this study.

51. Controls on interest rate levels are still in place in these countries. They now appear to be adjusted to reflect market conditions over time, but not necessarily on a month-to-month basis, which is the data frequency used in generating the estimates of ex post real interest rates shown in Figure 13.3. See Kemme (1994) for the current state of interest rate regulation in the transitional economies of Central Europe.

52. Subject to the caveat that ex post real interest rates need not be a good indicator of ex ante real rates.

53. This suggests that the so-called high real interest rate policy supposedly practiced by the monetary authorities may not be entirely effective. One caveat to this interpretation is that our calculations may be sensitive to the choice of interest rate series. We did try a variety of definitions and our inferences appear to be robust. Alternatively, what may be signalling the severity of the credit crunch is the differential between borrowing and lending rates at the commercial banks. More about this possibility below.

54. All figures reported below are annualized monthly rates of change in the consumer price index.

55. Bordo and Jonung (1987) and Siklos (1993).

56. In a quantity theory formulation, namely $MV = Py$, where M is the money supply, V is income velocity, and Py is aggregate nominal income (i.e., the price level (p) multiplied by real income (y)), if Py is stable then a release of the overhang should, other things being equal, signal a reduction in velocity. Thus, a monetary crunch could trigger a rise in velocity to offset its effects. Indeed, velocity in all three countries behaves as a random walk since tests fail to reject the null of a unit root in the logarithm of the levels at conventional significance levels. For Hungary the Dickey-

Fuller test statistic is -1.442 (four lags), -2.585 (four lags) for Poland, and -.864 (one lag) for Czechoslovakia.

57. This is consistent with the institutionalist model of velocity's behavior. See Siklos (1993) and references within. The regression of the logarithm of velocity (v), on a constant, the log of the currency-money ratio, and inflation (as a proxy for expected inflation) produced the following results: for Hungary $v = 4.75 + .53\text{CM} + .001\pi$ (R-squared =.28; sample: 1987.4–1991.2); for Poland $v = 4.99 + .65\text{CM} + .001\pi$ (R-squared = .66; sample: 1990.01–1991.12). There were too few observations to estimate a regression for Czechoslovakia, while the data for Hungary are quarterly because currency data were only available at this frequency. All coefficients were found to be statistically significant at the 1 percent level, except in the Hungarian case.

58. E.g., see Sundararajan and Baliño (1991).

59. It is only fairly recently that reserve requirements have begun to fall in the three countries considered here. The effects would not, however, be apparent in the available data.

60. See Bernanke and Lown (1992) for empirical evidence that the most recent recession in the U.S. (1990–1992) was one of the few not directly caused by a credit crunch but rather by a weakness in the commercial banking sector's balance sheets. Given the discussion in section 3 above concerning the Basel guidelines applied to banks in the transitional economies, the parallels with the U.S. situation are interesting.

61. Doubts have been expressed recently about both the quality of industrial production data and its relevance in analyzing transitional issues. On this question see, for example, Sachs (1993).

62. While we have followed previous practice for such tests there is the possibility that Granger-causality test results can be overturned because of omitted variables bias.

63. See Borensztein and Masson (1993).

64. See Sachs (1993).

65. The International Financial Statistics CD-ROM did not contain the relevant series for Czechoslovakia. Data for Czechoslovakia from *The Economist* ("Buy Now, While Currencies Last," June 20, 1992, p. 92) also reveal a rise in the real exchange rate of the crown since 1991. The undervaluation may, of course, have been a deliberate policy tool. It could be argued that such a policy acts as an insurance premium of sorts in light of the uncompetitiveness of the countries considered here along the quality or technology dimensions of their exportable products.

66. This is purely a substitution effect for losses anticipated on foreign exchange transactions that can be offset by gains in production costs savings due primarily to relatively low real wages in all three countries. Other factors influencing the supply of funds include fiscal and monetary policies in western industrialized countries, notably those arising from the costs of German reunification as well as deficit financing needs in those countries. Another side effect of a real appreciation, of course, is that the higher relative price of home goods leads to a reduction in aggregate demand. The resulting output loss makes investment in these countries still less attractive.

67. Ábel and Siklos (1994:Table 2).
68. The data for Poland do not reflect inter-enterprise arrears but rather ordinary trade credit. Hence, discussion of these figures would be misleading.
69. From data in Figure 3 in Ábel and Székely (1992a).
70. See Figure 6, Ábel and Székely (1992a).
71. National Bank of Hungary (April 1993:35).
72. There exists a vigorous debate about whether transitional economies should lift capital controls. The argument in favor of capital controls is the prevention of capital flight, while those who oppose such restrictions view the removal of capital controls as necessary to ensure a commitment to market liberalization and low and stable inflation.

References

Ábel, I. 1992. "Variants of Bankruptcy." *Eastern European Economics* 1: 47–54.

Ábel, I., and J. P. Bonin. 1991. "Two Approaches to the Transformation in Eastern Europe: The 'Big Bang' versus 'Slow But Steady'. " *Acta Oeconomica* 43(3–4): 213–30.

⎯⎯⎯⎯. 1992a. "Capital Markets in Eastern Europe: The Financial Black Hole." *Connecticut Journal of International Law* 8 (Fall): 1–17.

⎯⎯⎯⎯. 1992b. "Hungary's Loan Consolidation Program: Is It A Step Backward?" Manuscript.

⎯⎯⎯⎯. 1992c. "State Desertion and Financial Market Failure: Is the Transition Stalled?" Unpublished manuscript.

Ábel, I., J. P. Bonin, and P. L. Siklos. 1994. "Crippled Monetary Policy in Transforming Economies: Why Central Bank Independence Does Not Restore Control," in P. L. Siklos, ed., *Varieties of Monetary Reforms: Lessons and Experiences on the Road to Monetary Union*. Dordrecht, The Netherlands: Kluwer Academic Publishers, forthcoming.

Ábel, I., and P. L. Siklos. 1994. "Constraints on Enterprise Liquidity and Its Impact on the Monetary Sector in Formerly Centrally Planned Economies." *Comparative Economic Studies*, forthcoming.

Ábel, I., and I. P. Székely. 1992a. "The Conditions for Competition and Innovation in the Hungarian Banking System." Unpublished manuscript.

⎯⎯⎯⎯. 1992b. "Monetary Policy and Separated Monetary Circuits in a Modified CPE (The Case of Hungary)." *Acta Oeconomica* 44(3–4): 392–428.

Act on the National Bank of Hungary. 1991. Budapest: Ministry of Finance.

Aghlevi, B., E. Borensztein, and T. van der Willigen. 1992. "Stabilization and Structural Reform in Czechoslovakia: An Assessment of the First Stage." IMF Working Paper 92/2, January.

Balassa, A. 1992. "The Transformation and Development of the Hungarian Banking System," in D. Kemme and A. Rudka, eds., *Monetary and Banking Reforms in Post-Communist Economies*. Pp. 6–42. New York: Institute for East-West Security Studies.

Bank Research - Eastern Europe. 1991. Budapest Bank Rt., Hungary.

The Banker. 1992. London, July.

Bernanke, R., and A. S. Blinder. 1988. "Credit, Money, and Aggregate Demand." *American Economic Review Papers and Proceedings* 78 (May): 435–39.

Bernanke, B. S., and C. S. Lown. 1992. "The Credit Crunch." *Brookings Papers on Economic Activity* 2: 205–39.

Bordo, M. D., and L. Jonung. 1987. *The Long-Run Behaviour of the Velocity of Circulation: The International Evidence*. Cambridge: Cambridge University Press.

Borensztein, E., and P. R. Masson. 1993. "Exchange Arrangements of Previously Centrally Planned Economies," in Part II of *Financial Sector Reforms and Exchange Arrangements in Eastern Europe*. IMF Occasional Paper No. 102. Washington D.C.: International Monetary Fund, February.

Bruno, M. 1992. "Stabilization and Reform in Eastern Europe: Preliminary Evaluation." IMF Working Paper 92/30, May.

Calvo, G. A., and F. Coricelli. 1993. "Capital Market Imperfections and Output Response in Previously Centrally Planned Economies." Manuscript, May 20.

———. 1992. "Stagflationary Effects of Stabilization Programs in Reforming Socialist Countries: Enterprise-Side and Household-Side Factors." *The World Bank Economic Review* 6(1): 71–90.

Calvo, G. A., and M. S. Kumar. 1993. "Financial Markets and Intermediation," in Part I of *Financial Sector Reforms and Exchange Arrangements in Eastern Europe*. IMF Occasional Paper No. 102, February.

Cohen, D. 1991. "The Solvency of Eastern Europe." *European Economy*, special edition no. 2: 263–303.

Commission of the European Communities. 1991. *European Economy*, special edition no. 2.

Corbo, V., F. Coricelli, and J. Bossak, eds. 1991. *Reforming Central and Eastern European Economies: Initial Results and Challenges*. Washington, D.C.: The World Bank.

Cukierman, A., S. Edwards, and G. Tabellini. 1992. "Seigniorage and Political Instability." *American Economic Review* 82 (June): 537–55.

Duchatczek, W., and A. Schubert. 1992. "Monetary Policy Issues in Selected Eastern European Economies." SUERF Papers on Monetary Policy and Financial Systems No. 11. Tilburg, The Netherlands: Société Universitaire Européenne de Recherches Financières.

Fischer, S. 1991. "Privatization in East European Transformation." National Bureau for Economic Research Working Paper No. 3703, May.

Glück, H. 1994. "The Austrian Experience with Financial Liberalization," in I. Székely and J. P. Bonin, eds., *Development and Reform in Central and Eastern Europe*. London: Edward Elgar, forthcoming.

Grosfeld, I., and P. Hare. 1991. "Privatization in Hungary, Poland, and Czechoslovakia." *European Economy*, special edition no. 2: 129–56.

Hardy, D. C., and A. K. Lahiri. 1992. "Bank Insolvency and Stabilization in Eastern Europe." IMF Working Paper 92/9, January.

Hare, P., and T. Révész. 1992. "Hungary's Transition to the Market: The Case Against a 'Big Bang'." *Economic Policy*, April: 228–64.

Hrnčíř, M. 1994. "Reform of the Banking Sector in the Czech Republic," in I. Székely and J. P. Bonin, eds., *Development and Reform in Central and Eastern Europe*. London: Edward Elgar, forthcoming.

_____. 1993. "Financial Intermediation in Former Czechoslovakia (Lessons and Progress Evaluation)." Paper presented at the Conference on Company Management and Capital Markets, Prague, April.

_____. 1991. "Money and Credit in the Transition of the Czechoslovak Economy," in H. Siebert, ed., *The Transformation of Socialist Economies.* Pp. 307–25. Tübigen: J. C. B. Mohr (Paul Siebeck).

Hrnčíř, M., and J. Klacek. 1991. "Stabilization Policies and Currency Convertibility in Czechoslovakia." *European Economy,* special edition no. 2: 17–40.

International Monetary Fund. 1993. *Financial Sector Reform and Exchange Rate Arrangements in Eastern Europe.* Occasional Paper No. 102. Washington, D.C.: International Monetary Fund.

Jaksity, Gy. 1993. "Egy Nem Hàtékony Piac Alkimiàja [The Alchemy of an Inefficient Market]." Budapest: Lupis Bròkerhàz, January.

Jindra, V. 1992. "Problems in Czechoslovak Banking Reform," in D. M. Kemme and A. Rudka, eds., *Monetary and Banking Reform in Post-Communist Economies.* Pp. 43–71. New York: Institute for East-West Security Studies.

Kaser, M. C. 1990. "The Technology of Decontrol: Some Macroeconomic Issues." *Economic Journal* 100 (June): 596–615.

Kashyap, A. K., J. D. Stein, and D. W. Wilcox. 1993. "Monetary Policy and Credit Conditions: Evidence from the Composition of External Finance." *American Economic Review* 83 (March): 78–98.

Kemme, D. M. 1994. "Banking in Central Europe During the Protomarket Period: Development and Emerging Issues," in I. Székely and J. P. Bonin, eds., *Development and Reform of the Financial System in Central and Eastern Europe.* London: Edward Elgar, forthcoming.

_____. 1992. "The Reform of the System of Money, Banking and Credit in Central Europe." Manuscript, Wichita State University.

Kokoszczynski, R. 1993. "Money and Capital Market Reform in Poland," in I. Székely and J. P. Bonin, eds., *Development and Reform of the Financial System in Central and Eastern Europe.* London: Edward Elgar, forthcoming.

Lane, T. D. 1992. "Inflation Stabilization and Economic Transformation in Poland: The First Year." *Carnegie-Rochester Conference Series on Public Policy* 36 (July): 105–56.

Lipton, D., and J. Sachs. 1990. "Creating a Market Economy in Eastern Europe: The Case of Poland." Pp. 75–133. *Brookings Papers on Economic Activity* 1.

_____. 1991. "Privatization in Eastern Europe: The Case of Poland," in V. Corbo, F. Coricelli, and J. Bossak, eds., *Reforming Central and Eastern European Economies: Initial Results and Challenges.* Pp. 231–52. Washington, D.C.: The World Bank.

Lui, S., and K. Osband. 1992. "Can The Release of Monetary Overhang Trigger Hyperinflation?" IMF Working Paper 92/24, March.

Montias, J. M. 1994. "Financial and Fiscal Aspects of System Change in Eastern Europe," in I. Székely and J. P. Bonin, eds., *Development and Reform in Central and Eastern Europe.* London: Edward Elgar, forthcoming.

Nagy, M. 1992. "Nagybankok a Hazai Bankrendszerben [Large Banks in the Domestic Banking System]." Budapest Bank Tanulmànyok 8, Budapest.

Narodowy Bank Polski [National Bank of Poland]. 1993. *Information Bulletin,* 5/1993.

National Bank of Hungary. 1993. *Monthly Reports*, various issues, Budapest.
―――――. 1992. *Annual Report 1992*, Budapest.
New Banking Act in Hungary I and II. 1991. Budapest: State Banking Supervision, December 1.
Nyers, R., and G. Lutz. 1992. "A Nagybankok Portfòliòjànak Javitàsa [Correction of Large Banks' Portfolios]." *Bankszemle* 1–2: 34–43.
OECD. 1992. *Financial Market Trends* 51 (February): 15–30.
Owens, R. E., and S. L. Schreft. 1992. "Identifying Credit Crunches." Manuscript, Federal Reserve Bank of Richmond, August.
Peek, J., and E. Rosengren. 1993. "Bank Regulation and the Credit Crunch." Federal Reserve Bank of Boston Working Paper 93–2, February.
Phelps, E. S., R. Frydman, A. Rapaczynski, and A. Schleifer. 1993. "Needed Mechanisms of Corporate Governance and Finance in Eastern Europe." European Bank for Reconstruction and Development Working Paper No. 1, March.
Portes, R. 1993. "EMS and EMU After the Fall." *World Economy* 16 (January): 1–15.
Prust, J., and IMF Staff Team. 1990. *The Czech and Slovak Federal Republic: An Economy in Transition*. IMF Occasional Paper No. 72. Washington, D.C.: International Monetary Fund, October.
Rudka, A. 1992. "Reform of the Banking System in Poland," in D. M. Kemme and A. Rudka, eds., *Monetary and Banking Reform in Post-Communist Economies*. Pp. 72–153. New York: Institute for East-West Security Studies.
Sachs, J. 1993. *Poland's Jump to the Market Economy*. Cambridge, Mass: MIT Press.
Sanford, G., and M. Myant. 1991. "Poland," in S. White, ed., *Handbook of Reconstruction in Eastern Europe and the Soviet Union*. Pp. 167–82. London: Longman Current Affairs.
Siklos, P. L. 1994a. *Money, Banking and Financial Markets: Canada in the Global Environment*. New York: McGraw-Hill Ryerson Ltd.
―――――. 1994b. "Central Bank Independence in the Transitional Economies: A Preliminary Investigation of Hungary, Poland, the Czech and Slovak Republics," in I. Székely and J. P. Bonin, eds., *Development and Reform of the Financial System in Hungary*. London: Edward Elgar, forthcoming.
―――――. 1993. "Income Velocity and Institutional Change: Some New Time Series Evidence, 1870–1986." *Journal of Money, Credit and Banking* 25 (Part I) August: 377–92.
―――――. 1990. "Hyperinflations: Their Origins, Development and Termination." *Journal of Economic Surveys* 3: 225–48.
Siklos, P. L., and I. Ábel. 1994. "Real Exchange Rate Targeting in the Transitional Economies." Wilfrid Laurier University, in preparation.
Stanczak, K. 1992. "Inflation Stabilization and Economic Transformation in Poland: The First Year—A Comment." *Carnegie-Rochester Conference Series on Public Policy* 36 (July): 157–62.
Szabó, L. 1991. "A Pénzintézetek Gazdàlkodasa 1987 és 1990 között a mérlegadatok alapjà." *Bankszemle*: 29–46.
Székely, I., and J. P. Bonin. 1994. *Development and Reform of the Financial System in Central and Eastern Europe*. London: Edward Elgar.
Sundararajan, V., and T. J. Baliño. 1991. "Issues in Recent Banking Crises," in *Banking Crises: Cases and Issues*. Pp. 1–57. Washington, D.C.: International

Monetary Fund: 1–57.
Swaine, N. 1991. "Hungary," in S. White, ed., *Handbook of Reconstruction in Eastern Europe and the Soviet Union*. Pp. 113–46. London: Longman Current Affairs.
Székely, I. P. 1992. "Economic Transformation and the Reform of the Financial System in Central and Eastern Europe." Manuscript, United Nations, August.
_____. 1990. "The Reform of the Hungarian Financial System." *European Economy* 43 (March): 109–23.
Székely, I. P., and D. M. G. Newberry. 1993. *Hungary: An Economy in Transition*. Cambridge: Cambridge University Press and CEPR.
Wightman, G., and P. Rutland. 1991. "Czechoslovakia," in S. White, ed., *Handbook of Reconstruction in Eastern Europe and the Soviet Union*. Pp. 29–58. London: Longman Current Affairs.
Wyczański, P. 1993. "Polish Banking System." Economic and Social Policy Series No. 32. Warsaw: Friedrich-Ebert Foundation.

About the Book

There has been fierce debate about the optimal sequencing of economic reforms in emerging market economies. Many economists argue that for market-oriented systems to operate effectively, a reasonable degree of monetary stability is necessary. Rampant inflation, a common challenge for emerging economies, greatly reduces the chances that market-oriented reforms will be successful. In this comprehensive volume, a group of policy-oriented economists from North America, Europe, and the former Soviet Union explore the causes of monetary instability in reforming economies and evaluate alternative institutional mechanisms designed to reduce inflationary pressures.

Considering the latest theoretical and empirical research—as well as the experiences of former Communist countries, including Russia and the erstwhile Soviet republics—the contributors view inflation as a political issue and make a case for the creation of strong political institutions. They argue that although government actions that stimulate inflation tend to have low costs or even benefits in the sort run, they impose heavy costs on the economy in the longer term. Consequently, there is a strong need to develop institutional mechanisms to help ensure that decision makers place appropriate emphasis on the long-run consequences of policy actions.